D0667711

PIECES

[AN ANTHOLOGY]
BY SILAS WANJE.

PIECES

ISBN: 9781696458757

PROLOGUE

This is a book about RECONSTRUCTION.
These words are my attempt to repair after pain, time and life all had their way with me.

I don't have anything juicy or profound to say,
I emptied the tank in these pages.

To Noelle,
Thank you for listening to all the incomplete sentences and being the bouncing castle to my ideas.

And, in the words of every NBA/NFL player ever drafted,
Thank you to everyone who helped me through this process.
I wouldn't have done this without you.

This will last forever.
09/25/2019.

PIECES.

<u>PIECES.</u>

I am in pieces and I used up all of the
GLUE on you.

I am in pieces because of you.
Your empty words, stung,
And set off irreversible chain reactions
In my mind.
I let the memories play,
Like a weird slide show of bliss.

I am in pieces because of me.
I waved goodbye to who I was way too soon.

I never fully explored all of the chapters,
At least, not well enough to close them.
Closing doors is a lot easier than opening
them,
Closing has the pretence of finality,
But I am in pieces and I have CRACKS.

Fragments of my OLD self,
Are bleeding through the cracks,
They are yearning to be reconnected,
With my newly revivified self.

I have a chronic problem,
I never leave things behind,
It is a syndrome.
I still hold on to everything,
Just like I used to.

I am pieces of a poorly combined being,
With unsourced opinions, undefined traits,
unsteady emotions and too many words.

I am not sure if these fragments,
Will corrupt or help me carry my CROSS,
Even Jesus had disciples.

I am not sure if these fragments mean well,
Or they are attempting to crucify me on the
cross of my past.

I don't know if these pieces are permanent.
I do know that God is waiting on me,
But I am testing his divine patience.

I am taking the long, HELLISH, scenic route
to redemption.

I didn't ask him to mend me.
I can blame it all on Him though,
I *was* convinced that he made me.

I am in pieces because I let things latch
onto the tentacles of my spirit.
I am way too playful with forces I do not
fully understand.

I also don't pace myself,
I am always rushing to do WHOLESALE damage
to my pieces.
Self-sabotage should be my middle name.

I am in pieces.
I am constantly chasing after vices that
would pose nothing but an existential
crisis to my inner core.

I play hide and seek with romance.
My life exists as an elaborate maze,
architected and designed by my mind.
I write things.

I am in pieces because, I blindly followed
earthly rules.
I am in pieces because, I gave way too many
of them away.
I am in pieces but I wrote all of them.

I am in pieces because I lost touch with
the third member of my trinity.
I was lost but never found.
The PARABLES have significantly darker
endings in reality.
That is why I rarely read the bible.

In reality,
The floods never really sweep anything
meaningful way.
Some bad habits cannot be drowned out.

The same fear, insecurities, anger,
doubts, pessimism, worries,
and jealousy still germinate,
as soon as the water clears.

I can blame it all on HIM,
I *am* convinced that He created me.

I am in pieces.
I can't seem to pray well.
Each piece is a prayer,
That I am not ready to ask for or let go.

So, I keep bathing in my incompleteness.
Apparently, it is a good thing to be a
rough draft.

Maybe I am evolving,
But I believe in creation.
I create things.

I hear voices in my head,
Then I grab a pen and listen.
I swear that's one of the symptoms of
schizophrenia.
Stories haunt me.

I am in pieces because you were my
medication.
I have successfully self-medicated my way
through most of the foreign feelings.
I was not aware that you were doctor
prescribed.

You OOZE sex appeal.
You ooze sex appeal and I am infected with
desire.

You were one of the good ones,
But I am only good in very small controlled
doses.
I only have a hint of self-control.

I am in pieces and my heart is thirsty.
I have tried to quench it with rum,
I should have just gotten a juicer,
Now I drink both.

If you squeeze me now,
Nothing meaningful comes out.

And CUPID needs to calm the fuck down with
these arrows!!!
I am still working on dislodging the last
arrow he shot just last week.
How did he know that my heart was thirsty?

And he never misses.
Just like I miss u
Especially on the mornings,
After I have spent most of my nights,
Looking for someone like you.
Obviously, this cannot be healthy.

I swear I never wanted to write about you.
I started writing about LIFE and by the
fourth page,
The only words that came out were about
you.

I hope that touches you.
I am very touchy,
I remember that you like that.

I tried to hold the hand inside of you,
When all you needed was just a normal hand
to hold.
I am way too deep for my own good.
I go too deep,
I remember that you liked that.

Even God knows.
He heard his name being used in vain.
I broke some commandments and now I am in
pieces.

I am unstable, I cannot stand myself.
I am in pieces because of us.

Our souls were two electric ropes destined
to be tangled up,
But we formed a noose.

Deep, deep down,
I knew that you were the fabric that would
cloth my existence,
But I poured salt all over your wounds.

I did not even try to set you free,
You were shackled to the pain of your past.
Chains only break if you let them RUST.

I thought you needed saving,
But I was the sinner.
You could have been a MATYR for believing
in me,
It's the hope that kills you.

I am in pieces because you are a PISCES.
It's not just a zodiac sign.
I checked.

You were all the water I needed,
But my soul is not a well-oiled machine.
We never meant to mix.
Your soul-quenching water leaked through
the cracks of my pieces.

The cracks between my pieces expose the
flaws of my foundation.
I used the wrong materials to build me up.

I PATCHED up the new me using my old wilted
pieces,
Instead of undertaking the complete
overhaul my soul required.

I am in pieces,
But I used up all of the GLUE on you.

GENES AND UNBROKEN CYCLES.

GENES AND UNBROKEN CYCLES

I need to let go of the heaviness of being
a fatherless son.
I need to embrace what that has done for
me.
I need to accept how that has molded me.

I am an unwilling participant in unbroken
cycles.
I guess that's how much power a name can
have.
It is my understanding that, it is also how
genes work.
We are eternally tangled to whatever is
enclosed in those strands.

I made a promise to myself,
Even as versions of me were being gobbled
up by time,
I bookmarked these words to the home page
of my mind…

Though, I may get a lot of things wrong in
this life,
I will remain forever careful,
So as not to resemble him in any behavior
or in tendencies.
But I am closer than I thought I would be,
That is how genes work.

I promised myself that I would tap into
wherever strength comes from,
So that I could always proclaim,
I am not him.

I am better than him.
I can do better than him.
I can do life better than him.

That I could be there for people better
than he could.
That I could drink less than he did.
That I can be someone that my mother
doesn't consider a mistake.

That I could be known and remembered as the
new and improved version.

But I have his charm.
But I have his laugh.
But I have his reputation for leaving.
But I have his smile.
But his stubbornness has helped me
sometimes.
But I have his genes.

I wish I didn't know how genetics work,
Because then I could pretend that most of
my faults were his doing.

Then I could pretend that most of my good
traits were of my own making.
But that is not how genes work,
We become everything encased in those
strands.

I wish I didn't know how genetics work,
But I have his brain.
I also have his hair.

Even though he was never present,
My present is very much influenced by his
absence.
I never met this man,
But I long to have a conversation with him.
I never had a conversation with him,
But I sound like him.

I always think of this man,
I wonder how he thinks.
Then I wonder if I would despise those
thoughts,
God knows he was no angel.

I wouldn't want any chapter of my life to
be identical to his,
But I have his genes.

I am a fatherless son.
But I hope to learn from his mistakes,
Or I will keep making beds where I can't
lay.

I was born into his sins,
I grew up and confirmed this cycle.
I hope to avoid the sins of my father,
Or I will have a grave to dig.

I will make sure that no SON of mine ever
says that about me.
I never met this man,
But I wonder what he thinks of me.

I wonder if he would be proud of the person
I am,
I wonder if he would be pleased with the
paths I have taken,
I wonder if he would approve of my future
wife.

I wonder if I would have been a different man,
If he had any influence on me.
I wonder if I would even like him at all,
If he was around.

I wonder if I would show him these pages,
These waves of thought have swept me here.

I think about this man more than I should,
And I have never met this man.

I never met this man,
But I cried when he died.

PAIN.

PAIN

Pain is the absolute humanizer.
It demands to be felt.

I think every letter of the word deserves
to be CAPITALIZED.
It is an experience that not a single body
organ is exempt from.
It cannot be numbed or avoided, just
postponed.
As a result, we the people are at its
mercy.

Physical pain is just an appetizer.
What it is, are just a few nerves being
stimulated in an unfamiliar way.
It is my favorite kind of pain.
For at least it has the DECENCY to depart.

Pain by death is difficult to characterize.
We were never meant to come close to even
understanding it.
It signals the end of life,
Faces we will cruelly never see again,
But even that, in time, it dissipates.
We forget to remember.
Our distractions become our life.

God too, feels pain.
It hurts him when we stray.
He sheds a tear or two, when we take too
long to find our way back.
He is in pain as I write this.
He is howling for my wretched soul.

Amongst all kinds of pain,
Pain by heartache is the one I DREAD.
It is by far the worst kind of pain.

It is relentless and consuming.
It makes you physically sick without the
physical stimuli.
It leaves even our organs unaware of how to
react.

It is numbing and weakening.
It leaves most of us, even the self-
proclaimed strong ones,
Transfixed on memories.

It creates a pause button in our lives,
Or whatever is left of it.
It clouds our judgement, if we have any
leftover.
It perforates our hearts into many tiny
holes,
Or whatever part of it that is left
pumping.

It darkens most of our days.
It turns our smiles into whys.
It turns our fondest memories into
reflective tears.

You would think that the tears,
Would wash a fraction of that pain away,
But no, the tears are mostly
inconsequential and they DRY.
They leave all of the hurt still heavy and
intact.

Pain cannot be erased.
Time has been trying for years.

Pain leaves fingerprints all over our
essence,
When it is done touching us, we are never
ever the same.

We become shackled to it.
Drugs of choice only delay its
inevitability.
People may cause pain,
But it is a being on its own.

It is to be embraced, not fought.
It is to be appreciated as a source of
strength.
It is to be experienced.

For it is just like us in that way.
It just wants to be felt,
To be noticed.

A BROKEN
MAN.

A BROKEN MAN

Nothing else can break me,
I am already broken.

Nothing else can bring me sorrow,
My soul is already engulfed in sadness.

Nothing else can terrify me,
Everything I have ever been afraid of, has
already happened to me.

Nothing else can fuel my inspirations,
I am already numb.

My once fortitude of a mind, is now porous.
It carefully curated memories,
But now, most of what it remembers is
painful.

My once kind heart is now hardened.
It learned to love,
But now, it is failing its beating classes.

My once infamous smile is mostly lifeless
now.
It was meant to be everlasting,
But pain has a way of choking the life out
of things.

My eyes are tortured,
There is nothing I have not seen.
They have witnessed happiness and then
watched it flee.

My tear ducts are all dried up,
There is nothing left to cry for.
I have wasted most of my tears on the wrong
faces.

There is nothing I have not felt.
I am a rainbow of emotions,
I feel love and hate in the same visceral
way.

There is nothing I have not deserved.
Karma is relentless and unforgiving.
Everything that I have ever done,
Has been done to me.

Nothing else can break me,
I am a broken man.
I have lovers, but I don't have you.

TIME.

TIME

Time cannot be deconstructed,
It has no synonym.

Time is like a whisper in the wind.
Intertwined and moving way too fast, for
anyone to fully capture.

Time is precious,
It is a virtuous cycle.
I have tried to disobey its rules,
But time has a way of reminding you,
who is boss.

Time is a contract.
The consequences are permanent,
if breached.
Time is ruthless,
It claims all of its debt.

Time flies, but we are our own pilots.
As time passes by,
It will tear you wide open.
It will force you to take a look inside.

Time is coming to sweep you away,
Grow some wings.
The fragile will not endure.

Time has no symmetry.
Time is devoid of any form of BIAS,
It guarantees both pleasure and pain.

Time can leave you in disarray.
It will help you remember and also give you
amnesia.

Time refuses to be customized.
It is not malleable.

Time is a leash.
It will keep you controlled and contained.

Time is a regulatory agency.
Time will reorganize your beliefs,
Allow it.

Time will give you access to wisdom,
Allow it.
Time will cleanse you,
Allow it.

Time allows for redemption.
Time is a cure for isolation,
You realize that everyone is going through
it.

Secrets disintegrate in time.
Time reveals truth,
It is its gatekeeper.

Time needs an audience.
So take time to learn more.
Take time to embrace change.

Time will disrobe your genuine self,
No matter how many masks you wear.

Time cannot be deconstructed,
There is beauty in its complexity.
So take time to say yes,
Your options are limitless.

Take time to suffer the pain of discipline,
Use it as a shield.
The pain of regret is so much greater.

Take time to fail and fail again,
As you navigate your way to your goals.

Time has no use for your half-done dreams,
It will vacuum away any unfulfilled
potential.
Time will not wait for you.

Time is undying,
It does last forever.
Our interactions with it are the only
things that are short-lived.

Time keeps turning your *"LIFE PAGES"* daily,
You are just not consulted on their
content.

Take time to cry,
But for every tear be sure to smile.
Take time to let more love IN,
Especially after every heartbreak.

Dedicate time to create an optimal present,
Don't bookmark pages you've already read.

Time is a vivid illusion.
Before you know it,
It will be gone.
All that will remain are half scribbled
pages.
I thought I had more time.

DEATH.

DEATH

What if death is a ghost that will forever
haunt us?
What if, death is like a stranger but the
creepy kind?
What if, most the good musicians go to
hell?

What if, you met the love of your life,
After the death of your wife,
Who you thought was the love of your life?
These are just some of the many reasons I
am horrified by death.

Death has no good intentions.
Death is like a spell forged by all the
forces of the universe,
It has never been broken.

I am not afraid to die.
I am fully aware that someday, some moment,
Some minute will be my last.
Not knowing the how and when, is what makes
it unbearable.

If we knew when death will whisk us away,
Maybe we could prepare for it.
We could make time to curse some people out
for hurting us,
And maybe we could make time to say our
final goodbyes.

I know I am not ready, for whatever chapter
of reality comes next.
I think there are some places, I have yet
to lay my eyes on.

I know there are some people, I have yet to
make regret meeting me.
I think there are some things, I am dying
to accomplish.

I know there are some sins, my soul is
still itching to commit.
I think there are some questions, I still
need answered.

Why do we have to leave anyway?
What if, whatever comes next is not as
pleasing, as what we would be leaving
behind?

What if, there are no orgasms in hell?
Sounds like a garbage place anyway,
I hear it gets really hot down there.

I have been held down by angels,
Helpless, as life was slowly clipping my
wings away.
Feather by fucking feather, as death was
trying to take my soul.
And that was just my childhood.

I know what it feels like, to be in the
outskirts of hell.

Where the hell do we go anyway?
If our destination is significantly better
than this,
Why is it painful for all the people we
leave behind?

Why do we cry?
Are tears the only acceptable grieving
mechanism?
Is it OK to smile when someone dear dies?
Is death relief or is it punishment?

Timing is defined as the ability to select
the precise moment for doing something,
I think death is purposely not good at this
timing thing.
Most people are destined to perish
prematurely.

Why does it not wait until we find God?
Why does it not wait until we find love?
Or at the very least, why not wait until we
find ourselves?

Why can't we take the people we care about
with us?
As a way to avoid loneliness when we get up
there.
What if we like it HERE?

What if the thrills of life remain
enticing?
Is there a way we could get some kind of a
preview?
That would definitely guide some of the
mistakes I would choose to make.

Why can we not come back to our earthly
roots?
In case we find that the allure of eternal
bliss is overrated.

What if we have unfinished business in this
realm?
What if death stops you from becoming all
you could be?

After life is done putting us through its
unbalanced paces,
Why is it, that our hearts never gain
enough resilience to prepare us for death?
They are still shredded by every death.

What if when our time comes to take a walk
with death,
Away from all of life's impairments,
We are not quite done with the show.
What if we are still enjoying life's
performance?

What if heaven is just a replica of earth
but in a more mysterious realm?

What if our souls remain untouched?
Our souls are under-developed, because they
are still clutching at earthly straws,
trying to rest on solid ground.
It is all they know.

Death does not talk to us,
It makes us feel.
Death is the road to self,
Or somewhere close.

Will death actually grant our souls the
rest they yearn?
Is death punishment or is it divine relief?

The more I think about it,
All these pages could be about life.

The mystery.
The uncertainty.
The suddenness.
The pain.

The tears.
The drama.
The numbing.
The goodbyes.

Death is the shadow of life; it follows us
to the end.
It is fitting, that life ends with
something as dramatic as death.
I am not sure which I like better.

Death is the ruthless ruler of life.
Death has no immunity,
It is a necessity that is never reluctant.

Eventually, we all succumb.
That which cannot be avoided is to be
feared.

FUTURE SILAS.

FUTURE SILAS

Sorry I lost our tickets to heaven.
I hope you are stronger than I was.
My hope is that you will have learnt, most
of these lessons before you read this.

I hope you stay madly in love with your
pen.
I hope that my RAMBLINGS bloomed into
sentences,
That would maybe be the title of our book.

And since nothing exists until it has a
name,
I hope that you complete our book.
It will be our legacy.
Finally, the world will get a polished
glimpse of our thoughts.
Sorry, I did not leave you enough pages to
work with.

Life was hard for me,
I don't expect it to be any different for
you.

Life is harsh.
Please develop some resistance,
Even bacteria have figured that *shit* out.

I hope you are stronger than I was.
Strong enough to survive,
Even when things around you unravel.
Strong enough to be grateful,
Even when evil happens to you.

This world will give you nothing.
I hope you are debt free,
Not owing a single soul anything.

I hope you are stronger than I was.
Sorry I used up, most of our reserve of
tears.

Your soul is a marionette,
Please be careful who you give access to
those strings.
Be careful what you practice,
You may get good at it.

I begun the grueling process,
But I never learnt how to forgive myself.
I just scratched the surface,
Keep digging.

I was nothing but unrealized possibilities.
I was not who I could be,
Even by my own poorly defined expectations.
Be more than what you are.

Don't wait like I did.
Don't hide like I did.
Don't be scared like I was.

Everything that you are afraid of already
happened to me.
I took that bullet for us,
Karma should be on our side now.

Sorry I wasn't careful with our heart.
I know it's physically healthy,
I can't say the same about its insides.
Sorry I left a mess down there.
If it is any consolation,
I was also careless with other people's
hearts too.

I never learnt to love,
Good luck finding our wife.
I tried, but I was drunk on most nights.
I was also searching in the wrong
locations.

Sorry I lost your ticket to heaven.
I committed a few sins.
I may have accidentally, cleaned your slate
with God in the process.
You will have no new sin.

But promise me, that you will live life as
if everything matters.
Promise me, that I will be a worthy
sacrifice.

Promise me, that you will aim at something.
Promise me, that you will always keep
moving,
Wandering is worse than being lost.

I should know,
I was wandering aimlessly, until I stumbled
forward.

Live as if everything matters.

Every thought you consider is important,
Every conversation, every word matters.
I learnt the hard way.

Do not live life as if you don't exist.
Do not ignore what you have to focus on.
Do not walk in and out of people's lives,
STAY.
If you think that you will end up leaving,
Then don't get in.

Do not let darkness mold you,
It can corrupt your whole being.

Don't make excuses to do things that you
don't believe in,
Excuses compound over time,
And time will want its pound of flesh.

Excuses compound over time,
You will be able to justify any behavior,
You will able to sacrifice any principle.

Over time,
Most of your inner core will disintegrate.
Over time,
There will be hardly any of *"YOU"* left,
Just an exoskeleton and a sketch of your
past.

Never want anyone's life,
That is the evidence of your weakness.
Don't aim to be exceptional,
Radical success is unhealthy.
Seek wholeness instead.

Be a polymer,
Spread yourself out.

Be dependent and independent.
Try to be sane,
But have your crazy side accessible.
Try to be good,
But have your *"BADNESS"* lurking.

Be admirable in most situations.
See the meaning in objects.
Turn that camera outside.
Circulate peace within your inner circle.

Continue to learn as much as humanly
possible.
Please UNLEARN most of what I taught you,
Only then can you gain wisdom.

I killed most of our bad habits,
So you have a chance at revival.

Find yourself again.
Please, continue to evolve.
Evolve or evolution will claim you.
Love, above all else.

I AM
SELF-AWARE.

I AM SELF-AWARE

Windows and mirrors are alike to me,
Every time I look at either,
I never see myself.
How else am I supposed to do any kind of
self-reflection?

They say that there is ecstasy in paying
attention.
But how can we pay attention to each
moment,
When we have apps more addictive than
ecstasy?

How can we live in the moment?
When most of them are unscripted and don't
last.

Apparently, that is why we are here.
To notice things.
To witness time and its poetic constraints.

It speaks to God's sense of humor, that all
days have the same number of hours.
You would think we would get more time,
To enjoy the few blessings and otherwise.

That the joys littered amongst the
heartaches, would last longer.
You would think that we would get a few
more hours, to celebrate successes.

If I ever figured out how time works,
I would attempt to keep the good days
almost unending.
I would clock-out on my bad days.

My Mondays would only be two hours,
So I can escape the infamous BLUES.
But, it's mostly because I got to kiss you
on Mondays.

I would need at least four more hours on
Sundays,
To confess the sins of my weekend.

If I ever figured out how time works,
I would dedicate most of my week,
To allowing the passions to consume us.

Without any semblance of a fight,
I hope that you would let me fall inside
you,
So I can steal BACK my heart.

I guess, we could clean the STAINS of our
erotic voyages on Saturdays.
Some chore that would be.

Fridays have always been reserved for
dancing.
Dancing in the cinematic bubble,
To the soothing music our faulty souls
created.
It was their attempt at mending.

Most of the faces I encounter are
unremembered,
But you have left shadows and footprints in
my heart.

I can't keep fighting all these arrows,
Cupid keeps hurling at me.
But I don't trust him, he has misled me
before.

I realize that I should have used my words,
not signals.
Even road signs have letters.

I realize that I should have torn up the
checklist I wrote,
I write way too much for my own good.
I know that love should be template free.

I realize that bubbles burst.
I realize that most of what remained,
Even after the self-inflicted rupture,
Even when the savage lust was fading,
You were enough.
I was just fighting unnecessary battles
with myself.

I realize now that everyone else was a
waste of time.
I have to stop living like the short
stories I write.
I always wanted to be your constant.

I was ready to feel love, but I wasn't
ready for the process.
I realize that I was witnessing love,
But I am self-aware and I have radical
doubt.

My halo is rusty.
My heart is injured. It is bathed in pain.
It is mostly unexplored chambers and empty
vessels.

Yet, you stumbled into my life.
You snatched a starring role in it,
But the show was cancelled.
It was too good,
I knew it wouldn't last.

I let you in, but I didn't show you my
heart.
I promised you nothing,
At least I kept that promise.

I am sinking slowly.
I wish quicksand would live up to its name,
This hurt wouldn't last.

But I wish you stayed longer.
I wish I prayed longer.
I should have talked dirty to you, like the
mess that you were.
But I am self-aware and I wish I wasn't.

I shouldn't have watched you go, but I run.
That's the Kenyan in me.
I know I was not good enough for you
because you were all I needed.
Whatever part of my heart still beats,
Would lead me to yours, if it could walk.

I know I am like a cactus, prickly on the
outside,
But if you can get passed the thorns,
I swear, I am sweet.
It's a shame you didn't see that side of
me.

I wish I didn't bring my clones to life.
I wish I wasn't indifferent to my
instincts,
But I am its passenger now.

I keep having continuous conversations with
all the DARK versions of myself,
On ways I could overcome my lonely streak.

I wish I didn't walk with these devilish
thoughts in my pockets,
But those are the sins of my rebellious
past.

I am self-aware,
I was bound to repeat this pattern.
Most of my thoughts are rinsed by alcohol.
Those are the sins of my father.

I liked to play games, but I was never
really good at them.
I needed to recalibrate my world, so it was
all about you.
But I am self-aware, and I have radical
doubt.

I even questioned our first encounter.
For it was out of this world, celestial,
As if scripted by God and his glorious
helpers.

Heavenly intervention is the only
explanation,
For that symbol of perfection, you have for
a body.
For that angelic chuckle you have, instead
of a smile.

For that bewitching creation you have,
where your lips should be.
Your style was presidential,
Michelle Obama.

Our chemistry should have been coursework
for Chemistry 101.
You are what a complete package wants to be
when they grow up.

I should have realized I was witnessing
love,
Love and all of its demons.
But the problem with being self-aware, is
that you realize,
You are the only reason; you keep missing
out on your blessings.

My heart remains injured,
Those are consequences of being reckless
with it.
It's obvious that I miss you.
You were crafted in my dreams,
I met you in reality.

Your heart needed a place to hide,
But I have misplaced most hearts I cared
for.

I thought love was measured by the amount
of tears I made you cry.
I thought my cruel heart and cold kisses
Would more than make up, for all my other
faults.

I am self-aware.
I convinced myself,
That you will love the way that I intended
to hurt you.
If this doesn't make sense to you,
It shouldn't.

I dove deep trying to reach the depths of
my heart,
And I found treasure down there,
But I chose to leave it behind.
I am horrible at leaving things behind.
I still hold on to things, just like I used
to.

All the ghosts of my void would agree,
That you were the beginning of a beautiful
story,
But I always choose unhappy endings.

I am self-aware.
I tried to cry for you,
But my tear ducts were all dried up.

TIME refused to do its thing.
It was supposed to help me forget you,
But your memories still linger.

Your face is plastered, all over the walls
of my mind.
I am a mess, but its only karma.

Time keeps undressing my flesh.
But it refuses to do its duty, and help me
forget.
I cannot forget you,
Believe me, I tried.

It would take some kind of dark magic,
And I am the worst magician I know.
I am just a mostly speechless writer with a
rusty halo.

That dreadful feeling of losing you,
Has found shelter in my mind,
Next to where our bedroom Kamasutra
memories lie.

Life is when we were in bed together,
Everything else is just waiting.

But the problem with being self-aware,
Is that you realize,
You are the reason,
You keep missing out on your blessings.

I am self-aware,
I wish I met you, before I met me.

IF THEY CAN
FIND ME FIRST.

IF THEY CAN FIND ME FIRST

Self is what I crave.
My own me.
My own path that I can confidently follow.

My own values.
My own pleasing traits,
Right only in God's unerring eyes.

I want to be and stay well-adjusted,
Even in this profoundly sick society.

I want to keep my inner core intact,
Even when everything around me is changing.
I want to be changed by nothing.
I want to exist free from outside
influences.

I want to have fortitude,
So that no ONE event would be strong enough
to shift my self-concept.
I want to have excess determination,
So that no love would push me close to
folly.

I want perfect sanity.
I want complete alignment with my senses,
So I can teach them to act only logically.
I want to be choosy about every step I
take,
That way I may not falter.

I would like to understand most of what
floats through this brain.
I want to learn things, as much as humanly
possible.
I hope to gather some lessons from my
mistakes and copy/paste them to whatever
page I flip to next.

I want to experience uniqueness until I
feel no difference.
I want to see things through.
I want to strive for my superlative best,
as a means of keeping failure away.

I want to be strong, even when life makes
me weak.
I want to be careful, but carefree on most
nights.

I want to live in the now, no matter how
suffocating it maybe.
I am learning not to fuss about the future,
for it will surely come.

I would like to watch the lost souls make
mistakes so I can do the complete opposite.
But also make some mistakes twice,
Because they are way too fun to indulge in
only once.

I would like to meet my destiny,
On the road I will certainly take to avoid
it.
I would like to abandon the past,
In the concrete in which it is written.

I would like to keep my infamous smile
intact and share it with people in need.

I would like to see beauty in negative
spaces, goodness will certainly follow.
I would like to find peace and solace where
only unrest and aggravation exists.

I want to let pain go,
Into the dark of night where it belongs.

I want to let my scars heal.
I would like to shield my little excuse for
a heart,
It's mostly just muscle.

I want to find something to love,
That leads to someone to love.
Or if they can find me first…
I want to love people I have yet to meet,
Or if they can find me first…

I want to find God,
Or if He can find me first…

I would like to find destitute hearts,
Help them mend.
Or if they can find mine first,
That too would be nice.

I want to find good friends,
Or if they can find me first…
I would like to stumble into your life,
Or if you can stumble into mine,
That too would be nice.

I want to live ferociously,
So that death will think twice before it
takes me.

I want to be me.
My own definition of a man.

THEY[CARRY ON].

THEY[CARRY ON]

They say that damaged people are the
wisest.
They disguise their shatter with words.
They tuck in their sadness with hope.

They are wise because they learn.
They learn to put themselves first,
They realize that no one else will.

They learn to always be on the mend,
However undefined it may be.
They learn to unlearn most of what they
believe,
Only then do you gain knowledge.

They learn to add layers of complexity to
every fabric of their being,
Only then can you consider yourself strong.

They learn not to fall for the same
temptations twice,
Only then can you master your ghosts.

They say that the loneliest people are the
kindest,
They understand the far-reaching
consequences kindness has.
They understand that despair is just a
voice that needs to be left alone.

They realize that open arms are more
powerful than open eyes
They understand how simply joyful it is to
be in good company and how soothing than
can be for any achy heart.

They understand that there is more to life
than pursuing fleeting memories, things and
thongs.

They say that the saddest people smile the
brightest.
They appreciate the power of their smiles.
They understand that their smiles can take
them further than a frown ever could.

Their smiles keep them all stitched up.
Their smiles are smiles of remembrance.
Their smiles, however broken, keep them
accustomed to all the foreign feelings.

Their smiles, are enough to save them from
folly.
Their smiles, however broken, strengthen
them.
Their smiles grant them patience,
To keep waiting for their skies to clear
and for their clouds to scatter.

They seem lost,
Their compasses are faulty.

They are tourists in their own body, mind
and city.
They seem lost, but only in society's eyes.
They are always moving, even though the
destination is unclear.

They seem blind, but it's only because,
They got blinded trying to manifest
society's dreams.
Society is the blinding agent.
They cannot keep up with the moving goal
posts.

They are chasing after a poorly defined
life.
They are chasing after mostly uncertain and
unsatisfactory goals.

They are chasing after more and more
things,
While ignoring matters of the heart.
They are chasing after this riddle and
riddles,
That we were never meant to solve or
understand.

Yet, despite the appeal of psychotic
impulsivity,

They carry on.
Yet, despite the dark magnetism of death,
They carry on.
Even though they are tormented by their
thoughts,
They carry on.

Even though their path is inundated by numerous fault lines,
They carry on.

Even though the light at the end their tunnels is flickering,
They carry on.

Even though they are running out of guardian angels,
They carry on.

Even though the voice from their God is faint,
They carry on.

Even when their demons extinguish the
luminous lights of their soul,
They don't ferment in the darkness for very
long.
They carry on.

Even though their cries for help, only echo
in their own minds,
They find comfort in the noise.
They carry on.

Even when the only arms, available to wrap
themselves in are their own,
They carry on.

Even though their chemical balance isn't
what it used be,
They carry on.

Even when they have not been able to decode
their purpose,
They carry on.

Even when they are spiraling closer to the
ledge,
They carry on.

Even when there are no signs of life in the
depths of ruin,
They carry on.

Even when they are dying in slow motion,
They carry on.
Even when the only choice is walking away,
Please carry on.

WORDS.

WORDS

What is more powerful than words?
Words can topple even the most powerful of
kingdoms, faster than an army ever could.

What is more long lasting than words?
Words can outlive most kingdoms.

What is more powerful than words?
Words can divide a country faster and more
efficiently than tribes ever could.

In the wrong LIPS, words will have you
WRUNG.

In the wrong lips, words will have you
convinced,
That the gap between our differences and
similarities is wider than the inches
between our lips.

In the wrong lips,
Words can influence the minds of the
population more clearly than pop culture
ever could.
Words can shift public opinion more
strongly than a salacious scandal ever
could.

Words can blur the lines that truth depends
on.
And if repeated long enough,
These same deceptive words may become the
truth.

In the right LIPS,
Words can form religion.

Words can make you believe in the obvious
beauty of nature.
Words can make you fascinated in the
unfathomable glory of science.

But if you replace a few letters,
The same WORDS can have you questioning the
whole existence of the universe.
Words can lead you to faith, and the same
words can also ERODE most of it in the next
sentence.

What is more powerful than words?
The same confusing words, that would lead
some wandering souls into a cult, are the
same words that can guide lost souls into
the light.

Words can make history and record it,
better than a picture ever could.
Words can shape the future more clearly
than technology ever could.
Words can make ARTS timeless,
Movies and music are empty without them.

What is more powerful than words?
The same destructive words that can ruin
your reputation, will be the same words
that will help you reconstruct it.

Words that will give psychotic focus to
chase after life,
But if shifted, they will be the same words
to leave you stumped and hopeless.

Words can pierce the heart and cause pain,
faster than a bullet ever could.
Those same words, will heal you after time
does its thing.

What is more beautiful than words?
A beautiful combination of words can melt a
heart, faster than physical beauty ever
could.

Words can lead you to love, faster than SEX
ever could.
The same words that will nudge you towards
someone's arm,
In the next sentence will drive you away,
faster than an UBER ever could.

What is more confusing than words?
The same words that may have you recklessly
falling for someone, are the same words
that will make you rethink everything.

What is more beautiful than words?
Words will make you cry tears of sorrow.
Remove a few letters, and the same words
will then replace them with tears of joy,
faster than comedy ever could.

What is more powerful than words?
Words can send you spinning into
depression.
Those same words will medicate you through
it.
Those same words will give you hope.

What is more powerful than words?
Words can bless you with prayer,
Those same words can curse you for
generations.
The same words that will give you peace,
Can torment you more effectively than a
horror film ever could.

What is more powerful than words?
Words can help you find friends, faster
than any APP ever could.
The same words will walk you through the
process, as you cut them off.
Words can make a night out with friends
memorable more than a *selfie* ever could.

What is more confusing than words?
Words that you have plenty of, as you
linger in lust,
Will desert you and leave you speechless
when you are in LOVE.

The same words that may take your breath
away, can become fighting words in another
sentence.

What lingers more than words?
Hurtful words can give you sleepless
nights, more efficiently than insomnia ever
could.

Words can mold any tender mind.
Words will hold our hands through life,
But they are not enough to say goodbye when
we die.

GRACE.

GRACE

Days are irreversible.
You have lived every minute by unforgiving
minute, gracefully.
It is only fitting that your persona
somehow matches your name.
I think you came first,
They just decided to use you as a synonym
for grace.

You are not perfect, but you are the
perfect mother.
You are an emblem to that word, down to the
very last letter.
R is for resolve.

You nurtured us through sickness.
You guided us through the growing pains of
reckless infancy.
You filled the roles of 2 parents, when he
who shall remain nameless left.

You sheltered us from the world,
We were mindless toddlers, definitely not
ready for anything the world had to offer.
You did the work of multiple guardian
angels.
Thank you.

I wish gratitude were a tangible currency,
I would make it rain.
You would see how forever grateful I am.

You were strong enough to give us HOLY ass-
whoopings,
And still gentle enough to instill
discipline.

You were an African queen,
How else were you able to raise 4 kings.

You implanted in our psyche,
To use education as a way out of poverty.
So, we buried our brains in books to make
you proud.
But also, not to make you worry, you had
enough on your mind.

You taught us to pray,
Even when we didn't have a lot of reasons
to believe.

You lived a life of sacrifice,
So we could have an example.
We were wild teens underserving of your
sacrifice,
But you put us first.

You worked 2-3 jobs, to ensure we had
everything essential.
You lived a life of hard work,
To show us that it's possible.

No currency currently exists, for us to
reimburse you in.
Thank you.

I wish I could copy/paste some of your
traits into my being.
I wish I could copy/paste most of your
recipes,
You are a magician in the kitchen.

Your hands have saved many lives.
They have touched many more.
They have charmed a lot of pain away.
Everything you do matches your name.

I am proud to have been forged by parts of
you.
If only I had your grace.

LORD.

LORD

I am hoping that this is a safe page to
fall apart on,
For I do not know where to begin.

I have ignored your wise voice for years.
I have been buried in silence.

I am yet to speak to you earnestly,
Months in the dark have passed.
And even in those days I needed that light
you are famed for,
I still did not turn to you.

I ran away from your grace.
But no matter how many steps I took way from you,
You were right there with me all along.
Apparently, that's how GRACE works.

So here we are now.
You with all your glory,
Me, with whatever the opposite of that is.

I come before you,
Humbly, ashamed and regretful.
Regretful,
For all the choices I boldly made without consulting you.
For venturing into this bizarre roller-coaster we call life, without asking you to guide me.

It feels insane, that I attempted to do
things on my own,
When clearly I cannot.

And now, engulfed in some dark clouds,
I wonder if you still love me the same,
Despite all of these miles I have knowingly
strayed.

I wonder if the GODLY plans you had for my
life and soul are still intact.
Or did I stray too far even for your
limitless mercy.
I hope you can see me,
Despite all of this darkness that I let
cloud, me and my always flawed judgement.

I want you back.
Or if you can take me back,
That too would be nice.

I want you back my lord, my all.
I want your timeless forgiveness, and
especially your infamous mercy.
If at all, I am still worthy.

I want to be your child again,
I grew up way too fast.

I want to be in your circle of friends,
I want to love like you do.

I want that biblical favor,
For selfish reasons.
For me.
For I am a fragile creature, and only you
can strengthen me.

I need your GRACE.
I need two guardian angels this time
around,
So I can stay on the path you drew up.
So I can breathe in those moments, you had
in mind when you created me.

I know you are always trying to reach this
broken world,
It would be nice if you can use me.

Take me, LORD.
Mold me, alter my devilish alter ego.
Change me, only into what is fitting before
your unerring eyes.

My heart is pounding on those heavenly
pearly gates,
Please let me in.
Do what you will,
I surrender.

Have your way.
Love me again,
Control all this which I cannot.

Save me,
Lest I perish.

OLD TESTAMENT.

OLD TESTAMENT

I think Solomon either had ghost writers,
or he invented time management.
How else did he find time to marry 700
wives, and give all of them sufficient
attention?

How did he have time to go to war, somehow
acquire 300 more concubines, keep all of
them happy, and not even have a favorite?
Maybe OLD TESTAMENT women weren't that
needy.

He accomplished all of this,
While ruling a kingdom and [I'm assuming]
being a shitty father,
Because of, you know, logistics.

To top it off, he still somehow,
Managed to find time,
To thoroughly think about the human
experience and write PROVERBS, SONGS OF
SONGS and ECCLESIASTES.

Three very deep and very profound books.
How did he make time for all these things?
Or maybe Old testament minutes were longer
than ours.

He lived long enough,
To reach the realization that everything is
utterly meaningless.
He concluded, that everything is like
chasing after the wind.

His words, not mine.

He fought many battles, but none more draining than life.
He lived long enough,
To be trapped with the knowledge of not knowing what it all means.

He witnessed death, and accepted that it is inevitable.
He lived like a king, but still noticed that suffering was a common ingredient in life.

He was guided by GOD, sought after him, and walked with him.
But none of that erased any of the questions.

Questions of life, love, and time.
Questions of mortality, suffering, and
meaning.
Most of the same questions that
we still wrestle with, in this century.

If humans truly evolved,
How is it, that the same OLD TESTAMENT
questions are still unanswered?
And how did he know?

I think about these things, because that is how
my mind works.
It may not be normal.
I feel like I belong in the Old Testament,
But knowing my luck,
I would probably end up being an outcast.

I could never be a prophet.
You have to listen to GOD,
I am not a good listener.
I am not a good follower either.
I can't just get up and leave,
I don't like driving.
It also involved a lot of camping in the
wilderness and I am not a fan.

I could never be a prophet,
I don't handle rejection very well.
I have radical doubt.
I don't even trust my guardian angels.

I feel like an Old Testament lake
sometimes,
Surrounded by a religious mountain.
My lake is filled with thoughts that would
feel at home in Sodom.
These thoughts are uncontainable and I have
no dam.
So they flood out sometimes.

I couldn't even build my ARK on time, to
save me from the SELF destruction.

I gathered everything that was worth
gathering,
But I passed out.
I drank too much wine,
I thought it was water.
I thought my miracles would work.

They would never let me be a prophet,
I am always hungover on the Sabbath day.

I need to have an INTERNAL exodus,
Assemble all of my good soldiers,
And demand from my demons, to let my people
go.

But there is no burning bush,
No signs from GOD,
Just weird, unrefined ideas from my mind.

I would never have crossed the red sea
I have radical doubt.
I am also not a good swimmer.
Also, the red sea is really cold
And I don't like being cold.

I probably would have convinced some people
to stay behind,
Just in case the whole plan didn't go so
smoothly.

They would never let me be a prophet.
My people were never chosen,
We have been fighting oppression for years.

They would never let me be a prophet.
I am not good with directions.
I get LOST without GPS.

I would have wandered through the
wilderness with the ISRAELITES.
I have the worst luck,
I probably would never have made it to the
Promised Land.

They would never let me be a prophet,
Because I would have to engage all the
false prophets.
I would have to prove their false gods
wrong,
But I don't really like confrontation.

And knowing my luck,
I would probably end up praying to the same
false gods,
Because this world is theirs.
My mind and body are still chained to the
cravings of this world.
I cannot shake them off.
They are the only ones who can grant me
these earthly desires.

I could never be a prophet,
Because I want to live forever.

I want to be taken up to heaven, in a
chariot of fire like Elijah was.
But knowing my luck,
The gates of heaven would probably not
open,
The chariot would probably breakdown, and I
don't have [triple] AAA anymore.

I could never be a prophet,
I have trust issues.
I could never obey like Abraham did,
I am stubborn.

I would be trying to argue with GOD…

" Hey man, I am not really good with babies
Plus I feel like, you are more experienced
at this sacrificing thing than I am,
Also, I am not really good with knives.
So, maybe this is not a good idea."

They would never let me be a prophet
because I make excuses.

I would never have survived the things that
Daniel did.
I have the worst luck.
My angels would probably forsake me,
As I was being thrown into the pit of fire.

Also, I never really like cats
So, the lions would probably feast on me.
But at least it would be faster than
How life is presently eating me up.

I could never suffer through the
afflictions of JOB,
I was never a loyal servant to begin with.
Also, I don't really resist or fight any
temptation.
Plus, I am already bitter.
It probably wouldn't take that much
suffering, for me to blame God.

They would never let me be a prophet,
I don't have strong convictions.
My shame does not set when the sun goes
down.

I would go into SODOM and GOMORAH, with the
intent of leading a revival,
But knowing me, I would probably end up
fitting in.
I kinda like the party scene.
Also, I would probably get a lot of
material for my book.
But I would have been destroyed with the
rest of the city.

I could never be a prophet.
I am not that strong.

I could never be an Old Testament king,
I have never fulfilled my potential.

If being king was my destiny,
I would probably avoid it.
I would still be like David,
But the shepherd version.

I have the worst luck,
My sling shots would miss.
Goliath would still be alive.
The book of Psalms would be unfinished.

I would never have gone to battle,
I don't like conflicts.
I would be in some village writing,
Someone has to tell those stories.

I could never be determined like Solomon,
How else do you manage that many wives and
mistresses?

My heart never learnt to multi-task,
I still have trouble forgetting just the
one.

But I think I have his wisdom though,
I have passed all of life's tests,
That didn't involve you.

But I could never be a prophet,
Because I would have to leave you behind.

MAYs AND MAYBEs.

MAYs AND MAYBEs

I knew that MAYBEs will one day cost me
something real.
Nothing seems important since I lost you.

Maybe, it was the right time to lose you.
Maybe I should have let go sooner,
Before I got swept by your naval wave.
I should have learnt how to swim,
Before I sunk into your world of mays and
maybes.

Maybe it is just karma settling some debts.
Most of the things you are doing to me,
I have been guilty of.
I have broken many hearts, just for the
material.
Or maybe it was just cupid, and his damn
arrows.

Maybe, I should sit still and wait.
Wait until you remember,
Wait until you come to your senses.

They play tricks on us, our senses.
Our own eyes blind us.
We rarely see that which is good for us.

And even when we do,
Our minds trick us to ignore it.

And even when we realize it,
Our hearts trick us to disregard it.
We tremble instead of trusting.

As I attempted to trick your heart to fall
for mine,
I fell.

Now, if only I could get you out of my
mind.
I would erase all of these fingerprints,
That you've left scattered all over my
heart.

Maybe I will just sit still,
Wait for them to be washed away by your
naval waves.

Maybe it is just karma trying to even
things out in the universe.
If that is the case,
Then why do I feel so UNEVEN, now that you
are not in my days?
Why do I feel incomplete,
Now that I don't get to kiss those heavenly
things you have where your lips should be?
Rumor has it,
That you may be riding a new love wave.
I never really loved triangles.

I should have paid more attention in math
class.
Then I probably would have been able to
solve,
Whatever the equation was, that would have
led to you staying.

For the record,
This is not a plea.
Nor is it a wish,
Wishing is for incompetent people.

This is definitely not a prayer,
But I did ask GOD.
And yes,
He modified the human prototype, just to
make your body
Maybe, that is why I can't get you out of
my mind.

Maybe, that is why my nerves are aching to touch you.
Maybe, that is why missing you lights fires of biblical proportions.
And where I am from, they don't get put out.
Fires consume.

That would explain,
My fascination with all these ungodly memories we made.

That is why you are running wild in my mind.
And I am running wild,
To find out what it is that you want,
So I can have it ready when you come back.
And I can break your back,
With these ungodly tricks I learnt, in my rum soaked nights.

It's obvious that you are missed.
I know parts of me that would tell you so,
If they could talk.
I know parts of you that would lead you to
my bed,
If they could walk.

I knew you would be hard to forget, from
the moment I met you.
I knew I was in trouble, when songs started
reminding me of you
I knew you were not a short story,
I have written plenty.

Here I am now, these waves thought have led
me here.
Four pages deep, after I had promised
myself to not write about you.
It is clearly, not going well.

There aren't that many emotions,
That I can say with certainty I haven't
felt,
This is one of them.

I am always on the other side of this.
No one has gotten to know me, and walked
away.
I am always the one doing the running.

You know me.
There isn't a lot that I fight for,
But this feels like a battle for my life.
I cannot let you go, because part of you is
me.

Your beauty has essentially colonized my
mind.
You have infected my heart and psyche, with
some kind of incurable sickness.
The breath-taking mental pictures of you,
have me gasping.

So maybe I should sit still and wait,
Wait for you to find your way back.
And maybe then, it will be permanent.
I will be permanent.

Nothing pleasures my heart more than waking
up next to you.
I know you remember.

Again, this is not a plea.
I just happened to taste something
beautiful, and I want another quenching
bite.

Maybe it is just karma,
But I need you back in my days.

I SEE/I HEAR.

I SEE/I HEAR

I see nature's sail,
I hear its yawning winds.
I am nature's love child,
Of careless birds and unbroken cycles.

I see society's sustained chants for
change,
I hear the haunting stories.
I am a failed social experiment,
Of death leading to life.

I see their smiling eyes,
I hear their mumbling voices.
I am my heartbeat,
Of unexplored chambers and empty vessels.

I hear the prayers of the saints,
I see most of their failing devotions.
I am a disciple of most of the fallen
angels,
Of Kamasutra and ungodly acts.

I hear the warning of the lonely faces,
I see how uncertain the path seems.
I am the captain of stumbling onwards,
Of still shivers and radical doubt.

I hear the promises of youth,
I see time undressing my flesh.
I am the audacity of unfulfilled potential,
Of wasted mornings and harsh realities.

I hear the whispers of my conscious,
I see most of its goodness eroded.

I am a naïve attempt to escape time,
Of fun dilemmas and a lot of bad decisions.

I hear the quiet beat of a mending heart,
I see unworthy memories flooding back.

I am the culmination of a few blurry
lustful encounters,
Of drunken texts and carry-on luggage.

I see the beginning of a beautiful story,
Still I chose to direct unhappy endings.

I WANNA BE YOURS.

(An ode to the song I wanna be yours by the Arctic Monkeys)

I WANNA BE YOURS

I wanna be yours.
I wish I was the light that pierces your
room every morning.
That way, I would be the first thing you
see when you wake up.

Let me be the coffee in your cup,
So I can start my day by tasting you.

I wanna be yours.
I wish I was your day,
So you could never go through life without
me.

Let me be the ending of your day,
I would always make you finish.

I wish I was the moon and the stars of your
sky,
I would illuminate even your darkest
nights.

I wish I was the sun,
All of your planets would revolve around
me.

Let me be your dreams,
So I can spend every night with you.

I wish I were your pain,
You would always feel me.

I wish I was the lotion you use,
So I can explore every inch of your body.

I wish I was your brain,
So I can always be thinking of you.

I wish I was your thoughts,
So I can always be inside you.

I wish I was an amusement park,
You would always find pleasure in riding
me.

Let me be your heart,
I can give you life.

I wish I were your tears,
Every time I left you would get some
relief.

I wish I was your lips,
I would always make you smile.

I want to be your enema,
So I can help you process all your shit.

I wish I was your surgeon,
So I can put your pieces back together.

Let me be the muscle in your bones,
I would be strong for the both of us.

I want to be your instincts,
You would have no choice but to trust me.

I wish I was a new language,
So you can learn me.

I wish I was your values,
You would always keep me.

I want to be your goals,
You would always think about what you would
do to me.

I wish I was your puzzle,
So, you could put my pieces back together.

Let me be the pills you take,
So I can be the one to take most of your
pain away.

I wish I was the dust in your hometown,
You would settle down with me.

I wish I was your JOB,
I would always work for your affections.

I wish I was the stain on your dress,
You would be stuck with me.

I wish I was your detergent,
I would wash most of your fears away.

Let me be the walls in your room,
I would always be around you.

I wish I was a light switch in your room,
You would always turn me on.

I wish I was the plant in your room,
You would always water me.

I wish I was the stairs in your house,
You would always climb me.

I wish I was your kitchen,
So I can possess everything that you crave.

Let me be your tortilla,
I would have you wrapped up in my warmth.

I wish I was your wine glass,
You would unwind with me every night.

I want to be your charger,
I would never leave you on at 1%.
I would keep you charged up on most nights.

I wish I was the keypad on your phone,
That way, you would never take your hands
off me.

I wish I was your social media,
You would always check up on me.

I wish I was your TV screen,
You wouldn't be able to take your eyes off
me.

I wish I was your favorite song,
So I can always be on your lips.

Let me be your bank account,
I will always support you.

I wish I was a sign,
So you could read me.

I wish I was I was a stop sign,
You wouldn't leave.

Let me be your seat belt,
I would hold you tight and keep you safe.

I wish I was the driver seat in your car,
You would always seat on me.

I wish I was the gas pedal,
So I can make you come fast.

I wish I was traffic,
You would be stuck with me.

Let me be your GPS,
I would always guide you.

I wish I was like the weather,
You would think about me before you decide
on what to wear.

I wish I was a cyclone,
I would sweep you away.

I wish I was death,
You would experience me.

Let me be your pen,
You would never put me down.
I would grace all of your pages.

I wish I was your favorite paint brush,
So you can always use me.

I wish I was your story,
You would always talk about me.

I wish I was your birthday,
You would never forget me.

Let me be your summer,
I have the HOTS for you.

I wish I was the GOOD bacteria in your
guts,
So can always live inside you.

I wish I was your soul,
You would never lose me.
I dreamed you up myself.

I wish I was your guardian angel,
I would never stop caressing your soul.

Let me be your guardian angel,
I wouldn't have to save you.

I wanna be yours.
I wish I were your SINS,
You would have no choice but to commit to
me.

I was never selfish until I met you.
You are scrumptious, and I wouldn't want to
share you.

WE CAN MAKE MAGIC
WITH THIS LUST.

WE CAN MAKE MAGIC WITH THIS LUST

For all have sinned, and fallen short of
the glory of God.
This is going to be one of those nights.

My mind is in the gutter tonight,
We can make magic with this LUST.

We can be the authors of this exciting
anthology,
A compilation of all the artistic, lustful
episodes.

I can't make out the senses,
Of all the people that walked through your
life.
They must have been immune to your charm.

I have waited for so long,
For your face to be a nose away from mine.
I have waited for so long,
For your moans to be the soundtracks of my
nights.

I listen to my heart,
But only the chamber that leads me to
pleasure.
I am chasing after this lust,
It has been calling my name.

My soul will finally get to meet you.
My hands will finally relieve this LUST.
My heart will finally have a genuine reason
to pound faster.

I put your body against the wall.
Gently, of course
Even though I know you like it rough,
I am a gentleman.

I have already undressed you in my mind,
So I will know my way around that temple.
I will know the places to touch.
Your weak spots will be my weakness.

My hands will explore you thoroughly like a
laser guided drone,
On a mission to explode in the magic of
this lust.

My hands will embark on an expedition,
That will get you to lay your armor down
and give in to these Christ-like passions.

I will surgically incise you with my sweet
nothings.
I will not stop or slow down until I see a
spike in your vital signs.

I have had multiple recurring dreams about
this very moment,
But my eyes are overcome by the beautiful
reality.

You have left me both breathless and
speechless.
You are stunningly beautiful.
Your naked body is a masterpiece.

My lips are itching to be introduced to
your breasts,
I want to kiss you from head to toe.
I want to dedicate my life to those
succulent lips,
I have been dying to taste you.

I can't wait to fall in love with the
warmth of being inside you.
We can make magic with this lust.

There is no weaning from this lust,
It is in therapeutic range.

I have replayed these lustful moments.
I am married to this dream.
It is not divorced from reality.

Throw yourself in the fire pit of this lust
I call my bed,
Allow the flames to combust and burn our
fiery hearts,
We can wallow in the ashes of this lust
till the morning.
We can make magic with this lust.

The tears on your pillow will be replaced
by cum stains.
We can't even blame the wine,
We are drunk in lust.

My eyes will finally get to witness your
pleasure face.
My mind will get to capture new dirty
mental pictures,
For its lust album.

My ears will finally get to be blessed, as
you whisper my name.
My hands will be busy adoring your every
curve.
My legendary ego will be polished in this
lust.

You were an irresistible temptation, that I
was destined to fall for.
You were a midnight trap that I gladly
walked into.
I thrive in the dark.

Your breaths and groans of ecstasy fill the
air while I fill you up.
I have been dying for you to sit on me.
For you to take this ride and take your
place atop this throne,
Like the queen you are.

Your ass will have wildly crafted
handprints.
Your heart will be at peace.
Your body will be in pieces.
I will tear you up,
I can't wait.

Let me shake your insides.
I will be all over you,
INTRAVENOUS.

I can't wait for you to experience the
orgasm-induced naps in my arms, and how
revitalizing that will be for your sleep
cycle.

We will make magic with this LUST.

SOMETIMES, SILENCE IS FIGHTING.

SOMETIMES, SILENCE IS FIGHTING

Sometimes, silence is being lost in the
orbit of confusion.
But sometimes there is peace in silence.
If I can relinquish most of the fear,
Maybe I will enjoy being in the company of
silence.

I have no illusions of grandeur,
I know you no longer live in my heart.
I know that in my silence,
I will be surviving the wreckage missing
you has caused.

Because of your silence,
I only made it halfway to your heart.
Sometimes, silence is remembering.

When I have no thoughts is when I remember.
When my brain is idle is when you creep in.
It is in my silence that questions bombard
my mind.

How do I choose the faces I let into my
life?

What criteria to use to let people go?
So that my mind isn't eroded any further.
So that I can keep my inner core intact.

I am perched in stillness, my mind lives a
daze.
My thoughts are as blank as the sky I gaze
upon.
I am transfixed on NOTHING.

Even in the midst of the night crowd,
Even with souls buzzing, mine is still.
Noise occupies the air but I hear nothing.
Eyes open but I don't see a thing.
Missing you is blinding and sometimes,
silence is waiting.

In my silence, my smile gets broken.
Silence is a drag.

Minutes seem painfully slower than usual,
Hours seem unnecessarily drawn out.
Every part of me is begging to be where you
are.

I am aching to see you,
So my eyes can smile again.
I am longing to hold you,
So my hands can live again.

I am waiting to hear that voice,
So my ears can breathe again,
But sometimes silence is hoping.

Hoping that my charm overpowers your
doubts,
So I can annex your mind.
And just maybe, I would be stuck there,
Just like you are stuck in mine.

You camp in my mind now
Thoughts of you reluctantly reside there
now
Your silence weakens my fight for your
affections.
Please don't dissipate from my *"Love-sight"*.

I never really liked hovering around.
My desire was to entice you to be mine,
To be right in the epicenter of my days.
But sometimes your silence was bruising,
I should have shown you THESE pages.

Sometimes, silence is just a better word
for ACHING.
I hate the uncertainty of cross-roads.
I wouldn't have been comfortable,
If I knew I only had you for a few nights.

I wouldn't have been swallowed by your
vortex
It was accidental.
I never thought you would be important to
me,
It was accidental.

I was swallowed by your vortex.
My lust was there for the taking.
I was hopelessly falling.

But in my defense,
Actually, I have no defense.
It was pathetic.
But anyone who has seen you naked would
understand.
It is in my silence, that I have these
devilish thoughts.

Your body was crafted by a team of angels.
And I think they applauded themselves when
they finished.
Either that or GOD was just showing off his
magnificence.

Yes,
My days have always been incomplete without
you.
I gave up fighting your gravitational pull.

Yes, I like pulling things.
Even RAPUNZEL finds happiness after having
her hair pulled.
Yes, I can pull out.
I have taken food out of the microwave
before [on time].

Yes, you can sit on my lap.
But my face is much, much more comfortable.

Yes, I have an addictive personality.
In my defence,
You taste like wild strawberries and I
warned you I have a sweet tooth.

But, you didn't want to fix me.
I was just wishing for a pause button and
sometimes, silence is just waiting.

I think I may have used way too many words,
In this attempt to describe this feeling,
Of whatever LOVE becomes when it gets a
PHD.
Silence reminds me of you.

Of course, I would be wounded if I lost
you.
I would lose me in the ruins leaving would
form.
I shouldn't have depended on your smiles,
To make my days memorable.

It may be too late,
I warned you that I have an addictive
personality.
I am addicted to you
Most dresses are.

Please delay your departure.
Let me taste you again.

Please don't flip this page,
Stay on this beautiful and confusing page
with me.
I see a future in those eyes, but I can
only hope in silence.

My inner core continues to endure through
all of this.
It remains intact.
It remains beautiful, just like I remember.
Goodness still permeates through it.
Sometimes, silence is fighting.

OPPOSITE MAN.

OPPOSITE MAN

I am the opposite of man.
Not GOD but only a semblance of his
imagination.

My DNA structure was either cursed, or
intended to be that way,
Both of those prospects are terrifying.
My nerve center continues to be mysterious,
It has the nerve to be triggered by all the
wrong emotions.

My eyes always gaze at the wrong faces,
My face is always misunderstood.
My heart is always on the opposite end of
love,
And I still don't know what the opposite of
love is.

My hands have a tendency to grasp at
nothing but lost causes.
My feet keep leading me down untrodden
paths,
My legs can barely keep up.

My lungs are longing for a breath of fresh
air.
My hair longs for a new start.
My stomach is always craving SOUL food.

My thoughts, at least most of them,
I keep bound in these pages.

My mouth always gets me into trouble.
My consciousness has been untraceable
lately.
My virtues are nameless but not countless.

I am the opposite of men,
My EGO is fragile.

My pain receptors are under repair.
My memory has a lot of scars.
I miss you, but I don't really remember
you.

My life was like a dream,
But LIFE also woke me up.
My life has come full cycle,
But I still haven't found myself.

I know karma is an eternal BITCH,
But she is also my mistress.

The pain receptors are still under repair,
For I am young and filled with fear.
My days unfold,
Soon I will be OLD and filled with repaired
parts.

I am in a constant state of more,
My present isn't good enough,
No present memory fully embraced,
I am always in the next moment,
But hindered by the remains of time.

I stray from society,
But I still don't know what the opposite of
opposite is.

My pain receptors are still work in
progress,
I missed all the classes on strength that
pain was teaching.
I thought it was an elective.

Like everyone else,
I ignored the lessons on wisdom that
history was giving,
I thought they would be repeated.

I have told many tales,
I know it's not normal to have it all,
Even your smile was temporary.

My senses would agree with you,
I should have asked you to stay.
Especially on those nights that I miss you.

I gladly scribbled my name on the very long
list,
Of great men who were side-tracked by
beautiful women.

I question answers, and I still don't know
what the opposite of healing is.
Everything started and ended in my bedroom.

I am the opposite of most men,
My prayers are recycled.
I always prayed for the same thing,
Just you.

But my prayers aren't very strong,
I am not sure they reach the skies.
I have some goodness in me.
Enough to be a saint, but I am mostly like
CAIN.

My senses have a long history of being
careless,
That's how I ended up with a black heart.

Maybe I will learn to settle someday.
Unfortunately, I come from a long line of
NOMADS.
I never cared for mortal things, except for
you.

Maybe I will someday recover from the
midlife crisis I had in my twenties.
But what if I don't.
My life pages keep unfolding,
But they are all blank.

What if the only reason you were falling is
because you are sloppy?
And what if I was only falling for hearts
that I couldn't manage?
What if my LOVE is like a cult?
But there's only you and me in it.

What if, our love was strong, but we did
not belong?
Lovers come and lovers go,
But what if my lamentations don't empty out
all of the tears?

What if I was all that you needed, but you
don't see what I see.
What if I never questioned these answers?
I still wouldn't know what the opposite of
opposite means.

I am the opposite of man.
I was a ghost,
I breezed through my childhood.

My childhood did not mold me,
I had to grow up, I had to.

The walls I tried to build are INCOMPLETE,
The maps to myself have been blurred by
change.
The maps to my world just got torched by my
guardian angel.

My muscles are weaning, weathered and
TIRED.
Life is presently taking its toll on me.

My nights have given me a lot of material.
My indecision has me SPIRALLING.
My dreams are flickering.
My book is still UNWRITTEN.
My pen has left a lot of words unused
My words are all I have
And I still don't know what the opposite of
not healing is.

WHAT LIES
WILL WE TELL???

WHAT LIES WILL WE TELL???

What lies will we tell to try to explain
Why we are the reason our planet is on
hospice.

We have filled its lungs with toxic smoke.
We are tearing unrepairable holes in the
atmosphere.
And just to highlight to the peak levels of
insanity,
That seem rampant in this backward
iteration of reality,
We are wasting time launching money into
space,
In search of other habitable planets while
ignoring the obvious restoration that the
earth is longing for.

What lies will we tell?
When we try to cowardly explain,
Why we have been treating our oceans even
worse than our sacred lands.
Like a stepchild,
Except that we saved our worst for it.

We have been having our way with it,
Spitting in its mouth,
Disposing our trash in its personal space,
How much disrespect can one body take?

It is bubbling with anger now.
One of these days it will spill over.
It will swallow us as pay back for what we
did to her children and that would be less
than what we deserve.

We have facilitated the planet's decay,
when our only mission was to be its
caregiver.
What lies will we tell to try to explain
Why we haven't been able to leave the
planet better than we found it?
Instead, we embarked on a demolition job
but earth just happens to be resilient.

How will we explain, just how disheartening
it is
That a large sub-section of the media
landscape,
Is designed, with a very clear and sinister
purpose,
To discredit the competency of reality.

What lies will we tell to deflect and to
justify why we haven't improved on the
human experience?

How will we rationalize all of these
churches?
But not enough people being saved.
How will excuse all of these religions?
But not enough lasting peace.

How will explain all of this wealth?
But not enough people doing well.

What lies will we tell to justify all of
this technology
While most people still have to work more
than 2 jobs.

We will probably craft the lies,
From the corrupt, smoky air we exist in.
We have become the masters of false
equivalences,
In this era that is being overrun by
shameless hypocrisy.

What lies will we tell to explain
Why we haven't been learning from history?
We are repeating the same mistakes, like a
bad sequel to an already awful movie.

We are still killing each other for the
same archaic reasons, as the people we
considered primitive.
At least they did not know any better.

What weak excuse will we use to explain
Why we don't have any worthwhile advice to
pass on especially if they chose to listen?
We still haven't figured out how love
works.

Families are more broken now.
There is a whole new generation growing up
fatherless and in incomplete homes.

What lies will we tell in an attempt to explain
Why we still struggle with the concept of caring?
We are emotionally damaging each other and calling it love.
Our capacity to love is dangerously low.

What lies will we tell to defend just how abysmal our grasp on race is?
We have barely found words appropriate enough to use when we talk about it.
We still allow it to divide us.

What lies will we tell to explain
Why we have weapons capable of destroying the entire planet but not enough money to feed every child.
What lies will we tell to defend
That we haven't been able to heal the millions whose bodies have been overwhelmed by sickness.

What lies will we tell to explain
Why there are billions of us, yet half of
us are lonely.

What lies will we tell to explain
All of these pills currently available but
there is still no remedy for happiness.
We keep looking for it in things instead of
each other

There isn't a drug strong enough to numb
you from this reality,
That would not leave you lifeless.
What lies will we tell to defend the people
in power who have successfully hidden
information about the world?
How it was? The genesis of most religions?
People have gone through great lengths to
rewrite the imperfections of history.

I used to believe in the world.
We are born naïve.
I believed it to be a machine of competency
and efficiency.
I have lived a little now,
That illusion has been permanently unveiled
as untrue.

What lies will we tell
When we try to rationalize to our
daughters,
Why we MEN are the leading cause of death,
For all these women we claim that we cannot
live without.

How will we explain evolution?
If we are truly evolving as time erodes us,
Then why do we still hate, people who love
different than us.

We still kill,
People who pray to a different god than
ours.

We still look down on,
People who speak a different language to
ours.
We still hold steadfast opinions,
On topics we don't really full understand.

What lies will we tell to defend our so-
called leaders?
I use the word leaders, very loosely.
They are not worthy of that title.
They are mostly just useful puppets in
2019.

They are literally breathing life to the
narrative,
That nothing needs to fundamentally change.
They are preaching that there is nothing
wrong,
With this system and all these theories
that have led us to this critical, bizarre
timeline.

These so-called leaders claim that we
should be realistic.
Even in our hopes and especially in our
dreams.
Their motto is better things are not
possible.

The only ballot issue that is bi-partisan,
and in which the leaders are unified on are
tax cuts for multi-national corporations
and the wealthy.

What lies will we tell when we try to
justify
Why we haven't changed that much.

The bodies of unarmed black men are still
lying on unpaved streets.
They are still waiting, impatiently,
For any one of the police who were meant to
protect them,
To be convicted of anything.

There will be justice, but only if you can
afford it.

Our planet is on hospice because we are
addicted to cash.
It needs some TLC or CPR, but we are doing
the opposite.
We are actively stomping on its chest,
While it is gasping for its last breath.

We set the planet on fire.
Splashed gallons of gasoline on it.
We stopped making fire extinguishers.
Banned firefighters.
Pretended that the fires wouldn't be too
destructive.

You can't even have a conversation about
the fire, without being frowned upon.
We claimed that since other people are also
playing with the same fire,
We would only attempt to control the fumes,
when or if the others did the same too.
We watched the fire consume most of what we
consider beautiful and melt away most of
the ice we would have needed for the
cooling.

What lies will we tell to justify the
inaction?
As if we could survive any battle against
nature.
We will be rendered extinct, and the planet
will not miss us.

*T*aking
TRAUMA
out of Teen
Transitions

Larry Anderson

A MINISTRY OF THE NAVIGATORS
P.O.BOX 35001, COLORADO SPRINGS, CO 80935

The Navigators is an international Christian organization. Jesus Christ gave His followers the Great Commission to go and make disciples (Matthew 28:19). The aim of The Navigators is to help fulfill that commission by multiplying laborers for Christ in every nation.

NavPress is the publishing ministry of The Navigators. NavPress publications are tools to help Christians grow. Although publications alone cannot make disciples or change lives, they can help believers learn biblical discipleship, and apply what they learn to their lives and ministries.

Library of Congress Catalog Card Number: 91-61421
ISBN 08910-96353

Second printing, 1992

Cover illustration: Dan Pegoda

Some of the anecodotal illustrations in this book are true to life and are included with the permission of the persons involved. All other illustrations are composites of real situations, and any resemblance to people living or dead is coincidental.

Printed in the United States of America

FOR A FREE CATALOG OF
NAVPRESS BOOKS & BIBLE STUDIES,
CALL TOLL FREE 1-800-366-7788 (USA)
or 1-416-499-4615 (CANADA)

Contents

To my wife, Gina,
who brings such grace and hope
to each of life's transitions.
And to my three sons,
Caleb, Joshua, and Aaron,
who have given me the privilege
of walking through life with them.

Foreword

Even the strongest of us tends to get weak-kneed when it comes to certain transitions . . . from carefree student to full-time work responsibilities, from no kids to twins, from a sprawling home in the country to a squashed apartment in the city, from great health to hearing the doctor diagnose a serious condition.

None of us can avoid transitions in our lives, but during the teenage years, young men and women are often terrorized by them.

Almost without exception, we all go through more personal, relational, and societal transitions during the teen years than at any other time in our lives. From childhood to being young adults, from throwing rocks at girls to thinking about marrying them, from majoring in playground to picking a major in college. During these years most of us will make the decision of who our Master is, what our mission in life is, and what methods will get us there.

These are huge transitions! Many of which can set the course of a person's life. Without exception, before our children reach their twenties, they will either be enriched or defeated by how they face these twists and turns in their personal road map.

The task of preparing children to face transitions is one of the most important things any parent can do, but most of us need help in dealing with these turning points ourselves!

That's why I'm glad you picked up this book. When we drive into a large, unfamiliar city, it's great to have a road map. But it's even better to have a personal guide take us by the hand—past all the road construction, one-way streets, and detours—bringing us and our children safely to our destination.

When it comes to the subject of this book, Larry Anderson is just such a guide. He is a nationally respected expert on youth issues, having helped hundreds of teenagers *and adults* take the word *trauma* out of transitions. And he can do that for you in this book.

The Marines teach you to dig your fighting hole big enough for two people. That's because, when the battle comes, it's better to face that trial with a buddy next to you. In even the best of homes, times of transitions can often create a battle-zone atmosphere between parent and child. In all my exposure to youth workers across the country over the years, I can't think of a better, more qualified person to help you and your child win the day than Larry Anderson.

I hope you'll pause and linger over the words and stories in this book. The wise counsel you'll find here will not only help you face the changes your child is going through, but better prepare you to honor God through the transitions you'll face as well.

I'm honored to write this foreword and endorsement for this book, and trust you'll find it to be as helpful and valuable a resource as my wife and I have.

—JOHN TRENT, PH.D.

Acknowledgments

When one of my oldest and dearest friends, Dan Peddie, introduced me to Steve Webb, of NavPress, I had just about given up the idea of writing this book. From there Steve not only became a great editor but a good friend as well. As this book is prepared to be released I want to acknowledge a number of people who have influenced its production. First, I would like to thank Steve for his enthusiasm and support throughout the process of writing this book. He has lent great professional support and skill to a nervous, first-time author.

I would like to express my appreciation to John Trent, who initially challenged me to write a book like this. Without John's support and wisdom, this book would not have gotten off the ground. After John convinced me to go forward on this, he, Tim Kimmel, and Steve Lyon storyboarded the original book concept with me.

I am appreciative of the support of the Young Life family

for their collective support and wisdom over the last sixteen years. Many of the concepts proposed in this book are a result of some great mentors throughout Young Life. I want to especially acknowledge my appreciation to Bob Krulish, my "boss," for allowing me to pursue the completion of this book.

I really thought my first book would be in collaboration with my mother. I had decided that the title should be *Kitchen Table Psychology* for all the wisdom that both my mother, Billie Anderson, and my father, the Rev. Tommy Anderson, supplied me with as parents and continue to supply as parents and grandparents.

I am indebted to the wisdom and the work done by Brennan Manning and Tim Hansel, among others, who are quoted throughout the book. Their winsome style of writing and their personal encouragement has been both helpful and inspirational to me.

Next, a special thanks to Renee McKenzie, who runs the regional office out of our home. Her extra administrative support and computer expertise has been valuable.

Finally, to my wife, Gina, who is an untiring supporter and fan, and to my three sons, Caleb, Joshua, and Aaron, who make life so fun and provide great tests for Dad's theories, thanks, I love you.

• • • • • • • • • • •

CHAPTER ONE

The Trauma of Transition

It was May, and the Arizona sun was typically hot as I wheeled my little Nissan toward the church. But even the sun's piercing heat could not thaw the chill I felt in my heart. As I drove, my thoughts were clouded by doubt and a feeling of failure. Another young person had made the tragic decision that life was not worth living.

Kit came to Young Life all through high school. He went to camp with us and regularly attended our Bible studies. We were good friends. He was such a likable guy. He breezed through high school appearing to enjoy every minute. Somehow, though, after graduation he was unable to make a successful transition to early adulthood and dropped out of college without telling his parents. On the day he should have been graduating he took his life. Without the courage to face his family he chose a harsh and permanent way out of his trauma.

Now I was driving to Kit's funeral feeling pain over his

death and guilt that maybe I could have done more. I knew he was attending a good church and seemed to have some Christian friends there. I continued to play the tape of our relationship over and over in my mind, always searching for a clue to Kit's actions that I was not so sure I wanted to find.

Young people like Kit are not unusual today. Many are unable to contend with the various directions life takes as they grow up. Without the tools to make good decisions they turn to harmful alternatives like drug and alcohol abuse, partying, and sex. They often lash out at their parents or society, looking for someone to blame, or they withdraw because they are afraid to face perceived failure.

My eyes began to glisten and my sight blurred as I caught sight of the book the pastor was holding as he led the service. It was the Bible I had given Kit early in our friendship. As he opened the Bible he began to comment on verses that Kit had underlined. Verses of hope and direction, words of life and joy.

My tears were flowing freely as I fought for understanding in the midst of tragic circumstances. I knew that committing my life to youthwork would mean days like this. I have counseled with many young people from junior high to beyond college who were confused by the changes they were experiencing in their young lives. I have sat with broken-hearted parents lamenting the choices their children had made. Many of these were good and conscientious moms and dads who dearly loved their kids.

As boys and girls approach middle school or junior high, a mysterious metamorphosis begins. Their hormones go into high gear and as their bodies experience enormous change a search begins for two things: *identity* and *independence*.

Mostly, we see the struggle for identity in the way young teens dress and try to "fit in." They can be moody and belligerent. They are children growing up in a culture moving so fast it threatens any sense of stability in their lives. Teenagers' need for acceptance is a natural drive and one that everyone must face. They have been loved by their parents; now they feel the need to be accepted by the world.

In the midst of this, just when many parents would love to shelter and protect them, teenagers begin to pull away. They need some space from their parents. They need to experiment with being on their own. This independence often surprises parents and can leave them somewhere between bewildered and hurt.

As the young person approaches high school, the search for identity and independence becomes more social. I once heard a sociologist claim that high school created a mini-society where a small percentage succeeded and everyone else spent the rest of their lives making up for it. If you doubt how powerful these years are in the life of your child, take a moment to reflect on your own high school experience. Were those years wonderful—full of achievement and popularity—or are your memories a painful and grim reminder of what you dreamed of being but were not?

Perhaps this exercise of memory seems to oversimplify things, but such reflection is intended to provide clues to the transitions your own young people must face during the teen years.

College is a good example. The college years represent the final transition from childhood to adulthood. Unfortunately, this transition is too often only symbolic. In many ways college students, or young people of college age, are the most hard pressed. They know they are approaching a time when they must take on adult responsibilities. The wild parties and recklessness often associated with these years represent either a last fling at childhood with its lack of responsibility, or rebellion at the notion that as young adults they are being forced to grow up. Today, this is often carried over into adulthood in the fast-paced, get-rich-quick attitude of so many young folks just starting out.

I couldn't fathom the tunnel Kit had stumbled into or comprehend how he had gotten so lost. I had served as a compass for a part of his journey. But, in the end, he chose his own route. When Kit had realized he had taken a wrong turn so soon on his life journey, he was afraid to stop and ask for directions. Unable to face the consequences of his decision, he got out.

Perhaps I was too consumed with my own sense of failure. As I sat on the smooth, varnished pew I felt rough and tarnished. My thoughts strayed to how others more capable, or more spiritual, might have changed the course of Kit's life. This is always the game we play. Someone else could have done it better. He or she would have prayed more, had the right words to say, appeared at just the right moments. I wondered how many more Kits I would come in contact with in days and years to come. I wondered how many parents would feel the same sense of failure.

I was startled out of my reflections when the pastor began to speak. At that point in the funeral service he gave me a great gift. He spoke with fondness of the change and impact that Young Life had on Kit and read from the Bible I had given Kit—words of hope Kit had marked during our studies together. Then he said, "The only problem was that Kit didn't wait for God to fulfill His promises." Waiting isn't easy for young people. Yet waiting is part of learning to deal with life's inevitable transitions. And none of us deals effectively with change all of the time.

I realized then that the pastor and I were a team. We had not made an official agreement, but nevertheless we were on the same team, with the same hopes and goals and prayers for young folks like Kit. Now he was supporting me in the same way both of us had sought to support Kit. Sometimes it is crucial to know that we do not battle alone.

TOOLS FOR TEEN TRANSITIONS ARE AVAILABLE

As a parent I have a strong desire to give my children the tools they need to face the transitions of adolescence and early adult life. But as someone who has been in youth ministry all of my adult life, I also have a strong desire to see parents and their kids develop a strong *team* to support and guide them through the tricky and often perilous times in their teenagers' lives.

Too many young people race through their early years unaware and tragically unprepared to deal in healthy ways with the *inevitable* changes they must face. Suddenly, they find themselves in previously uncharted waters with no navigational system and no anchor. They are adrift in a sea of change with no land or hope in sight. These are not necessarily young people from bad homes with difficult lives. Even for successful children from the best of families, the current of transition can carry them to perilous waters. Many will not stay afloat.

Life is never static. It is always changing, moving forward, dynamic. How many times have we as adults felt like screaming, "Stop the world and let me off!"? But time will not stop. No matter how we attempt to alter it or simply slow it down, it marches on. We cannot shield our children from change, therefore we must prepare them for it.

We really have only two options. We either prepare ourselves and our kids for the inevitabilities of transition and the march of time, or we watch as we and our children are pushed, jostled, and occasionally trampled as life surges ahead.

Transitions are points in our journey where we pass from one phase to another. In a novel, transitions can make the story easy to read and enjoyable; poorly done, they render the book choppy and hard to follow. The same is true in our lives and in the lives of young people. The passage of each phase of adolescence can have a lot to do with whether they experience success or failure handling change as adults.

As a high schooler, Kit hadn't anticipated the need to know how to face transition. He had never considered the impact time and change would have on him. When the reality of his choices finally caught up to him, he lost all hope and in his own way he struck back. He wasn't prepared for failure and couldn't bring himself to ask for help.

This is not a book of pat answers and easy antidotes. Nor is it a scientific experiment. I really hope to accomplish two major tasks. First, I want to share what I have observed and learned through years of walking the passages of adolescence and young adult life with hundreds of kids and their parents. And second, I'd like to help draw you closer to the One who desires to reveal Himself in the midst of the storms and changing tides of our lives. He is the One who gives comfort and hope. For He enables us to navigate the perilous waters of transition.

Deeply imbedded in the lines of this book is the conviction that the closer we walk to the heart of Christ, the more we experience His love and mercy—and the more we are able to dispense such love during the tides of change in our families.

To hear of the birth of Christ and then learn of His resurrection is a wonderful thing. Those two events changed the course of human history. Yet, without the stories of His life from childhood through the cross, the account is woefully incomplete. We see something of Jesus' passage from childhood to adulthood when we read of Him as a boy in the Temple courts asking the rabbis questions (Luke 2:41-49). We are filled with wonder when we think of what this event must have meant to Mary and Joseph as they began to glimpse the change that was about to hit their lives.

Another critical transition comes in John 2. A wedding celebration Jesus and His mother were attending was about to come to an abrupt end because of an exhausted wine supply, and Mary began to sense in her heart that maybe this was the moment Jesus would be catapulted into public ministry. Up to this point He had quietly begun to gather disciples and teach in the synagogue. But, if He now did what His mother asked Him to do, His life would never be the same. He would become a miracle worker, a hero, a religious celebrity.

One must wonder if Jesus paused a moment there. This miracle would start in motion a chain of events that would eventually lead Him to the cross. One must also wonder how Mary had perceived that this indeed was the time of a significant transition for her Son.

What a moment!

It is one thing to read the words describing the miracle Jesus performed that day. It is altogether different to try to grasp the significance of this transition in the life of our Savior and the role Mary played in recognizing the necessary turn of events. When He was a child she had protected Him from perceived dangers, now she could not protect Him from the inevitable—the Father's plan.

In a similar sense, we must realize there is no way to protect our children from change. They must eventually face the realities of their growing up, as must we. But we all desire to walk through the phases of our lives with less surprise, less fear, and less sense of failure.

This is a book about growth, about the realization that growing pains are as much a part of maturing as are lost love or lost security. It is about dealing with the trauma of these inevitable teenage transitions.

THE TRANSITION TEAM

In an election year the first place the president-elect turns his focus is to his transition team. The team's job is to make sure the new president has as smooth a transition as possible. They scout ahead for potential disaster, help him choose his administrative team, make sure he shakes the right hands and speaks to the right people, and in general, assure the public they made the right choice. How well the team members do their job will have great impact on how well the president makes the transition to his new role and responsibility.

Perhaps a team like this is exactly what Kit, or his parents, needed. In the following chapters we will be assembling your team. It is my prayer that these tools will provide help and confidence for you parents as you sail the often-troubled sea of transition with your children on their voyage to adulthood.

• • • • • • • • • • •

CHAPTER TWO

Teen Passages

"There is no reason for you to be embarrassed about S-E-X," I told my daughter. "Sit down and I will tell you all I know about it. First, Lassie is a girl. Second, I lied. Sensuous lips do not mean fever blisters. Third, I did not conceive you by drinking the blood of an owl and spitting three times at a full moon. Here is the bra and girdle section from the Sears catalogue. If you have any questions, keep them to yourself."

ERMA BOMBECK

I n this chapter we explore the various stages of adolescent development. This will give you a framework by which you can view the transitions your son or daughter will face.

Each of us has had to deal with the changes between childhood and adulthood. We challenged the ideas of our childhood and stretched the patience and wisdom of our parents. To say that adolescence is a complex time for parents and children often seems like an understatement. The period of adolescence is not static. It will begin earlier for some children than others. It will be more painful for some than others. But, it is a pivotal time in children's lives, and how they handle it is directly linked to whether their adult development is healthy or not.

THE TWO PHASES OF ADOLESCENCE

For our examination of the adolescent experience we will break the broader period of adolescence into two primary categories. The first is *early adolescence*, those years generally associated with junior high school and running from age ten through age fifteen. The second phase we will call *late adolescence*, which approximately corresponds to the senior high and college years, or ages sixteen to twenty-two. Because the time and intensity of adolescence will vary with every child, it is difficult to be more specific. But these two divisions of adolescence are widely adhered to by experts in sociology, psychology, and education.

Early Adolescence

"Adolescence" comes from the Latin verb *adolescere*, which means "to grow," or "to grow to maturity." While we may be most conscious of the physical changes in our children during early adolescence, this transition in their young lives is far more radical than mere physical change. To aid us in our discussion of this period, we will look at the two most dramatic types of change of the *early adolescent* period: *physical* and *emotional*.

Physical: The Great Awakening. Generally, the first thing that comes to mind when parents think of early adolescence is puberty. That is when we brace ourselves for everything in our family to come unglued. Puberty may be a prelude to confusion and disarray in your home, but that is not always the case.

It is difficult to predict the beginning or the end of the pubertal process. There is about a *six-to-seven-year* range in both boys and girls for both pubescence and puberty. *Pubescence* is the stage of physical growth marked by the maturation of reproductive functions and the primary sex organs and by the appearance of secondary sex characteristics (breasts, pubic hair, changes in voice and skin, and so on). Pubescence lasts about two years and ends in *puberty*, the point at which a person is sexually able to reproduce—and the time of life when the greatest sexual differentiation since the prenatal stage takes place.[1]

Judith suddenly seems glued to a mirror. She is always looking at herself with a critical yet curious eye. For the first time she is recognizing the new contours of her body, and while she is entranced by her body in private, she is very nervous and self-conscious in public.

Many young girls who mature quickly experience a time of insecurity. They may feel conspicuous and out of place among their peers. Parents and teachers may treat them differently, even appear as if they disapprove of the way they look. This can be a very trying, but productive experience for young women as they learn to face differences and challenges for later life.

The same is true for young boys. While sometimes it is fun for them to "look older" than their peers, often they are not mature enough to handle the expectations resulting from their mature appearance. It has been my experience that the "late bloomer" often develops better coping skills as an adult because of the challenges of early adolescence.

Emotional: A Roller Coaster Ride. Adolescence is a period of tremendous emotional upheaval. Transition and change are challenging for any of us, but for a young teenager experiencing the emotional challenges of adolescence, they can be even more difficult.

Here is a list of some of the most prominent causes of emotional tension in teens:

- Coping with physical change
- Setting aside childhood habits
- Lack of social (adult) skills
- Dealing with the opposite sex
- Family stability (or lack of)
- Environmental changes (moving, new schools, new church)
- Failure in school
- Parental conflict (stretching old boundaries)
- Moving from dependence to independence

Any or all of these emotional challenges are bound to bring behavioral consequences with them. Often this is a result of teens' feelings of insecurity and fear.

Here are some of the typical behavioral side effects:

- Aggressiveness
- Self-consciousness and ego-centeredness
- Withdrawal from others
- Aloofness
- False courage (macho)
- Moodiness
- Daydreaming
- Sudden outbursts
- Irritability
- Demandingness
- Materialistic

In *early adolescence* each child experiences these emotions differently and at various times. There is a great deal of moving back and forth. One moment your teen will seem grown-up and you have a feeling of a job well done, then the next moment you will be wondering if that teen will ever grow up. But as we will see, the challenge continues into *late adolescence*.

LATE ADOLESCENCE

While physical maturity and emotional stability are still issues among older teens, two other transitional developments often rush to the forefront: *intellectual development* and *identity*.

Intellectual Development. When a young child is told that his father is no longer going to live with the family, many times he will assume it was because he was bad. This is because children are *concrete thinkers*. They take everything at face value. Teenagers going through *late adolescence* have developed the ability to think *abstractly* to the point where they can weigh various bits of information and draw an independent conclusion regarding the situation.

Developing this skill allows teenagers to take information gathered in the past and apply it to current situations. Young people are therefore capable of hypothetical-deductive reasoning.

Egocentrism. Experts believe that this new ability to reason in adolescence brings with it a unique sort of egocentrism. The teenager begins to act as if others are as preoccupied with her behavior as she herself is.[2]

Although teens are rarely aware of this egocentrism, they act out their need for being "center stage" in numerous ways. Romantic interests, conformity to peers, and even peer relationships can be part of this new attention-getting style. Part of this transition for teens relates to the discovery of *ideals*. This new thinking can inspire and repulse adults. It is a mode of thinking that often forsakes the practical for the adventurous and romantic.

David Elkind describes some adolescent behaviors behind this new thinking:

- Finding fault with authority figures
- Argumentativeness
- Self-consciousness
- Self-centeredness
- Indecisiveness
- Apparent hypocrisy[3]

Parents must view these behaviors as natural and consistent with all adolescent development. This does not mean unacceptable behavior should simply be tolerated in the home, but knowing that these behaviors are generally part of the growth process will help parents take a more objective view of their teen.

Identity. As teenagers begin to view themselves from this new vantage point, a search for identity begins. Ideals often begin to emerge. Teens begin to wonder how their lives can really count in the world. By now they have established some personal views of success and fulfillment.

The entire adolescent period is one of great influence. We often call them "wet cement" years because adolescents are formulating so many views about life. The battle to mold these young minds and hearts is a fierce one. The competition is tough.

One way kids discover who they are is by what Elkind calls *markers*.

Markers are external signs of where we stand, in Kierkegaard's lovely phrase, in "the stages on life's way." Markers can be as simple as the pencil lines on the kitchen wall that mark a child's progress in height from birthday to birthday, or as complex as a well-deserved promotion after years of hard work and dedication. Markers are signs of progress to others as well as to ourselves.

We all have a "sense of becoming," of growing and changing as individuals. Markers confirm us in our sense of growing and changing.

Giving up old markers also helps the young person become aware of his or her progress toward maturity. There is a direct parallel between the child of six or seven who says, "I don't believe in Santa Claus anymore," and the car-driving sixteen-year-old who says, "I don't ride bikes anymore." In both cases there is a pride in a new accomplishment and in a certain disdain for an earlier skill marker that is now seen as part of a period one has left behind.[4]

If as parents we work hard to recognize the markers in our children's lives, and allow them the privilege to move from one to another, we will help our kids stay on target and give them a better chance to make good decisions.

It is easy for parents, especially fathers, to become emo-tionally distant or separated from their teenagers. Busy with careers and adult activities, moms and dads often continue to think of their children as just that—children. Sometimes this means thinking of them as still six instead of sixteen; at other times it means comparing them when they hit age eighteen to themselves at that age.

But times have changed and so have kids. They have been exposed to more of the world than we were at the same age. They have more choices to make in school than we did. Sex is an open topic, and drugs and alcohol influence every campus.

While they seem less ready to accept responsibility over-all, they are more aware of what adult life is like socially. They have been tutored by the media on all the vices avail-able to the adult, and each lesson is pushed by handsome men and beautiful women eager to get them to try these vices out.

If parents are not able to communicate with their chil-dren during this time, it can be a crushing blow for both. For parents it generates a great sense of failure, for kids, a sense of frustration and alienation.

Complicating late adolescence is a strong sense of ideal-ism in young people. Whether they live it out or not, they have a strong sense of justice and right and wrong. This idealism comes from a new view of the hurt and injustice in the world. They become aware that half the world goes to bed hungry every night. While it may not slow down their junk-food habits, it may cause them to criticize their parents for tossing those leftovers when so many are starving.

Often they are very judgmental. This can hurt parents and at times make us angry. Yet of all the generations of parents, we should be the most sympathetic to this phase of growing up. All of us are at least aware of the upheaval of the sixties. The riots and student protests of that era were led by some of you reading this book. Materialism was *out* and all adults, especially parents, were not to be trusted. The lesson we learned in the eighties is that idealism without truth never leads to lasting change. The famous protesters of the sixties became the ravenous consumers of the eighties. If the music of the sixties was protest songs, the sound of the eighties carried a beat that could be exercised to by all those graying hippies seeking youthful bodies again.

Young adults want answers—now! Patience is not very high on their list of virtues. They spurn the well-worn solutions offered by their parents and seek the truth for themselves.

To make matters worse, the questions and struggles of our kids during late adolescence sometimes bring to the surface unresolved issues of our past. We are imperfect people. Recognizing and accepting the gaps in our own lives will make us more tolerant toward our children.

Yet, one of the great gifts of adolescent idealism is that adolescents will not be comfortable with our "brand" of religion if they sense it is not real in us or impacting the world. They will push us to examine our own relationship to Christ. I have seen many families renewed in Christ because of their teenager's witness.

ONE TEEN'S WITNESS

In the desert, surrounded by the affluence and luxury of Scottsdale, Arizona, two lonely people lived in a rented shack. Some college-age volunteer leaders for Young Life noticed Fritz's loneliness. They could not articulate his needs scientifically or academically; they simply saw a young person in need. As Fritz slowly got involved in the Young Life program he began to discover a place of acceptance and nurture. He loved the meetings and the leaders who showed such kindness toward him. He responded to virtually every opportunity for camps and outings, always learning afresh that this was a place he belonged. Acceptance wasn't an issue with these friends, it was a given. Soon Fritz had given his life to Christ and was committed to weekly Bible studies.

As the leaders talked one evening, the subject of Fritz came up. They were all encouraged by the growth they saw in his life, yet there was a nagging feeling that something more was needed. Their sense of justice and their energy for doing it was still in high gear. They discussed numerous possibilities and finally came to a conviction that Fritz now needed a dentist to complete the metamorphosis occurring in his life.

They approached a sympathetic orthodontist, who agreed to greatly discount the cost of the dental work. Some parents, hearing what these young people had in mind, chipped in on the bill. The next time I saw Fritz he gave me a wide smile showing off his new braces. He was proud of the hardware in his mouth. It represented a significant step in his life. Those braces would be a marker he would always look back to.

On a Sunday morning a few months later, our pastor asked if anyone there would like someone to pray with him or her to find Christ. I noticed two hands in the front row go up. To my surprise one hand belonged to Fritz and the other to a gray-haired gentleman next to him. It didn't take me long to figure out who the man was. He was Fritz's dad.

As I made my way toward the front of the church to stand with them, I couldn't help but consider the events that had led to this moment. Fritz had experienced the love of Christ through a group of young volunteers. He had discovered the identity and acceptance that had long eluded him. Now that he had some clear markers to guide his way he had found another important one. He had moved from follower to leader. His father, overwhelmed and intrigued by the changes in his son, had agreed to visit church with him The Spirit of God did the rest.

CONFLICT

Conflict is an inevitable part of adolescence. As teenagers begin to develop their reasoning skills, they will look for opportunities to make decisions on their own. They will challenge our values and take an idealistic approach to our practical advice. While conflict generally escalates during *early adolescence*, it is often not until later that parents suddenly think the disagreeing will never end.

Most arguments between parents and their adolescents focus on normal, everyday goings-on, such as schoolwork, social life, peers, home chores, disobedience, sibling fights, and personal hygiene.[5] Within some normal range, then, conflict with parents may be psychologically healthy for the adolescent's development. A virtually conflict-free relationship may indicate that an adolescent has a fear of separation, exploration, and independence.[6]

It is important to remember the impact of youthful idealism on the world. Much is done because of adolescents' convictions and zeal. They challenge old ideas and force us to defend or discard our positions. In that way, they are good for us, and we must allow reasonable room for them to grow and think for themselves. Listen to General Douglas MacArthur's thought on this.

Youth is not a period of time. It is a state of mind,
a result of the will, a quality of the imagination, a
victory of courage over timidity, of the taste of adven-
ture over the love of comfort. A man doesn't grow old
when he deserts his ideal. The years may wrinkle
his skin, but deserting his ideal wrinkles his soul.
Preoccupations, fears, doubts, and despair are the
dust before death. You will remain young as long as
you are open to what is beautiful, good, and great;
receptive to the messages of other men and women,
of nature and of God. If one day you should become

bitter, pessimistic, and gnawed by despair, may God have mercy on your old man's soul.[7]

HIGH SCHOOL

One parenting expert says this about high school: "High School is the central organizing experience in most adolescents' intellectual lives. It offers basic day-to-day learning, a preview of career choices, and opportunities to participate in sports and get together with friends."[8]

This prime social and academic environment is where many of the adolescent transitions blend together. In high school, puberty, abstract thinking, independence, and identity all merge in the teenager. You may well see many of the behaviors associated with adolescence in your child at this point. At the same time, there are some important decisions being made. As most young people begin to think about college and careers, they are forced to ask, "Who am I going to be?" and "What am I going to do?"

I think today we have allowed too much focus to land on "Who will I *look* like I am?" There has been so much emphasis on having money, cars, nice homes, and spectacular vacations that teens are often more concerned about finding a job that will net them a desired lifestyle than they are about living a productive and fulfilling life. While it is obviously true that both fulfillment and financial reward can be attained together, the wrong focus can keep teens from taking a realistic view of what they should get out of life.

My son Josh is in elementary school. He wants to be a pro football player someday. There is very little doubt in his mind about his chances. The elementary school years are generally the fantasy period. My son Caleb is in his junior high school years. He often rebukes Josh for his optimism about a future in football. Caleb would love to play pro basketball someday, but he has begun to admit it may not happen. He is in his tentative period. Before they graduate from college they should move into the realistic period and begin to look seriously and realistically at what they want to do with their lives. In my opinion, the media blitz on young consumers, increased foreign competition that impacts jobs and services, and the frantic rush for financial success in the 1980s has caused many young people to avoid this realistic period. For many the "appearance" of success has blurred their view of fulfillment, the establishment of realistic goals, and the notion of God's call—the most important element in anyone's vocational outlook.

WORK—AN OPTIONAL TEEN TRANSITION

More young people are working today than ever before. While there are a number of positive aspects to this, there is a down side as well.

On the positive side, working can influence your teen's self-image. It can help the teen develop some independence, time management, and a positive attitude about work and authority. If the manager or employer is willing to give thorough training and be sensitive to a teen's other responsibilities (such as family time), working can be a rewarding experience.

In a survey of high school seniors, three out of four had some kind of job income. But on a negative note, the same survey showed that tenth graders who worked more than fourteen hours per week suffered a drop in grades. A similar drop was found among eleventh graders who worked more than twenty hours per week.[9]

DEVELOPMENTAL TASKS

Every culture makes certain expectations of those who are to be considered adults. Certain tasks should be learned if a person is to function adequately in our society. During the adolescent years, the following skills should be developed:

1. Achieving new and more mature relations with age-mates of both sexes;
2. Achieving a masculine or feminine social role;
3. Accepting one's own physique and using the body effectively;
4. Achieving emotional independence of parents and other adults;
5. Achieving assurance of economic independence;
6. Selecting and preparing for an occupation;
7. Preparing for marriage and family life;
8. Developing intellectual skills and concepts necessary for civic obedience;
9. Desiring and achieving socially responsible behavior; and
10. Acquiring a set of values and an ethical system as a guide to behavior.[10]

Helping your teen acquire these skills is a big job. You'll need every member of your *transition team* to help you and your child through this important passage. It is also critical to keep in mind that the adolescent period will go to at least age twenty-two and sometimes later. If your eighteen-year-old has not mastered all of these skills yet, don't start worrying that he or she will never grow up. As we learn to understand the various stages of adolescent development and discover how to make our transition team work, we will find the whole process less intimidating and more enjoyable.

SPIRITUAL DEVELOPMENT

Often as we raise our teenagers the most frightening thought is that they might not choose to follow Christ. The idea of them rejecting something we hold so dearly is a painful thought. But the fact is, teens must "choose" whom they will follow. It is not a decision we can make for them. I am encouraged by Kevin Huggins when he says,

I believe God is at work in kids' hearts. And I believe He is summoning them to nothing less than a life of servanthood for Him. My goal is to provide the kind of environment in the relationship and responses I offer kids that makes them both aware of and accountable for why they do the things they do. When my strategy majors on getting them to just change their behavior to get out of trouble, or just change their circumstances to get out of pain, then I am actually making it easier for them to enter adulthood without grappling with the main issue of life: *Who are they* intending to serve through their actions?[11]

Most people in youth ministry agree that the adolescent years are when kids are most open to committing their lives to Christ. They may challenge the "religion" of their parents and even complain about our "old-fashioned" values, but they are still looking for truth and their hearts are hungry for a sense of wholeness and love. We must give our teens the freedom to choose, while we provide an environment that encourages them toward Christ.

The adolescent period is complex and challenging. There are many points along the way where things can go wrong. But if we can begin to prepare ourselves for what is ahead, we can help our kids set a course for a productive and useful adult life.

From Brennan Manning's book *The Ragamuffin Gospel* come these words from the Indian poet Tagore:

No, it is not yours to open buds into blossom.
Shake the bud, strike,
    it is beyond your power to make it blossom.
Your touch soils it.
You tear its petal to pieces
    and strew them in the dust,
But no colors appear and no perfume.

Oh, it is not for you to open the bud into blossom.
He who can open the bud does it so simply.
He gives it a glance and the life sap stirs
      through its veins.
At his breath the flower spreads its wings
      and flutters in the wind.
Colors flash out like heart longing,
      the perfume betrays a sweet secret.
He who can open the bud does it so simply.[12]

• • • • • • • • • • •

CHAPTER THREE

Managing Expectations

Will was one of the finest basketball players ever to grace the courts of our city. He had superb physical tools and the mental tenacity to be a winner. He could score, rebound, block shots, and play defense. In short, he was a coach's dream. He was also a parent's dream.

When our basketball team took the court, invariably most eyes were on Will. He had become a near legend. Most people overlooked the fact that he wasn't a great student. And hardly anyone knew how sensitive he was. Here was a great big kid with unbelievable talent who basically wanted to please everyone.

It was no surprise to any of us when dozens of colleges began vying for Will's basketball talents. Some schools wanted him so badly they were willing to offer some of his less talented teammates scholarships just to get Will to attend their school.

Those were heady days for such a sensitive young guy.

As the time approached for choosing a college, Will asked me for advice. Knowing that he wasn't an outstanding student and just how vulnerable he was by nature, I encouraged him to stay close to home. Several good schools close by could offer him everything he needed, including the support of good friends. The weight and pressure of the decision was beginning to slump his shoulders and slow his step. He could no longer enjoy the simple pleasures of his peers; his was a life of notoriety and constant attention. All eyes seemed to be on him and everyone was guessing which school would be the recipient of his considerable talent. I hoped and prayed he could relax after the decision was made.

Finally, one major event changed the course of his life. He talked to his parents. They had been so proud of his accomplishments and so sure of his future that they actually told him that if he didn't go to a big-time basketball school they would never speak to him again.

I couldn't help feeling it wasn't Will's future they were most concerned about. Will obediently chose the school they recommended.

Everything seemed to go well at first. On the surface, Will was adjusting to college life and contributing to the team. He had grown even taller after he arrived at the university and his potential now seemed limitless. That is, until a series of injuries cost Will his athletic career. No one had noticed along the way that he was barely able to stay in school academically. The average upperclassman playing football or basketball spends thirty hours per week in practice and preparation for games and only twenty-five hours per week in the classroom and studying.[1]

Will was unable to finish his degree. This failure, coupled with the loss of his athletic career, caused his self-esteem to plummet. As a result, he couldn't bring himself to come home for a visit because he couldn't face the family and friends he felt he had disappointed. Can you imagine a young man thinking that a whole community had pinned their hopes on his success? The wave of adulation and the soaring expectations he felt from almost everyone he knew made it impossible for him to face the folks in his hometown.

When I flew out to spend some time with him, Will was smoking one cigarette after another and taking an anti-depression drug prescribed by his psychiatrist.

The addiction to applause had become too great a habit for Will to kick. The disappointment was too heavy a burden to bear. In his adolescent heart he wanted to please. He had developed a chronic need for the praise and respect that had come so early in his life. Nothing had prepared him for this sudden fall from grace.

His parents had an equally hard time adjusting to the change. They grew tired of answering questions and found it impossible to hide their disappointment in Will. When disappointment gave way to resentment, the entire family structure collapsed. Will's mom and dad, now divorced and living in separate cities, rarely see their son and barely know his wife and children. Parental expectations and peer pressure had infected and destroyed a family.

BALANCING OUR EXPECTATIONS FOR OUR KIDS

As parents we all run the risk of expecting too much from our kids. But this does not have to be the case. Often the problem stems from *what* we are expecting. Athletics are not an important enough gauge of a person's worth to shape a life over it. Neither is academic achievement. These are simply convenient measuring sticks to see how our kids stack up against the "competition." We hope our kids can excel in something, and when they do we reward them for their performance. But to major in "outdoing the competition" reveals values that are not rooted in the Scriptures.

Young people want to be valued. Yet one of the greatest frustrations I have heard from kids over the years is that they don't measure up to the expectations of their parents. They seldom hear a "way to go" or "I'm proud of you" from Mom and Dad. Too often, it's, "Why did you get a B in that class instead of an A?"

While we want our children to succeed and develop a work ethic that always strives for excellence, none of us wants to set them up for depression and anxiety down the road. We know the world is rough, and we want them prepared for the hard knocks they must face. So we must be very careful to choose what to focus our expectations on. Somewhere there is a balance. As parents we must be committed to discovering what that is for each of our children.

FOCUSING ON VALUES AND CHARACTER
Tim Kimmel in his book *The Legacy of Love* highlights some important character traits for us to pass on to our children.[2] I appreciate the fact that he didn't give us guidelines for successful-looking children or something like that. He points out rather clearly that our children are in need of the right character, not the right style.

Faith, integrity, poise, discipline, endurance, and courage are the values Tim recommends.[3] If we keep these building blocks in mind, we won't need to worry what *our* peers are thinking. If we want our kids to remember it, we must remember that reputation is a byproduct, not a goal. If you want a good reputation in business, start by planning well, working hard, and showing integrity in your dealings with others. You will find little need for a public relations firm if you start out the right way. When parents focus on helping their children develop character, their reputation will reflect that character.

I have often quoted a little poem penned by an unknown author regarding character.

    Sow a thought
      Reap an act

Sow an act
    Reap a habit
Sow a habit
    Reap a character
Sow a character
    Reap a destiny.

Kids today are conspicuously conscious of what others think, especially their peers. But they often have a difficult time thinking through the consequences of their thoughts and actions. Part of the growing-up transition is learning to think. As parents we will give enormous aid to our sons and daughters if we affirm them as people while asking caring questions about their thoughts and feelings. At the same time, we must be careful to manage our own expectations of them. Our expectations, after all, reveal our own true values.

One of the toughest experiences I have had to face came from an extreme end of the spectrum of parental expectations.

By the seventh grade Mike had already experienced a tough life. His father was convinced that he would grow up to be a good-for-nothing and told him so frequently. If something came up missing at home, Mike got the blame. He rarely received any praise from his folks.

Mike was one of those kids who wasn't really a trouble-maker; he just hung out with some of the wrong kids and seemed to be the one who always got caught. I would look at him with his straight brown hair nearly covering his eyes and he would shrug his shoulders and tell me he really didn't mean whatever it was they were accusing him of this time. Mike was never belligerent. I never saw or heard of him hurting anyone, but he was living out an expectation that he would never amount to anything.

I am convinced Mike committed his heart to Christ, yet he struggled with the wrong set of expectations. At the age of sixteen Mike turned in front of a car while riding his motor-cycle and was killed instantly.

He had fulfilled a tragic and unnecessary prophecy. Ulti-mately he lived up to the expectations that had been pro-grammed in him. I guess I had hoped he could have lived long enough to prove them wrong. When he was killed on the motorcycle, his parents treated the tragedy like it was "one more dumb mistake by Mike."

We can be sure that whatever our expectations are, our kids will probably live up to them.

Because this is so true, parents of adolescents caught in the trauma of transition must be committed to building the character of their children and not simply their person-alities. The question should not revolve around how popular, or accepted by your friends, or even by their friends, they are. The key issue is, do they reflect the kind of character that is consistent with their faith?

In today's culture kids have become part of parents' résumés. The success of the child is too often seen as a reflection of the success of the parent. Therefore, teenagers are not allowed to make choices that might change the per-ception held by their parents' friends and associates. Will had been an important part of how his parents viewed them-selves. They loved the attention they received as a result of their son's success. It proved to be as much an addiction for them as it had become for him. Later, when he needed their unconditional acceptance, all he found was disappointment. In their eyes he had squandered a wonderful opportunity. He would never rise to his real potential. As an adult Will is still working through the pain of that ordeal.

THE ART OF ENCOURAGING TEENS

Encouragement is an art. We must work at it constantly.

Young people facing the transitions of adolescence need encouragement. They also need recognition, but we must carefully keep these two separate. By encouragement I am referring to *building up our children for who they are and not for what they do*. As parents we want to reinforce our love and commitment in ways that have nothing to do with their performance. Recognition means acknowledging their accomplishments and hard work.

To really excel at encouragement, we need to move beyond worrying about what our peers may think. If your son or daughter is not the "best" at something, that does not mean he or she will never achieve great things as an adult. In the long run, if your child reaches adulthood with faith intact and a clear sense of right and wrong, I'd say you have a very successful child. The world judges people by the cars, houses, and toys they can purchase. As Christians, we have a much better gauge for our lives. It is to be conformed to the image of Christ.

Telling your children things like "I love you," "You are a great person," and "I am proud to be your parent" for no apparent reason will create a mountain of confidence and security for kids trudging through the valley of adolescence.

Be spontaneous in your praise of the teenager in your home. If you wait for the "right" moment, you will lose a lifetime of opportunity. When your teens succeed at something, be quick to congratulate them, but don't tie "I love you" to those events. Children feel enough pressure to perform without the added suspicion that our love for them is wrapped in a package of performance. Instead, tell them how proud you are that they chose to work so hard to accomplish what they did and that the end results were great.

THE PRODIGAL PARENT: A MODEL FOR MANAGING PARENTAL PEER PRESSURE

The story of the lost son in Luke 15:11-24 is one of the best-remembered parables in Scripture. The father's unsurpassed love and acceptance is a lasting reminder of our heavenly Father's commitment to us. Here a young man had squandered his inheritance and had forsaken the morals and teachings of his youth, put his father through incredible agony and grief, and then was accepted back by his dad without a second's hesitation. It's more than we can fathom.

If this father had been more concerned about his reputation, he would never have allowed his son back so easily. Proper penitence and reparation would have been required. But this father didn't base his action on how he would be perceived by the religious in the community. He was responding to his son who was lost and now was found. Had this father been in a modern church, he may have had to deal with losing a position of leadership in the church because he was not managing his household in a manner "suitable" for someone in his position. He would have had to endure the humiliation of public acknowledgment of his failure as a parent.

We often decry the impact of peer pressure on our children and deny its impact in our own lives. Many times in the Christian community we feel the pressure to raise successful and trouble-free kids. We don't know what to do with those creative free spirits in our home who challenge every rule and thought. We want them to represent the family in a positive way. But we don't want to kill their spirit, either.

We need more parents like the prodigal's father—unashamed of their love for their children and unafraid of the perception of others. As parents we must become more and more confident in our relationship with our Father and less dependent on the approval of others. Our sons and daughters need the freedom to fail in the context of a loving home so they will not become addicted to the drug of pleasing people to gain acceptance.

TEEN PEER PRESSURE

Peer pressure may be the biggest challenge your teenager will face. Never minimize the strain of peer pressure. It is one of the constant forces of the adolescent life. Peer pressure tests the strength of young people. With the onset of adolescence, acceptance by one's peers becomes a need of titanic proportions.

As we learned earlier, most teenagers lack a sense of identity in one way or another. During adolescence they discover a new social order. They begin moving into adult activities and situations. They date, drive, make decisions about what kind of friends to have, and begin to compete for a place on the social ladder. During this pivotal time they are often somewhat closed to the comments and advice of their parents. This is a discovery time and a time to test the turbulent waters of the adult world.

In 1968 only 7 percent of driving-age teens owned cars. Now the figure is 35 percent.[4] A 1988 survey of twelve- to nineteen-year-olds conducted by an advertising firm revealed that 69 percent considered themselves to be adults. Independence was the greatest desire of 69 percent of the sample.[5]

As concern for status and acceptance escalates among our kids, so do other pressures. Playing on these needs, corporate America bombards them with the latest gimmicks for achieving the attention and acceptance they strive for. Teens now spend $55.9 billion annually on their day-to-day needs. This figure is up from $25.3 billion in 1975, even though the teenage population has dropped 15.5 percent since 1980.[6]

As parents we must recognize the needs of acceptance and identity within our teens. We cannot battle nature, but we can create a framework for help in the midst of this chaos. We know that the timing of these transitions and when they peak will be different for every young person. We also know each will respond to the challenges differently.

PREPARING FOR PEER PRESSURE CHANGES

So how do we face the dark clouds on our child's horizon? How will we prepare for the changes ahead?

First, remember that every child does not experience a grave crisis at each intersection of adolescence. Many will integrate most of the changes gracefully and without a great deal of drama. So let's not create a crisis if one is not there. At the same time, let's have our transition team in place and ready in case the need arises.

Pray for your kids. Each day give yourself anew to your heavenly Father, then leave the burdens of parenthood in His protective embrace.

If your household has both mom and dad, work hard together. Discuss the issues ahead of time and try to reach a consensus on the direction you want to take.

Everyone needs to think through the available resources. Ask, who can I call for help? Which institutions and organizations can I network with? Parents who are raising kids without considering every reasonable resource will feel like they are baking a cake with only half the ingredients. No matter how much sugar you add, if you don't add the flour and the rest of the ingredients, you won't have a cake.

If we are making decisions based on the long view of who we are and who we believe our child can be, our emotions and perspective can be healthier. The father of the prodigal son was able to look beyond the filth, both inwardly and outwardly, and embrace his son. He did not do it out of appreciation or even acceptance of the young man's lifestyle, nor was he responding out of fear that he might lose him again. His reaction was one of love and hope. Love for a son who though once lost had now been found and hope that the future would find them in relationship together.

Love is not a matter of public opinion. It is an attitude that recognizes the needs of acceptance and identity and provides the necessary room and the right resources for a son or daughter to find acceptance as a person and identity in Christ.

Let's strive to make the priorities John Baillie sets down in the following prayer our own.

O Lord—let me put right before interest: let me put others before self: let me put things of the Spirit before things of the body: let me put the attainment of noble ends before the enjoyment of present pleasures: let me put principle above reputation: let me put you before all else. Amen.[7]

• • • • • • • • • • •

Chapter Four

Making Transition Your Ally

I n many ways growing up has never been more difficult. Kids are faced with more choices and are required to make more decisions at a younger age than ever before. It is no wonder that stress and burnout are now observable in the lives of many young people.

Our kids are a product of a high-tech world, and the name of the game in technology is change. By the time they get the latest CD player it is out of date. On top of that, marketing strategists have discovered that kids are a highly profitable consumer group. So young people are being bombarded with ads to buy more and more.

A recently published survey provided this insight:

Teens have money to spend—girls go for make-up, boys spend more on entertainment. Girls' weekly average: clothing, $10.65; food and snacks, $6.50; entertainment, $3.45; cosmetics, $3.35; records and tapes, $1.80. Boys: food and snacks, $10.10; clothing, $6.19; entertainment, $4.35; records and tapes, $1.55; grooming, $1.10.[1]

But these are not just statistics. These are our children. Stacy, a senior who has been involved in Young Life all through high school, juggles school, dating, and Young Life and holds down two jobs to pay for her car and clothes.

Never before have junior high and especially high school students looked and dressed older than they do today. And with the clothes, cars, and money come other things. Surveys taken in 1988 show that 52 percent of seventeen-year-old girls had sex, up from 47 percent in 1979; for boys, it was 66 percent in 1988, up from 56 percent in 1979. Although AIDS cases among teenagers account for only 1 percent of the nation's total, the number of cases doubles every fourteen months, and many AIDS victims who are now developing the disease in their twenties got it during sexual activity in their teen years. The syphilis rate for teens aged fifteen to nineteen has jumped 67 percent since 1985, and condom use among teenagers doubled between 1979 and 1988. About one million teenagers have become pregnant every year since 1973—that's one out of ten fifteen-to-nineteen-year-old girls getting pregnant every year.[2]

We are aware that such activities are reinforced by media influences. Teens watch an average of twenty-two hours a week or about three hours a day of television.[3] And that includes MTV. They're also going to movies, listening to the radio, and reading magazines that are *explicit* and *influential.*

How does all this affect our college students?

A 1989 poll of first-year Harvard students revealed their three highest goals and values in life:

1. Money
2. Power
3. Reputation[4]

BUT THERE ARE STILL "GOOD KIDS" AROUND!

Now you may be thinking, "Things are not as bleak as all of that. There are still plenty of good kids around. After all, somebody's making it!" But the point is that the number of challenges today for those "good" kids has escalated dramatically. If you add to that the children living in single family homes or dealing with the breakup of their parents' marriages, the latchkey kids and young people facing the typical debilitating factors of their age, it paints a very challenging picture for all of us.

Jeff was an early bloomer. From age six until the ninth grade he was one of the best athletes in the city. During his junior high years he became a Pop Warner football legend. The high school coaches couldn't wait for him to arrive. Jeff didn't disappoint them. He was big and strong and had a great attitude. Through the season he rarely got a rest during a game.

By Jeff's sophomore season things had changed considerably. Jeff was still hardworking and aggressive, but other boys had caught up with him physically. He could no longer dominate a game, and it looked like the glory days were over.

I watched Jeff closely. He continued to work as hard as ever, yet by his senior year he barely made the team. I waited for the deep disappointment and rebellion to set in. It is difficult enough for adults to come to grips with their physical changes, but in a kid like Jeff it had to be impossible.

I was wrong.

Like almost everyone, I had underestimated Jeff. Athletics had never been his whole life. By graduation he was one of the top students academically in the school. It wasn't until his athletic career began to wind down that people noticed his other qualities. He made a very difficult transition with remarkable ease because he was prepared. I didn't know his parents well, but I had great respect for their encouragement of Jeff's growth in various areas. It would have been very easy for them to begin in junior high to push Jeff toward a college football scholarship.

I have had the father of an eight-year-old boy tell me that he was gearing his son for a college scholarship in one particular sport. That kind of pressure rarely works.

TEENS CAN OVERCOME PERCEIVED SHORTCOMINGS

Acceptance and identity are too important to teenagers for parents to set them up for failure in these areas. Teens can accomplish so much if we will let them pursue their areas of giftedness and interest.

One of my favorite characters in Scripture is Zacchaeus. His story can be found in Luke 19:1-9. One day Jesus was passing through Jericho, that ancient city rich with the history of God's miraculous power. The city around which Joshua marched the triumphant nation of Israel several hundred years earlier was now filled with disciples and gawkers as Jesus moved along her dusty streets.

One of the spectators that day was Zacchaeus. We are given only two brief but very revealing insights into this man. First, he was a wealthy tax collector (19:2). In the next verse we discover that he was short (19:3).

Let me tell you a secret about Zacchaeus. He was short before he was rich.

Perhaps it was his physical stature that drove him to achieve political and economic success. He certainly had clout. He could charge whatever tax he wanted, and the Roman army helped him collect. He could line his pockets with the hard-earned money of his oppressed and impoverished countrymen and there was nothing they could do.

I have seen hundreds and hundreds of kids in my years of youth work who are driven to make up for perceived shortcomings in their lives. Whether it is physical, social, or economic deficiency—real or perceived—they are working as hard as they can to develop some kind of acceptable stature among their peers. They must find a place in their lives where they measure up.

Like so many of our kids today, Zacchaeus thought he had found his place. He had attained the wealth and power he craved. But somewhere along the way toward recognition and stature, he lost himself.

Loneliness and isolation will sometimes make us do desperate things. Zacchaeus was desperate to see Jesus. Because he was unable to see Jesus over the crowd, he risked his stature and certainly whatever dignity he had in the community and climbed a tree. Above the heads of that throng of people he had his chance not only to see, but to be seen by the Savior.

I have a theory. I believe that Zacchaeus wanted to be found. Not only did he want to see Jesus, but his heart was bursting to be known, to be loved, to be understood. Today's kids want to be found as well. Part of our job as parents, ministers, educators, and youthworkers is to help them be found.

We can imagine how the scene played out. As Zacchaeus crouched among the leaves and branches the crowd was stunned to silence when Jesus approached. The amused chuckles of the followers suddenly became sighs of wonder as Jesus stopped the whole procession to call Zacchaeus by name and start a life-changing relationship with him.

For Zacchaeus the transition was swift and dramatic. The results of being found aren't always that spectacular, but they can be just as miraculous and just as real.

There are obstacles between Jesus and young people today. Their vision is blocked by the towering challenges of adolescence. It is more difficult to see Him than ever before. Money, sex, and fame loom high over our adolescents' heads. The pain of their own deficiencies or those around them keeps them bowed too low to see their Hope. They simply lack the view that comes from experience to see Jesus on their own. Consequently, they are unable to see the only Source of life.

Somehow we must find ways to help these young people

up the tree. Make it possible for them to see over the crowd. Give them a chance to be found.

DEPEND ON YOUR TEAM RESOURCES

This is not a job we can do alone. We must utilize every resource at our disposal. Fortunately, we have an abundance of resources—though we may not have taken the time to assemble those resources.

Let me introduce you to your team.

TEAM MEMBER 1—KNOWING GOD

Nothing in your life as a parent quite matches the experience of losing control over your children. For the first twelve years you have the dominant say in what they think and do. You work hard to set the patterns you believe are necessary to carry them through life. But while you are a flurry of activity for your kids, who is preparing *you* for the changes ahead?

The first step in our journey is to find ourselves in the Lord. Knowing God is the foundation of our team.

When Jim committed his life to Christ as a fifty-year-old, it was largely due to change he had seen in his kids. Several times he talked to me with tears in his eyes about the pain of watching his college-age son rebel and then drop out of several universities. As God began to work in his son's life, Jim was forced to take a hard look at his own. Today Jim is leading a household whose center is Jesus Christ. The family is facing the challenges of transition with new perspective and new hope.

In the next chapter we will discuss how to make your family journey a spiritual one. How we feel about ourselves as people and parents begins with how we view ourselves in Christ.

It has been said that the Bible is as necessary to our safe passage through this lifetime as oxygen is to sustain life. Yet, it often seems that the spiritual disciplines are first to go when transition brings rapid change and panic. I have often said in our Young Life ministry that it is very difficult for people to claim God's promises in their lives when they don't know what those promises are! We must learn to plant God's Word in our hearts and let Scripture change our perspectives.

TEAM MEMBER 2 — REALISTIC GOALS
Most people learn early to set goals. They want to get good grades, to excel in a sport, to learn the piano, etc. Then somehow later in life they either set the wrong goals or they allow their goals to be set for them by their jobs or by others. We need to know how to chart a course. We all want certain things in our lives and for our children, yet we are not sure how to start and we become lost in making midcourse corrections in our families. Consequently, we live in a state of panic, or simply survive.

We not only need goals in regard to planning toward our future, but also for the spiritual health of our families and who *we* want to be in the years ahead. Goals are a reflection of our values. They are where we begin to put "legs" to our convictions.

There's a well-worn story of a man who approached a laborer who was laying bricks and asked him, "What are you doing?" The laborer replied, "Can't you see I'm laying bricks?" The man then walked over to another bricklayer and asked, "What are you doing?" And the workman answered with pride, "I am building a cathedral."

Physically, both were doing the same thing. But the first laborer was occupied with the present task, while the other had in mind the ultimate goal. Setting clear and measurable goals will help get you beyond the pain or confusion of the present transition and back on track.

TEAM MEMBER 3 — MAXIMIZING RESOURCES
Another invaluable team member is your ability to muster your resources. Who do you call for help during specific

times of need in your life? Do you have the right compass and map to help you navigate the unknown terrain of transition?

None of us can make it alone. We must learn to gather around us those people and instruments necessary for our journey. It is inevitable that at some point you will need another adult to come alongside your young person. So often someone else can offer advice and direction that would not be heard coming from you.

TEAM MEMBER 4 — INTIMACY THROUGH COMMUNICATION

Far too many men and women today struggle to communicate their feelings during critical times in their lives. Some communicate well because they have always felt the need to maintain an image of strength for others, yet far too many simply have never learned the proper skills to share stress, burdens, fear, or happiness and fulfillment. These skills are a critical part of your team. These communication skills help you draw closer to young people during times of transition and help provide a framework for you to understand more fully what others are going through.

Communication is not a team member that simply helps you talk. It is the tool to help you *get through to those* you want to communicate with.

TEAM MEMBER 5 — PRAYER

One of the old hymns I remember singing often as a child ended with the warm refrain, "Take your burdens to the Lord and leave them there." The gift of prayer during times of change in our lives is an enormous one. Prayer can be the difference between being totally overwhelmed by our circumstances or seeing the hand of God in every situation. If we lose the ability to pray, or never develop that part of our relationship with Christ, we are woefully incomplete.

It is true that the first thing that changes through prayer is the one who prays.

TEAM MEMBER 6—MANAGING TIME FACTORS

Time is like a bank account that does not carry a balance from day to day. What you don't use is lost. Each of us has been given the same amount of time in our day. The challenge is to use it efficiently and wisely. There are many time management tools on the market today. But, as a member of your transition team, time management is not just a tool but a perspective bringing peace, hope, and energy. If you feel stressed by the lack of time in your life or your inability to manage all your time commitments, you need a team member that aids you in balancing priorities and commitments and helps you live each day to the fullest.

At the same time you need to be able to get a feel for how long these changes may take. If for example, you have a son or daughter going through junior high and all the changes that period brings, how do you plan for the next stage?

TEAM MEMBER 7—LAUGHTER AND FUN

Laughter is the music of hope. For the Christian it rings of faith that is not bound by circumstances. The ability to laugh says I will choose joy today because I know my God still lives. A family's transition team would be sorely incomplete without laughter. This is not a mirth that is unrealistic about problems and blind to pain. This is a gift to look at life with hope and to experience healing by allowing ourselves to see humor in the passages of our lives.

None of us wants to laugh at hurt. Yet, we need to learn to laugh in spite of hurt.

Not all of your transition team members will apply to each change in your life, or the life of your child. Nor is this an exhaustive list. But if you choose to use this team, you will find great help and hope for your teenager and yourself as you navigate through the various passages of family life with adolescents. Best of all, you will discover you are not alone.

• • • • • • • • • •

CHAPTER FIVE

Team Member 1: Knowing God

Anyone who knew Sarah would confirm that she was both charming and intelligent. Always fun and entertaining to be around, she quickly became one of my favorite people. Sarah could run a PTA meeting and then lead the youth group at church with equal grace and skill. She was one of those ladies that many kids wished they had for a mom.

That is, except for one of her own.

Sarah called me in despair. Her oldest child, sixteen-year-old Heidi, had run away, and Sarah believed she was staying with a man of twenty-one who had questionable values.

For the next two years I walked a painful road with Sarah and her husband, Ed. They applied tough love and tender love; they took Heidi back and asked her to leave. It was a nightmare for this successful and high-profile Christian couple.

Sometime during her eighteenth year Heidi settled down and began that long process of making peace with her parents and herself. Each time Sarah and I discuss those painful days, she always mentions the moment her faith began to rise above her torment.

Before Heidi's very open rebellion Sarah had been the queen of Christian moms. She was loved and admired and emulated by many. But at times during the family turmoil Sarah felt worse than a failure. More like a leper, she would say. She no longer felt fit to lead the PTA or try to teach other parents' kids right from wrong.

TWO GREAT TRUTHS

Yet, sometime during her grief two great truths emerged. First, Sarah recognized that her hope was in Christ and not in her success as a mother, or as a Christian leader for that matter. When all else failed, the Lord was truly all she needed. Sarah realized that her experience with Heidi spurred growth in her own life that she probably would have otherwise missed. In the midst of sorrow and pain she learned to enjoy the presence of Christ and discovered a joy that was not related to circumstance or environment.

We live in a world starving for that kind of joy. It is a joy that the world can neither give nor take away. It is the joy that comes from knowing God.

The second important truth that Sarah discovered was that Heidi, with all her anger and rebelliousness, was still more important to her than all the committees and boards and ministries she could think of. Her new discovery of God in the face of lost prestige had begun to remold her thoughts. She no longer aspired to be supermom and super Christian. Her heart now simply longed for Jesus, and she was eternally grateful to rest in the arms of her heavenly Father.

Sarah is living proof of a hard reality: Being a parent is tough. No question about it. In the midst of coping with life and all that confronts us as people, we are forceu ir raise another generation and prepare them for the road ahe,

It is no wonder that many people live with the stress and guilt of not being the parents that they perceive their children need. If you have ever experienced the fear of not being the perfect parent, I have great news!

You can't be one.

No one can meet all of the needs of his or her children, or even of a spouse for that matter. At best, we commit ourselves to hard work and growth. We must recognize that perfection is not for this world and our hope must lie in another place.

For this reason, we commit ourselves to One who is capable of meeting our needs. We have a heavenly Father who loves us. We are His children. He desires to see us whole and happy.

STEPS AND MISSTEPS IN SUCCESSFUL PARENTING

The first step to being a successful parent is *not* to become a "successful person." Many parents today are living under this tragic assumption. They equate worldly success with all its whistles and bells to their potential to parent success-fully. In the end they achieve, at best, an attractive family, but not necessarily a healthy one.

When a scribe asked Jesus what the greatest command-ment was, the Lord answered, "Love the Lord your God with all your heart and with all your soul and with all your mind" (Matthew 22:37). That is the call to men and women every-where. The greatest commandment is not to accumulate things, or to acquire prestige and power. It does not relate to any of our abilities. It is an act of the will: Will you love God above all else?

If educators are correct, 70 percent of learning is model-ing. We can talk about values and morals all day, but unless our young people are seeing them lived out in vital fashion, they are merely words, void of any real meaning in their lives.

We have discovered that most kids believe in God. They just can't seem to figure out why it matters. For years in Young Life we have said, "You gotta walk your talk." We have said something else as well, "You can take a kid only as far as you are in the Lord." As parents we must make our own growth in Christ our first goal. We can only lead and model what we hope our children will embrace from a posture of submission and love for Christ. George Bernard Shaw once commented that the only tragic thing about the Christian faith was that it has never been tried.

WHY WE DESIRE TO KNOW GOD

There are really two reasons to desire to know God. First, it is commanded. God has called us to Himself and He has prepared the way for us to have fellowship with Him through Jesus Christ. We do not come to Christ to be better parents. We do not yearn after God in order to change our kids, or our spouse. We follow Christ because He calls us to Himself and that is enough. Change, we discover painfully, usually begins with ourselves. As we draw nearer to Christ, our parenting will improve naturally. Why? Because God turns our attention from the faults and foibles of others (especially our teenagers) to our own need for Him. We are struck by the great forgiveness we have received and experience a new capacity to dispense forgiveness to others. The more we seek and yearn after Him, the sharper our focus on who *we* are as parents.

My pastor recently said, "God does not react to the *pressure* of faith, but to the *presence* of faith." In other words, we cannot manipulate Him to action. He is not a machine, He is the King.

Second, we all were created with a longing for God. We were made for that relationship, and we are destined to live aimless and unfulfilled without it. You may have heard the old illustration from Pascal that within each person is a God-shaped vacuum. Nothing else will fit, try as we might to find a substitute. Every attempt is akin to forcing a square peg in a round hole. Substitutes just won't do. It may strike you as illogical, but when our eyes are focused on Christ we will see our teenagers more clearly.

FIVE PRINCIPLES TO GUIDE YOU IN KNOWING GOD

If Sarah could discover God in a new way through the turmoil in her life and family, you can too. In the next several pages we will discuss the following five basic principles. These will guide you as you seek to know God.

- You are a product of God's grace.
- God is near.
- You can do all things through Christ.
- The Spirit—your source of power.
- Being heavenly minded.

YOU ARE A PRODUCT OF GOD'S GRACE

"Amazing Grace, how sweet the sound"—familiar words, but often for us an unfamiliar experience. As a high school student I was given a definition of grace that has stayed with me through the years.

God's
Righteousness
At
Christ's
Expense

We experience the grace of God through His unmerited favor toward us. This paints a graphic picture of God's sacrificial and unconditional love. We have such difficulty accepting that love at times. We have grown up in a number of competitive love situations. We competed with our siblings for love, and we competed with various demands on our parents' time. Then we competed at school for the attention and acceptance of our peers. We need to feel loved and accepted in various environments, and that means learning how to act and respond correctly. Finally, when we come to Christ we are struck by the fact that He isn't interested in our acceptance games. He won't force us to prove our worthiness time and time again. We don't perform for Him in order to earn His favor. This is hard to get used to!

As we grow, we discover that by working to earn God's love we are really working against ourselves. The real key is humility and contrition, as King David, the writer of the following psalm, knew so well.

> You do not delight in sacrifice, or I would bring it;
>> you do not take pleasure in burnt offerings.
> The sacrifices of God are a broken spirit;
>> a broken and contrite heart,
>> O God, you will not despise. (Psalm 51:16-17)

Youthworkers will often tell a child that if he or she were the only person on earth, Christ would still die for him or her. His love and commitment to us cannot be earned. His forgiveness is complete and permanent. I have struggled many times with this concept. As much as I recognize my need for God, I often strive to meet Him on my terms. I find that just as I competed for the attention of others as a child, I now compete to prove myself a spiritually sufficient person as an adult. I act out my Christianity for my peers and charges rather than simply loving Christ for what He has done for me. Unfortunately, when troubles come, this self-sufficient lifestyle is woefully insufficient. The apostle Paul summed it up beautifully in 2 Corinthians 12:9: "My grace is sufficient for you, for my power is made perfect in weakness."

The Lord's grace is the key to sustain us. Our transition

team will provide resources, but we experience peace in our heart because we know God's love is unconditional. He is not waiting to see how well we handle transition or struggles before He affirms us. It is often only in weakness and distress that we see His hand in our lives. Most of the time we are simply too busy to notice.

The secret to experiencing God's grace and peace is to daily, moment by moment, give your thoughts and dreams to Christ. It is not an ethereal or mystical concept, but as simple as saying, "Lord, please carry this burden."

Listen to the words of Isaiah.

> But now, this is what the LORD says—
> > he who created you, O Jacob,
> > he who formed you, O Israel:
> "Fear not, for I have redeemed you;
> > I have summoned you by name; you are mine."
> > (Isaiah 43:1)

The next time you find the swelling tide of teen transitions threatening to wash you away, first affirm to yourself that you are saved by grace. You are loved and accepted regardless of your circumstances. When within your heart you have a rock-solid conviction of who you are in Christ, you will not be swept away, regardless of the circumstances you face.

GOD IS NEAR

> Rejoice in the Lord always. I will say it again: Rejoice!
> Let your gentleness be evident to all. The Lord is near.
> (Philippians 4:4-5)

When was the last time you felt the Lord was far away and unconcerned about the hurt and trouble in your life? Yesterday, right?

The apostle Paul has good news for you—"Rejoice." He

is *not* talking about being glad for calamity and stress. He is saying that *in the midst of the battle the Lord is near*. The Lord has not left you. *You* may have turned from Him. The obstacles you are confronting may be crowding out your view of Him, but He is there.

Look at the next two verses in Philippians 4: "Do not be anxious about anything, but in everything, by prayer and petition, with thanksgiving, present your requests to God. And the peace of God, which transcends all understanding, will guard your hearts and your minds in Christ Jesus" (verses 6-7).

The peace of God can be ours. He is near.

From his beautiful book *God Came Near*, Max Lucado gives us this challenge: "Would you like to see Jesus? Do you dare be an eyewitness of His Majesty? Then rediscover amazement. The next time you hear a baby laugh or see an ocean wave, take note. Pause and listen as His Majesty whispers ever so gently, 'I'm here.'"[1]

Can you see Jesus in your teenager? The next time your son or daughter laughs, the next time you touch him, or watch her lounge around the house—see His majesty there, in your child, His creation.

YOU CAN DO ALL THINGS THROUGH CHRIST

We're all familiar with stories of men and women who have overcome enormous odds to achieve great things. These heart-warming tales of courage fill us with warmth and encouragement. But then we walk back into our ordinary world where the challenges aren't so clear and obvious.

That is why the apostle Paul left us some very valuable and practical advice in 1 Corinthians 9:24: "Do you not know that in a race all the runners run, but only one gets the prize? Run in such a way as to get the prize."

The last part of this verse is an admonition to run the race with the goal in mind. Most people run the race with the obstacles and challenges foremost in their minds. Paul says run to win. Our goal is usually just to finish the race.

My two brothers both ran the hurdles. I would watch them practice, and in so doing, learned an important lesson. Just as important as speed in running the hurdles is getting your steps down. There are a certain number of steps you need to take to make the transition between hurdles smooth and fast.

To run a strong race the worst thing you can do is watch the hurdles as you run. It always throws off your timing and gets you out of step. The best way to run the hurdles is with your eyes fixed on the finish line.

When we are focused on the hurdles in our lives, our view of the race isn't clear and we are sure to get out of step. Yet if we can keep our eyes focused on Christ during the race, we will see more clearly and the obstacles will not loom so large in our minds.

In Philippians 4:13, Paul says, "I can do everything through him who gives me strength." There is no obstacle too great for those who get their strength from Christ. Such focus requires discipline and commitment. It means every day renewing your pledge to keep your eyes on Him. Then quickly asking forgiveness, not allowing sin to get a permanent foothold in your life, and refocusing when you become aware of taking your eyes off Him.

With each change in our teenager's life we will face a new hurdle in parenting. Keeping a clear focus in our lives doesn't mean we know what to do in each situation. In the midst of unpredictable days we aren't consumed by the hurdles we must go over; rather, we keep our eyes focused on Christ and we run the race to win.

THE SPIRIT—YOUR SOURCE OF POWER

Jesus said to her, "I am the resurrection and the life. He who believes in me will live, even though he dies." (John 11:25)

The Resurrection. Not since Creation had the world seen such a display of power. That Jesus Christ would conquer death and usurp its authority in the world represents a power of proportions we cannot comprehend.

But God does not stop there. He makes that power available to us through the Spirit of God who inhabits us. It is His desire to provide the strength we need to wage the battles of our lives. Paul says it well in Ephesians 3:16: "I pray that out of his glorious riches he may strengthen you with power through his Spirit in your inner being."

We will be talking about appropriating this more in a later chapter, but the primary point here is: *Power is gained by waiting on the Lord.* There is no shortcut and no substitute. If we desire to be strengthened by the Spirit of God, we must wait before Him. Remember, it is not by pressure that we experience the Spirit; it is by presence.

Waiting will not always mean being still. If, as we walk through the transitions of adolescence with our kids, we have waited before the Lord, we are prepared and empowered to wait *on* Him. We live with the peace and knowledge that God is at work even during the busiest times of our lives.

BEING HEAVENLY MINDED

A great part of my spiritual tradition lies in the teaching that Heaven is our home and this earth is merely a stop along the way. I can remember as a child singing about Heaven. Those songs gave me two great truths about life.

First, they said, "Don't take this life too seriously." That doesn't mean to be flippant or irresponsible but simply that we are not to be consumed by the cares of this world.

I have heard it said that the life of a Christian in the hands of God is like a bow and arrow in the hands of an archer. God is aiming at something the Christian cannot see.

Being heavenly minded simply helps us leave the shooting to God. He sees things from a vantage point simply not available to us. He knows exactly where to aim.

Second, being heavenly minded means we are focusing on an eternal God and not the temporal things of humankind. Our values are based on eternal commitments and not the fleeting things of this world.

A few years ago, I heard James Dobson share a touching story of a little boy who was dying. One day when his mother arrived at the hospital, the nurses attempted to prepare her for the worst. "He has been hallucinating," they told the mother. "He has been muttering something about the bells."

"Oh," she said as she gently lifted her little one. "I told him that when the pain got too difficult to stand and he didn't think he could take any more to look up in the corner of the room and he would see Jesus. Then to listen very carefully and he would hear the bells of Heaven."

Most of us are too busy to distinguish the bells of Heaven from the noises and sounds that assault our hectic lives. Knowing God means to look for Him. As often as we can we need to be quiet. Quiet enough to hear the bells of Heaven.

There may be no greater gift we could give our children than the picture of us waiting and listening to the Lord. At the same time, as adults we need to be more heavenly minded. Our home is not of this world, therefore we are not overwhelmed by apparent failures or successes. With our focus on Christ we draw on the power God bestows on those who wait on Him. We do this knowing we are here to serve Him until He calls us to be with Him.

I have learned much from watching parents like Sarah live through the trauma of parenting a troubled adolescent. If her despair could turn to peace, so can yours. If her faith can rise above her torment, that strength is available to you and me as well. To know God is to experience His peace and strength. It involves daily taking your cares and fears to your loving heavenly Father. Then in the midst of struggle and challenge you can learn to enjoy the presence of Christ and discover a joy only He can give.

• • • • • • • • • • •

CHAPTER SIX

Team Member 2: Realistic Goals for Traumatized Parents and Teens

What lies behind us and what lies before us
are tiny matters compared to what lies within us.
OLIVER WENDELL HOLMES

J ack sat in my office an angry and confused dad. His son, Mike, had just wrecked his new Trans Am during a high-speed frolic with some friends. "I suppose I should be grateful that no one was killed," he said, as he slumped in the chair. Suddenly, he threw up his hands in a sign of surrender and in a broken voice asked, "Where did I go wrong?"

It would be impossible to count how many times I have heard those words spoken by confused, angry, or frustrated parents. They love their children and have attempted to do everything they can to provide for them. Yet, in the middle of the adolescent storm there is an overwhelming sense of fear and even failure.

My first reaction to Jack's question was to encourage and not let him blame himself. But, I also felt that it was necessary to ask a few questions. "Jack," I asked, "what is your major goal as Mike's father?"

"Well, I guess I just want him to be happy," was his reply.

As I continued to ask Jack questions, it became apparent to me that he had never really considered his goals for raising his son. He knew how to set aggressive goals for his company, and he was well covered for his future retirement. Still, he could not provide a clear blueprint for raising his son.

Finally, I shared with him one thought I had heard from James Dobson a number of years ago: Most people try to pave the way of success for their children rather than preparing them for the bumpy road of life.

Jack was ecstatic. He had been thinking about the process all wrong. He wanted Mike's life to be successful and he worked hard to ensure that. But when Mike failed to live up to his expectations or didn't seem to appreciate his efforts, Jack was often angry and hurt.

I encouraged him to develop a different pattern, one that focused more on character and less on "success." He recognized this trial as a great opportunity to understand the deeper meaning of goals. At the same time it was a great opportunity to guide Mike through a traumatic experience and show a Christlike attitude. Mike, as a person, and especially as his son, was far more valuable than the Trans Am.

GOALS THAT REFLECT DEEPER VALUES

Goals reflect our values. They tell us what our priorities are and help us put "legs" to our beliefs.

There are really two functions of this chapter on goals. One is to make sure you have clearly thought through your own goals. At this stage in life, you may not be able to establish goals for your son or daughter, but you can set personal goals regarding who you want to be and how you will respond to your family. The other is to recognize that "doing" the right things is not as important as charting a course to "be" the right person. You may not be able to "control" the actions or attitudes of the adolescent in your home, but you can respond according to some carefully laid out principles that guide you during difficult times.

There is no greater nor more tender example of clear goals than the story of Jesus healing the sick woman in Luke 8:40-48. Jesus was on His way to the home of Jairus, an influential and powerful religious leader. The notoriety from a miracle on behalf of this man would be significant. Jairus was beside himself. His little girl was dying. The crowd, sensing something special was about to happen, poured into the streets and made it almost impossible for the Lord and His disciples to move.

Jesus stopped. His brow furrowed in concentration, and scanning the vast crowd of people, He asked, "Who touched me?" Only one person really knew what He was asking. For a sick and destitute woman had just touched the hem of His garment and had suddenly been freed from her years of torment.

Now perhaps the most remarkable thing of all happened. She fell down before Jesus and shared why she had touched Him and how she had been healed. With Jairus wringing his hands, and the disciples fretting over the schedule, Jesus stood and listened intently while this little woman who had suffered so much told her story. Then before she got away, and before the crowd could separate them and force Jesus on His way, He blessed her.

He said to her, "Daughter, your faith has healed you. Go in peace."

Nowhere else in the recorded words of Jesus do we find Him calling someone daughter. She must have trembled at those words. The overwhelming joy at the words and warmth of Jesus would have surely burst her heart had not deep and abiding peace filled her soul at that moment. It was a moment when peace and joy were partners.

Jack didn't see instant results in Mike's behavior and attitude. What he did experience was a revolutionary change in how he viewed life and in particular, Mike. Good behavior was no longer Jack's number one goal for Mike. In fact, Jack realized that before he could entertain any thoughts about goals for Mike, he had to make some clear decisions regarding how he would live his life and respond, regardless of the circumstances. He knew that his first goal must be to know Christ personally and to become more like Him. Jack began to find a new peace and joy inside himself. I believed it would only be a matter of time until Mike would begin to experience Christ, too.

GOAL-DRIVEN PARENTING

As we learn to set goals for ourselves and attempt to guide our children in theirs, we must bear in mind the example of Jesus.

First, He is not only our hope, He is our model. He showed us how to love and how to care during those awkward intrusions in our lives that seem so unnecessary and out of place. He knew His goal was not to get to the next meeting as fast as possible. It was to touch people, lost and forsaken men and women, and to touch them one at a time. He valued the individual and, because He knew His ultimate goal, He didn't see the woman as a distraction, but as an important stop on His journey to the Cross.

Second, we can never be too busy to stop for our child. Jesus didn't see the woman as an intrusion, He saw her as a "daughter." His goal was not merely to use His time efficiently but to use it effectively. Too often we attempt to make our household efficient at the expense of effective relationships. While a certain amount of efficiency is helpful, whether it involves household chores or a specific dinner time, these activities must not become the goals. Rather, *our activities must be driven by our goals*. For example, if your goal is to have quality time as a family, you may have to adjust if a common dinner doesn't work.

The most powerful result in setting a goal is that it tells

you what *you* think is significant and puts you in a proactive position to follow your convictions. Instead of waiting around for life to "happen" to you, being proactive means to chart a course for your future.

Jack set a goal for his life that people would see Christ in him in every situation. He began to take some steps in his devotional life, and in his relationship to his son, to see that goal begin to take root in his life. If Jack's goal had remained to change Mike's behavior, he probably would have faced a long and frustrating battle.

GOAL-DRIVEN TEENS

In challenging young people to carefully consider the direction of their lives, we youthworkers often ask them to write their own eulogy. The idea is that they think about how they want to be remembered when they are gone. What will their children say about them? What will their coworkers believe they lived for?

In his very helpful book *The Seven Habits of Highly Effective People*, Stephen Covey does a beautiful job challenging adults with the idea of writing their own eulogy. He calls it "beginning with the end in mind." Covey says that if you carefully consider what you want said of you at your funeral, you will "find your definition of success."

I ask kids to put their thoughts into one phrase that they can memorize and apply to any situation in their lives. For example, "She was a woman after God's own heart." That little phrase says volumes about how you want to be remembered and what your values and goals are.

After we have talked about how they want to be remembered and they have decided on their "life phrase," we can begin to work backward to set some goals for achieving the desired end. We talk about what they need to be doing right now to set the course of their lives.

It is not my intention to tell you what goals you should

set for yourself or your children. People are different, and the best goal is the one you think of and apply to your particular situation and life. Ownership is the key here. Please don't hand your young people a set of goals for their lives. Give them most of the ownership. As children make the transition from junior high to high school, they are beginning to make decisions on their own and won't simply adopt your goals, no matter how valid they appear to you. And if they were to adopt your goals, you must ask yourself if you've helped them achieve even the basic level of independence necessary to survive in high school or college.

Help them ask the right questions. Ask them how they want to be remembered. Sometimes you may feel that they're incapable of thinking that far ahead. Ask how they want to be remembered by their classmates when they come back for their ten-year reunion. I have asked my boys how they want to be remembered after soccer season. I try to avoid letting them get away with cliches like "He was the best player on the team" or even "He was a real example for Christ." Instead I continue to ask what their statement means until we get to *values* like teamwork, working hard, and listening carefully. Then I ask them how they think they will work toward that end. Now the question isn't, "How good are you?" or "How did you play?" Rather, the question is, "Did you see some growth in the areas you established as priorities?" That is almost always a goal they can achieve. And it puts the emphasis on *who they are* and not on *what they do*. It allows them to set goals based on their own values and doesn't limit it to performance.

I am not trying to take away the value of healthy competition or to reward mediocrity. But when you work the hardest, listen the closest, and give the necessary respect to coaches, teammates, and opponents, there is bound to be an impact on your performance.

With this in mind, I would like to point you toward five values you may want to discuss with your son or daughter when setting goals. You can also use these values to guide your own goal-setting and thus provide a model for your adolescent and give you more patience as they pursue their own.

VALUE 1: LOVE GOD

"Love the Lord your God with all your heart and with all your soul and with all your mind and with all your strength" (Mark 12:30).

"Too easy," you say? Then obviously you haven't tried it. But try it you must if it is to be a goal for your child. Remember, your goals are an expression of your values. You will communicate those first by your lifestyle.

We are not talking about going to church here. We are talking about a devotion to Christ that commands the attention of your whole life (and your kid's!).

This is the foundation for the rest of the goal-setting process. Encourage your young people to give it some thought. Ask them what they want their children to say someday about their dad or mom's relationship to God. Ask them how they would verbalize that conviction.

Be content to set small goals. Make promises to yourself that you can keep. For example, one objective in reaching a goal in this category might be to commit to five minutes a day alone with the Lord. Now that may not seem very spiritual, but it is a promise you are able to keep. After ninety days you may want to increase the time.

So, while loving God with all our heart, soul, mind, and strength is no small goal itself, to live with such a high value requires that we start small and set achievable objectives to demonstrate our commitment to it.

VALUE 2: LOVE PEOPLE

"Love your neighbor as yourself" (Mark 12:31).

From his popular book *All I Ever Really Need to Know I Learned in Kindergarten*, Robert Fulghum shares the following thoughts:

ALL I REALLY NEEDED TO KNOW about how to live, and
what to do, and how to be, I learned in kindergar-
ten. . . . These are the things I learned:
- Share everything. Play fair. Don't hit people.
- Put things back where you found them.
- Clean up your mess.
- Don't take things that aren't yours.
- Say you're sorry when you hurt somebody. . . .
- When you go out into the world, watch for traffic,
  hold hands and stick together.[1]

Fulghum gives us a clever description of our attitude
to those around us. Our children are growing up in an
increasingly violent world. That world desperately needs love
modeled in tangible ways. The very first place we demon-
strate this attitude is in the home. And it begins with love
for our spouse. Our children's values will be established by
what they see lived out in the home. If love is lived out in a
home, whether or not both mom and dad are living there, the
impact will be far greater than all the sermons and lectures
in the world. As a teenager I would always notice when an
"older" couple held hands. I told myself I wanted to still be in
love like that after years of marriage. If you begin with your
"neighbor" at home, you are well on your way to reflecting
this value in your goals and behavior.

As junior high- and high school-aged kids make the tran-
sition from dependence on you to independence, you may
not get the response to your suggestions that you think you
deserve. But the key issue cannot be their response. If your
goal is to love, success is not dependent on their response.
Nor can you demand a response. The issue is who you are,
not how your children respond.

Psychologists tell us that most anger is related to unful-
filled expectations. If you are expecting a certain response
from your son or daughter, you will undoubtedly get angry
over his or her failure to respond. In truth, as boys and

girls pass through adolescence they often *don't know* how to respond. They are searching for a socially acceptable way to relate to others. Their world is changing so fast they may be incapable of responding in a manner acceptable to us.

This is not to say we overlook rudeness, but simply that we can't afford to view no response as necessarily a bad response at the time.

We must learn to share and play fair. And then we must certainly learn to stick together.

Here is one way to express the value to love our neighbor as ourselves. Stepping back, we encourage kids to define who their neighbor is. Then we ask them how they want to live out loving their neighbor, and finally where or with whom they will start. If they have seen a model of that happening in their family, they may start there. But they may choose to start with their peers. That is okay. They will own an objective; that goal will guide them. Don't panic if they don't respond the way you anticipated.

Finally, learn to serve. Demonstrate for your children what the Lord meant when He said, "Whatever you did for one of the least of these brothers of mine, you did for me" (Matthew 25:40). Sometimes our children need to see us serving outside the home in places they wouldn't expect. They need to be exposed to the world around them, which doesn't live the way they do.

VALUE 3: DEVELOP INTEGRITY

In his book *Legacy of Love*, Tim Kimmel has this to say about integrity:

> When I think of a legacy of love, I picture parents who carefully develop a child's integrity. All other skills and talents, regardless of how carefully defined, must submit to the demands of integrity.
>
> That's because integrity protects us. We never have to keep lies straight or catalog the deceptions. There's

never a worry about what we said or what we did. Integrity shines out of our life like an inner light, and people find it easy to place their trust in us.[2]

These are important words about integrity for all of us. Unfortunately, at about the junior high level integrity gets mixed up with another important word: *reputation.* This is a mistake that is too often carried over into adult life. Reputation, whether good or bad, is a by-product of our lifestyle and integrity. Typical junior high students will most often define their reputation in two ways. How they believe they are perceived by their peers is one definition. This used to begin in high school, but is now a junior high or middle school issue. Second, they are influenced by what they see in the media. Much of their view of beauty, masculinity, or success is a product of advertising and the media. A $170.00 pair of basketball shoes may never be on a basketball court, but it can be a symbol for many kids that they are "in."

In reality, we cannot control our reputation any more than Jesus could control His. He was often maligned as a friend of sinners. But many people cultivate a reputation. They strive to look "just right" to those around them. And often this is at the expense of their own personal integrity and spiritual health.

If we have a life goal that places Christ in the center of life, we must allow obedience to Him to supersede our obsession with reputation. By establishing personal goals we can teach ourselves and our children to draw approval from God and not others. That's *real* integrity!

Value 4: Work Hard

E. M. Gray once said, "The successful person has the habit of doing things failures don't like to do." Hard work is easily one of the most difficult values to communicate. The concept of hard work is very confused today. Most people think hard work and long hours away from home are one and the same. That is an unfortunate view of hard work. I have often wondered what kind of values in regard to work I am communicating to my sons if they never see me do any. If most of our work is done outside the home, their view will come from hearsay, or even worse, television and the media.

How do your teenagers think you earn money? Do they have an idea of how hard you work and how long it took you to get where you are today? Most of the time they don't really understand what you go through to provide for them.

I want to encourage you to do a couple of things. First, if at all possible, take them to work with you. Show them around and let them see you in action. Let them see the kind of accountability you face at the job. You could give them a great gift by letting them see some of your life. If it wouldn't be appropriate to visit your job, call on someone who can help you. Maybe a friend has a career that your teen has shown some interest in.

Second, share with them your thoughts about your career. Are you happy with it? Do you wish you had done something different? What are some of your major fears about your future? While you are at it you can let them see some or all of your budget. Let them see where the money goes. When they see the link between a full-time job and family financial commitments they will have a more balanced view of work and money.

Finally, as you model and share about work don't forget to let them know when you stop working. This is extremely difficult in my life and for most of us in the ministry. Too often, I am not able to distinguish between what is work and what is personal time. There are so many needs and so many relationships that seem to overlap. My sons are very aware of not having my full attention even when from their perspective I am not "on the job." To combat this I have always coached one of them in soccer and tried very hard to do things they like on a regular basis. Making time for this is an ongoing challenge.

VALUE 5: PLAY HARD

Do you know the art of leisure? Much of my early under-
standing on this subject came from Tim Hansel's book *When
I Relax I Feel Guilty*. There is something very central to our
health as individuals and families in learning how to play.

Tim expresses our dilemma with leisure like this:

> Part of our confusion about leisure is the result of
> using as synonyms a number of overlapping and
> ill-defined terms such as *play, game,* and *recreation.*
> Another difficulty lies in the fact that some define lei-
> sure as a certain type of *activity,* while others define it
> as a *state of mind.* One tradition conceives of leisure as
> free time not devoted to paid occupations. The other,
> much older, classical tradition conceives of leisure as
> cultivation of the self and a preoccupation with the
> higher values of life.
>
> If you will excuse me a moment for not speaking
> English, I think you will find it helpful to know the
> background of the word leisure. It comes from the
> Latin word licere, which means "to be permitted." More
> today than ever, we need to learn how to give ourselves
> permission to relax, to play, to enjoy God for who
> he is.[3]

Of course, defining leisure in a way that the whole family
can agree on can be a challenge. Leisure is different from
"kicking back," although that may be a part of it. Watching
television can provide a piece of your family playtime, but it
can have the detrimental effect when it is done in excess.

Young people like variety. They will do simple things if
the setting is right. Too many of us have an expensive view
of play. We buy expensive toys, go on exotic vacations, and
in general see play as something extraordinary that happens
on holidays. But play can be almost a daily occurrence. It is
part of what brings joy into life.

AFFIRMATION AND GOALS

After Jack had finished establishing goals for himself and had begun to talk to Mike about his goals in life, we discussed one final detail. Jack was going to need to learn to affirm Mike and any new goals he might come up with.

This isn't to say Jack could not ask questions and even challenge Mike's position, but he needed to affirm Mike's values, not his performance. He had to look at whom Mike was becoming and not just what he was doing. This would take lots of work and require patience. He would need to genuinely affirm Mike's goals and specifically point out things he appreciated. It would also be very important for Jack not to use these goals in moments of anger to embarrass or humiliate Mike.

Jack was energized and encouraged. He had a game plan now and not only hope for Mike but convictions about his own life as well. If your goals are an expression of what you value, what are they telling you right now?

I pray you will establish goals that will guide you through life and provide a proper model for those who follow.

• • • • • • • • • • •

CHAPTER SEVEN

Team Member 3: Maximizing Resources

O ur society loves celebrities. Folks watch their every move and dream of living their life. With the close attention famous people get from the media, we often get more information than we ever wanted. Most of our would-be heroes are tarnished and brought down by their own actions. Few can pass the test required by a public who likes its heroes bigger than life. As a parent I am constantly paying attention to successful athletes and other celebrities to discern if there is one my sons can latch onto as a role model. Certainly, I am always grateful for the ones who hold high standards and take their role in society seriously.

Parents know that successful role models are not all our kids need in developing a view of who they want to be and in making good decisions about life. The most important role models are right at home. Yet the influence other adults can have on our kids can be critical to their development.

Too many young people are facing the world today without enough resources to guide and support them. They are facing an increasingly hostile and competitive world with only a narrow view of life to guide them. It is in adolescence that these young folks need our help in mustering the resources necessary to aid their passage through these trying years.

Our children need to know that they are not passing through this life alone and that there are resources and helps they can turn to.

When you as a parent think about caring for your son or daughter during the transitions from junior high through young adulthood, you need to know where your resources are as well. You must know whom to call and where to go for help.

SIZING UP THE SITUATION

The first thing you will want to do is take a hard and honest look at what you are facing. No matter what phase your child is going through, there are five basic questions you can ask yourself to begin your assessment.

1. How do my kids view themselves?
2. What is the state of my teenagers' faith?
3. Do my kids have the social and mental skills to handle life on their own?
4. Are my kids surrounded by healthy people inside and outside the family?
5. Are they capable of making healthy independent decisions?

I would encourage you at this point to recruit someone who knows your children and has your trust to help you answer these questions.

Too many people in the United States still hold the view

that they must be self-sufficient. They believe that to accept help is a sign of weakness. They confuse fortitude with solitude. Nothing could be further from the truth. We were created by God to work together. The Body of Christ functions *best* when we are all pulling together. To refuse help is to cripple the plan of God in creation. Even the business world today is coming to grips with the need to work together. The business community expresses it in terms like networking and team building, but the point is, *we need each other.*

One strong resource can offset many deficits or setbacks in the life of a young person. A close family or a strong role model outside the family can carry someone through trials that might otherwise be debilitating. At the same time let me caution that resources need to change and adjust as kids grow up and circumstances change. We must always be ready to seek new resources when necessary.

We can say with a great deal of certainty that our teenagers are going to experience setbacks and failure. These may come in the form of some deficiency or finding they cannot compete and succeed in a certain area. It may be as common as being a jilted suitor, or as painful as missing the prom.

These setbacks are going to occur. The challenge is to have the resources in place to aid your teens through trying times.

TAKING INVENTORY OF YOUR RESOURCES

The second step in maximizing your resources is evaluating what you already have available. Make a list of who you can turn to for support and help. Write down other assets and tools at your disposal, including outside agencies, books and periodicals, and financial resources. And don't forget the all-important asset of *time.*

Let's look at some available resources.

PERSONAL FAITH

This is critical for both you and your son or daughter. Do you have confidence in the Lord? Are you committed to the work that God is doing in your life as well as in your child's?

Personal faith is our number one resource. We may not be able to force our convictions on our children, but we can remain true to these convictions ourselves in spite of all adversity.

FAMILY

Is your family in a position to be a resource? If so, use it. You can't *demand* that your teenager or young adult stay close to the family, but you can work at making the home a warm and comfortable place for your child.

I have often told my mom that she should write a book. I even thought of a title for her, *Kitchen Table Psychology*. I can remember our home vividly from my childhood. When we came home from school, Mom would always have something in the kitchen to eat—cookies, brownies, cake, etc., with an unending supply of milk. When one of us (I had one sister and two brothers) would wander in, she always managed to be around. Then while we were enjoying the treats, she would gently ask us questions about our day and how we were viewing life at the time. Our kitchen table was a secure place and many seeds of maturity were planted right there.

OTHER ADULTS

Significant others are some of the most crucial parts of your transition team. These are adults who have some kind of special relationship with your son or daughter. They may or may not be related, but they hold a place of love and trust in the family. As young people grow up, they reach certain points along the way where they experience some need to be on their own. This may not be a physical separation, but simply an opportunity to make independent decisions. This newfound independence is often frightening and painful for parents. You have made all the major decisions for years and now your teenager either isn't listening or is pressing you constantly for more autonomy.

In your heart you may doubt your teen's ability to make good decisions, but you recognize his or her need to do so. The adolescent environment may not be conducive to healthy choices, so we become concerned about the teen's choice in friends.

At this point you may want to call on another adult who has a strong relationship with your child and who holds to your values and commitments about life. As a Young Life leader, it has often been my job to fill that gap for parents. It is not any youthworker's goal or desire to replace parents or families; instead we prefer to come alongside families in times of transition and need. More important might be an uncle or aunt who has watched your child grow up. Extended family can be an invaluable resource.

The important thing is to be prepared. *Take a minute right now and list the resource people in your life.* Who would be in position to step in if your son or daughter needed an outside voice in his or her life?

A number of folks already know that I may call on them at any time, and they would be ready to spend some time with one of my sons or even have the boys over for a weekend or longer if necessary. One of the most difficult aspects of moving our family a few years ago was separating from the people who had surrounded our boys. If we hadn't been moving closer to a grandma and grandpa, plus uncles and aunts, we might not have moved.

If you don't have much of a list, I would encourage you to talk to your youth pastor. If that is not possible, look for another Christian organization such as Young Life, Youth for Christ, Student Ventures and others, and don't forget Christian coaches or teachers who might take a special interest in your child.

One warning. These people are resources and as such are to *supplement* and *support* you as the parent. Make sure you keep your expectations realistic as to their potential role. Never blame them if things don't work out the way you hope. They are resources and may be part of the team. They cannot be your whole team.

I think the first time I met Doug he was in trouble. I think the last time I saw Doug he was in trouble. In fact, he showed up at my apartment with two friends, all of whom were going to camp under duress. They had gotten in trouble with drugs at school, and I had convinced the vice principal that part of their sentence should include a Young Life camp. I had known the other two guys for a couple of years and they were dragging Doug along.

That week at camp forged a strong relationship between the four of us. Doug made a commitment to Christ and began to make some real progress in his life. Needless to say, his parents were encouraged by what they saw happening.

That is why I was so stunned one day when his dad called me and started to chew me out. In his mind I was the sole key to Doug's health and future. He was seeing a few slips in Doug's life and concluded that I wasn't right on top of the situation. I tried to explain to him the role I felt I played in his son's life, but he had a very different view. I suddenly found myself needing resources to deal with an unexpected problem.

I got together with Doug as fast as I could. We spent a good deal of time together and his attitude started to improve. A couple of weeks later his father called and apologized for his anger. He said some nice things, but the truth of his earlier call still bothered me. I had given all I could to Doug and I knew I couldn't keep it up. Already my relationship with him was costing me more than I had anticipated. As I thought through my options I realized there weren't many. From the day Doug walked into my apartment, I had worked hard to build our relationship. Now that I needed some help there was no place to turn. His father did not want the responsibility for his son's attitude and behavior back, and I had not developed any other resource people. Doug drifted away from the Lord in college and over the years we have lost touch, but I will never forget the lesson I learned early in my ministry. None of us can meet the needs of an adolescent by ourselves. We must develop a network of caring people to come alongside us.

Many friends and relatives out there would probably love to be a resource to you and your family. They have a great desire to see your family succeed. But they cannot replace you. One of the hard lessons we are learning as a nation is how to use our resources wisely. We have squandered so many of the beautiful gifts that God gave us. Our air is polluted, we are short of water, and many animals are living with the threat of extinction. By the same token we must be good stewards of the resources God has placed around our family. They are part of our team.

PEERS
This resource is a very tough one to orchestrate, but easy to encourage. If your child has good friends, be grateful. Conversely, if you are concerned about those friends, you may want to talk to a youth leader about getting some ideas and even some help.

Peers are extremely important during adolescence. They provide much of the social network for kids. One way to influence your child in a healthy way is to make your home a place where kids can hang out. Offer some incentive like food and take advantage of the opportunity to get to know your child's friends. For example, my mom got my friends to hang out at our house for two reasons. First, there was always good food around. Many of my buddies preferred eating dinner at my house to eating at home. Second, she was warm and a good listener. Most of my good friends saw her as a second mom. They would talk to her about things I didn't even know they were worried about. They knew she cared and would listen.

It would have been fun if we owned a pool table or had our own weight room, but you don't have to spend money to make your home a place where kids will hang out. Things like those can be very attractive, but they aren't the most important thing.

One of my favorite people is Jeff. He was a good kid from a good home. It has surprised no one that Jeff has grown up to be a highly respected young man and entered the ministry. But I have seen a number of good kids from good homes who did not turn out like Jeff. After weighing the evidence, I have reached the conclusion that Jeff's success stemmed from a group of buddies he surrounded himself with at Coronado High School in Scottsdale, Arizona. These young guys held each other accountable and hung together. Almost every one of them has done well. It is my opinion that one of the major reasons for the maturity and integrity of this group of young men is the commitment they shared as high schoolers to follow Christ together.

The younger your children, the more influence you can have here. I am not encouraging you to try to pick your children's friends, but make sure you encourage them, especially when they find a friend who is obviously a good influence.

SCHOOL

For some, this is a great source of encouragement and success. If you sense that school is a positive reinforcer, you don't necessarily need to do more than tuck that information away for future reference. On the other hand, if you can see that your teenager is not finding any healthy niche at school, start working with teachers, counselors, and others at the school to build a more positive environment. I know failure is often a better teacher than constant achievement, but an adolescent who doesn't discover any reason to stay in school may become difficult to deal with.

JOB

Again, a job may give a young person a sense of pride, responsibility, and accomplishment. If your son or daughter has a job or is pursuing one, make sure you get to know who he or she is working for. Not every place that hires younger folks worries about the environment they are creating. A new job can provide a very good opportunity to discuss goals and to learn responsibility. Ask questions like "What influence do you think this will have on school?" or "How do you think you will spend your money?" This may be a great time to show your child your family budget.

Having a job doesn't guarantee teens will learn responsibility. Yet, if you have thought it through, a job can be an integral part of your transition team.

BOOKS AND PERIODICALS

A great deal of resource information is available today in books and magazines for kids, young adults, and parents. Do your homework. Many resources deal with specific issues relating to parenting. If you have a daughter going into middle school or junior high, I would recommend you learn something about eating disorders. It may never be an issue in your family, but a little information early on could save you a lot of grief down the road.

You don't need to read everything, but you should regularly be seeking resources to help you grow as a Christian and a parent. A visit to your Christian bookstore or a call to your church or simply to another parent could yield a wealth of information about what is out there. I have placed a short bibliography at the end of the book. While it doesn't contain all of the helpful resources available in print, I trust it will get you started.

PROFESSIONAL COUNSEL

Another important resource is the Christian counselor. There are times when we simply need extra help. You may reach a particular point in your own life where your resource team has dwindled to a dangerous level. At these times I would encourage you to seek the help of a professional. It is important to pick someone who shares your values and has some experience in the situations you are facing.

PROVIDING A SAFE HARBOR IN THE STORM

You are your child's greatest resource.

No one can replace the role a parent has in the life of a child. And none of us should ever minimize our importance as a parent. Here are five things you can do to serve as a resource to your kids.

Pray

You have no greater tool at your disposal. As we will discuss later, the first thing prayer does is change the one who prays. Be faithful in your prayers for your children.

Encourage

There are a great many things in the world that will discourage and break young people. We need to learn the art of encouragement. Not praise for what they do, but appreciation for who they are. This is not applause without accountability. Rather, this is a building up and a recognition of the valuable inner person.

Trust

When possible, demonstrate to your children that you trust them. Give them opportunities to earn more trust. Whenever possible, treat them as adults.

Share Openly

One of the most effective ways to demonstrate trust and build your friendship with your children is to share how you feel about them and about life. They need to see how adults work out difficult issues in their lives and feel how adults cope with pain and disappointment. This is not to say that you should burden your kids with every detail of your life, but begin to let them in a little more. This is not simply sharing about how they make you feel. It must include more of your life than that.

LISTEN
They may rarely be in the mood to talk, but when they are, be prepared to listen. Ask good questions and maintain eye contact. Most kids are spontaneous emoters. They will talk when they are in the mood. At that point you will want to be ready to listen. They may not be looking for an answer from you. So be prepared to listen hard for the message *behind* the words. Most of all, show by your body language and your thoughtful questions that *what they are sharing with you is vitally important.* If you do, they will come back again and again.

The average American family moves every four years. It is common for kids to attend six or more schools while growing up.

Americans are taught to be individuals. Our society is hungrily consumed with grabbing for a piece of the American pie. Consequently, young people find themselves isolated and without clear guidance. They are trying to survive through the storms of transition without the necessary resources to keep their young lives on a steady course. Teenagers desire some independence, but there is often a need to find a safe harbor in the storm.

One of those lost in the storm of adolescence was Dottie. Her father was an alcoholic and her mom simply survived. There was virtually no resource team at her disposal.

I met her when she was a sophomore in high school. She faithfully attended our meetings and even went to camps. But she always seemed to be on a collision course with trouble. There were simply not enough people or resources around her to make up for the deficits she was experiencing.

Dottie and I have been friends now for fourteen years. Nothing much has changed. When we are together I can sense a real desire in her to be different. She continually renews her determination to make life work and to follow Christ. But she has never had a resource team in place. Try as I might to pull other resources together for her, she fears failure and won't risk a radical change. Dottie is now an adult who may never have the strength to follow her convictions.

A lot of people are like that. But we can muster resources for our children and give them the opportunity Dottie didn't have. It is going to take some work, but it is worth it.

Finally, one writer had this to say about our ultimate resource:

> The Lord works from the inside out. The world works from the outside in. The world would take people out of the slums. Christ takes the slums out of people, and then they take themselves out of the slums. The world would mold men by changing their environment. Christ changes men, who then change their environment. The world would shape human behavior, but Christ can change human nature.[1]

In the trauma of transition our teenagers face, we mustn't try to meet their needs alone. We will find great help and encouragement by gathering resources to aid us. Trusted adult friends, peers, school, a job, books and periodicals, and most importantly prayer are some of the resources at our disposal. We can be certain transitions are ahead. How they affect our children and our lives could be significantly improved with some well-planned help.

• • • • • • • • • •

CHAPTER EIGHT

Team Member 4:
Maintaining Intimacy
in the Midst of Transition

One of the great cries of teens today is for intimacy—the joy and security of closeness and trust with another human being. Too many have been robbed of the potential of real intimacy because of stress, busyness, pride, fear, and more. The lack of intimacy young people feel often causes a panic that forces them into misguided and even tragic relationships.

Marriages and families face great danger from the loss of intimacy or closeness. So much of our children's identity and sense of worth comes from relationships in the family.

What makes intimacy so difficult as kids go through their adolescent years comes from parents' lack of time and energy and teens' lack of response. For many parents, careers are peaking and there are more demands on our time. We are working more and beginning to discover we have less energy than in years past. At this point, we are often as insecure about what is going on as our kids are. We may have felt in control when they were younger, but now we don't know how to read them. Boys' responses are usually monosyllabic and girls' responses can range from chatter bordering on the frenetic, to sullenness with sudden bursts of tears.

When we parents expect the warm and expressive dialogue associated with preadolescence or mature adult conversation (which teens are sometimes capable of), we are generally let down and often feel disappointment, failure, or even anger. We may want to demand an adequate response and use negative reinforcement to accomplish it.

In this chapter we are going to offer some guidelines on maintaining intimacy during these trying times. Our goal is not to control the behavior of our teens, but to determine our response based on our security in Christ, and to develop some additional communications tools.

REMEMBER YOUR GOAL

If your goal is to achieve some preconceived "proper" response from your teen, then you have set the stage for ongoing tension between you and your child. If your goal is intimacy with your son or daughter, then you will look at the situation from a very different perspective.

The first objective is to remember who you are. You are a person who has set your eyes on Christ. Your identity and sense of worth come from your relationship with Him and don't depend on anyone's response.

If we can stay committed to this view of ourselves, the battle will not focus on our children's response. We will operate from a position of strength in Christ. Our own relationship with Christ becomes the foundation for our relationship with our teenagers. The peace and confidence we get from Christ will guide our emotions and responses to the teens in our family. This gives us the power to be proactive.

We can listen to the words being said, and we can listen with our hearts to our teens' silence, moods, or body language.

Gary Smalley and John Trent, in their very helpful book *The Language of Love*, quote current research about the communication of children.

> Researchers have found that from the earliest years little girls talk more than little boys. One study showed that even in the hospital nursery, girls had more lip movement than boys! That propensity keeps right on increasing through the years, giving them an edge at meaningful communication![1]

They go on to report that researchers found that 100 percent of the sounds coming from girls' mouths while on the playground were audible, recognizable words. The girls spent a great deal of time talking to other children, and nearly as much talking to themselves! Yet for little boys, only 68 percent of their sounds were understandable words. The remaining 32 percent were either one-syllable sounds like "uh" and "mmm," or sound effects like "Varooom!" "Yaaaaah!" and "Zooooom!"

This information should give you comfort. Now you know that the grunts that have been frustrating you are genetic and not simply a plot by your son to drive you crazy.

From a position of security and focus in Christ, you don't have to view the grunts and groans of adolescence as a threat. You can begin to develop the perspective that inside the heart of that young person there is a deep need to be loved and understood. God is doing a work in your teen's life just as He is doing a work in yours.

LEARN TO BE AN EMPATHETIC LISTENER

In the movie *Star Wars*, Obi Wan Kenobi tells Luke Skywalker to use his laser sword with his eyes closed. "Trust the force," he admonishes Luke. Luke didn't trust something he couldn't see until he experienced some success in wielding his sword with his eyes closed.

Parents generally put too much stock in what they see with their eyes and hear with their ears. They may even base their success as a parent solely on this criterion. This often creates conflict when they don't see or hear what they perceive as acceptable from their kids. Young persons on the other hand get frustrated because they sense conditions on their parents' love. They think they are loved only if they look and speak a certain way. These kids usually turn to a peer group for acceptance.

As parents we must be skillful listeners. We must constantly ask ourselves questions like, "Do I really understand what my son is saying?" "Am I forming my answer in my mind rather than carefully listening to the question?" "Have I just given my daughter another standard parental cliché?" "Do I present my ideas in ways that my kids can understand?" and "Am I communicating to convince or to understand?" These and other questions help us reflect on our communication style.

When Shawn came by my house one night I could tell things weren't going right. "My dad just blew up at me again," he explained. "He just won't listen when I try to explain how I feel!"

We'd had this conversation before. Shawn was a typical kid in many ways. He wasn't always very communicative, but he had a good heart. His father had great hopes for him and yet found it very difficult to listen to Shawn's hopes and fears.

There are always two sides to every conflict, and I worked hard with Shawn to help him own up to his responsibility in the relationship. But I could never get his dad to engage in a discussion about his own communication style.

"Kids are just spoiled," he would reply. Often he pleaded that what Shawn needed was another camp experience. It had made him so easy to live with for a while afterward.

Shawn's dad based his judgement of Shawn on a certain behavior. Consequently, he often missed what was really going on *inside* his son.

To be an empathetic listener we must step outside ourselves and attempt to view what our adolescent is saying from his or her point of view. The critical need for kids today is not our sympathy; it is our empathy, our understanding.

CLUES TO WHAT'S INSIDE A TEENAGER

The world of young people is one of constant change. Even when it's not apparent in their words or swaggering style, a lot of insecurity is creeping in. Often their words attempt to disguise their feelings. It is a difficult thing for them to admit they are insecure and unsure of themselves. At the same time, these young folks may not have the capacity to clearly express what is going on inside. To really understand them we must look for clues.

Boredom—This is one of the common stereotypes particularly seen in young males. They have a look about them that says the earth could be collapsing all around them and they really wouldn't care. We want to call them zombies, and we fret that they will never amount to anything.

Physical change—The truth is that many times these kids are in a growth phase or physical maturation phase during which their energy is used up from the inside. They may be walking around looking the way they look because it is how they feel. This phase also uses up much of their emotional energy.

Confusion—On the other hand, these teens may be at a point where they really don't know what to do or how they are supposed to feel. So at the moment at least, it may seem best not to worry about it.

A doctor would never prescribe a remedy for a patient without carefully considering the illness. Parents should not prescribe a remedy for their child without doing everything possible to discover where the teen's problems really lie.

Obviously, this involves some risk and a major effort at intimate communication. First, when we work hard to understand another person, we open ourselves up to being influenced by that other person. Our ideas and thought patterns are challenged. But, if our image of ourselves is centered on Christ and not our opinion of ourselves, we will always be open to change. We will see the communication risk as a way of being conformed to the image of Christ.

Second, we risk being wrong. What if after all this effort we misjudge what is actually going on? In response to that concern, I simply want to ask you this question: Wouldn't you rather someone work hard to really understand who you are and what you are feeling, and then with the best intentions be wrong, than to never have had another person risk that kind of love? But these risks must be taken to clear up teenage confusion. Only intimate communication can help teens face their doubts and fears.

Here are four other steps in empathetic listening for you to keep in mind.

1. *Choose a good setting.* If you are ready to listen carefully to your son or daughter, choose a setting that will facilitate communication. Make sure you are not likely to be interrupted. If possible, ask your child where he or she would like to meet.

At the risk of contradicting myself, I must say that even in the best setting communication doesn't always happen. We need to be ready to talk (or just listen) when our kids are ready. That may be in the car, while watching a movie, or just before bed.

2. *Keep your eyes on your teen*—and I don't mean spying. Often you may wonder who your teenager is talking to because of the way he or she looks down or around during a conversation. But your teen is aware if you are not totally with him or her. Work hard to stay focused on your teen. Eye contact is the key to this.

3. *Repeat back to them what you are hearing* in ways that acknowledge and express the content and feelings they are sharing. This will require you to set aside your own judgments on the matter long enough to really hear what they are saying.

When your college student says, "Mom, I hate school!" a typical response might be, "Well, everyone hates things they have to do sometimes. You'll grow to appreciate this opportunity." A more appropriate response might be, "You are really frustrated, aren't you?"

By a simple statement that acknowledges your teen's problem, you are not judging the outburst, and it allows your teen to clarify if "frustration" is an accurate description of how he or she feels.

4. *Respond from their vantage point.* When the opportunity presents itself to share your insight or wisdom, do it from your understanding of *their world*, not from the perspective of how the adult world functions. Show them that you have listened carefully to them and you understand the situation from their point of view.

When your seventh-grade daughter comes home crying and asks why no one likes her, don't say, "Nonsense, you are very popular." Instead, you may want to respond with, "Do you think it's your problem or their problem?"

Her response may tell you how she feels about her looks or how someone hurt her feelings. From here you may let her know that if she feels that way about her appearance there might be some possible solutions the two of you can explore.

To summarize, we must remember to demonstrate that we value our teenager's feelings and perceptions. We do this most effectively when we feel valuable in our own hearts because of what Christ has done for us. Then we work hard at listening and avoid forming our response while our son or daughter is sharing a feeling or trying to make a point. It takes a lot of energy to be an empathetic listener. We may often feel unappreciated by our teen for the effort we are making. But his or her response is not the key. Our commitment and faithfulness will pay off in time.

BEGIN TO MOVE FROM PARENT TO FRIEND

Grandparents will tell you that you never stop being a parent. Yet, in the course of raising children there comes that difficult point when we realize that we must begin to see our child as an adult. Even earlier than that, we must recognize when to begin to communicate more like a friend than an authority figure.

This is a very difficult transition to recognize. Also, we must remember that as our kids go through some periods in the teen years they may need the security of that authority. Beginning to share as a friend can be very intimidating because it may reveal some weak communication habits that we have not been aware of. Following are some tips to make the transition as smooth as possible.

Be Honest

All of us struggle with communication. Tell your teens how you feel and ask for *their* advice. Make sure they know how much you want to be an available friend as well as a parent. Be clear that you are not giving up your parental role and leadership, but you want to recognize their maturity and growth.

Say You're Sorry

If you recognize that you have not communicated in a helpful manner, apologize and make adjustments. By doing this you demonstrate your respect for teens' feelings and perceptions.

Give Them Space

Adolescents need room to grow. They need privacy. Becoming their friend does not mean acting like another adolescent.

It means demonstrating an attitude of respect. This means giving them some privacy and independence.

DEVELOP FRIENDS YOUR OWN AGE

Have you ever learned how to be a friend? Have you worked at it? All of us need to learn the art of developing strong peer relationships. Many times parents need the friendship of their young adults more for the parents' sake than the kids'. This can often lead to disappointment and frustration.

DON'T BE AFRAID TO TOUCH

You need to discover appropriate ways to touch your children. This is very important. It may mean a firm handshake instead of tousling their hair. Or a quick hug may be more apropos than plopping the kid into your lap. If you stay committed and observant, you will find out what works and you will discover that, even though kids need change, their need for touch will grow. A standoffish junior high boy can easily become an affectionate collegian.

DON'T TRY TO BUY INTIMACY

You cannot spend enough money to create intimacy. It must come from time, commitment, warmth, and love. It will come from kids who know you both care about them and also provide accountability and parameters. It will come when they discover that you have been on your knees on their behalf.

STAY CLOSE TO YOUR SPOUSE

The trauma of teen transition in a family often exacts its biggest toll on the parents' marriage. Unfulfilled expectations, disagreements about direction, and a preoccupation with the kids can leave wives and husbands feeling left out and jealous. The stress created by children can leave moms and dads bankrupt emotionally and unable to address each other's needs.

We have talked about finding our focus and center in Christ. Next we must guard and nurture our relationship with our spouse. Marriage is hard enough work without the added stress of adolescents, but it can become a great source of strength and encouragement when facing tough times.

Intimacy with our spouse gives us the experience and some of the framework for intimacy with our children.

Shawn and I are still good friends. His father left the family a few years ago and has been remarried for some time. Shawn's mom fought to hold the family together and make life as "normal" as possible for the kids. Shawn has slowly forged a relationship with his dad and has been a great help to his mom. He will never know the kind of intimacy with his dad that he wishes, but they have found some common ground to share interests and opinions.

Shawn remains very close to his mom, and she will tell you he has been her closest friend through everything. Intimacy is often the result of pain and struggle. Many times it is born out of desperation and failure. When we don't have all the answers, we become more human, more approachable. We are forced to admit that the best relationships aren't perfect. The deepest relationships aren't always the ones that are the most trouble free. Intimacy comes from dependence when we recognize our need for each other. It comes from commitment, that willingness to roll up our sleeves and to keep working on our relationship until we see some change (usually in ourselves). And it comes from endurance, our commitment not to give up on each other, but to stay committed through the hard and painful times.

Intimacy is much more a discovery than a feeling. It comes from a journey with many twists and turns along its path. But, if we can stay faithful to the direction set before us, we may discover intimacy along the way. As we move ahead with our transition team, the emphasis from this chapter will be continually underscored. The peace and confidence you have in Christ will empower you to make good choices. This will be important to using each team member well. Also, each additional member of your team is offered to help you respond to your children and not to manipulate a response from them. Then in the midst of your journey through adolescent transitions, you will discover the joy of intimacy with Christ and with your teen.

• • • • • • • • • •
Team Member 5:
Prayer—Healing Strength
for the Stressed

To say that prayer should be the first rule of parenting can be frustrating and convicting. We are a society raised on the premise that we need to be self-sufficient and independent. Therefore to reduce our parenting to prayer takes too much power out of our hands. We are unaccustomed to that position.

Far too many Christian parents simply trot down to the nearest bookstore for the latest guide to "successful" parenting. While these books are helpful and encouraging, they were never intended to replace the activity of prayer.

Whether we are aware of it or not, prayer impacts our lives. It may be the *lack of prayer* that results in stress and uncertainty, or it may be the *evidence of prayer* resulting in peace and confidence. There are few things in life more demanding and at the same time more necessary than prayer. It is our greatest resource in the battles we face, yet the most difficult one to master. It is the transition team member we should most often turn to, yet the one we usually find the most troublesome to face.

Throughout history when God's children have faced disaster, insurmountable odds, or tragedy, the common thread of their survival has been prayer. In Exodus 3:7, God told Moses, "I have indeed seen the misery of my people in Egypt. I have heard them crying out."

No one could express the sentiments of a broken and contrite heart like King David:

> Have mercy on me, O God, have mercy on me,
>   for in you my soul takes refuge. (Psalm 57:1)

TRANSITION AND TRANSFORMATION
FOR THE ONE WHO PRAYS

It has been said that the first thing prayer changes is the one who prays. When parents come before the Lord on behalf of their children, they may often walk away with peace in their own hearts. When we ask the Father to change the behavior of one of His children, we are generally confronted with our need for grace and change.

Such was the case with Herb. We had talked often about the rebellion of his oldest son. Herb was a successful businessman and was very embarrassed and hurt by his son's actions. His wife, Marilyn, was a woman devoted to Christ and with a clear understanding of the need for prayer in this situation. As Herb resisted her invitations to prayer, tension grew in their relationship as well as in their family. Their son was being swept away in an angry current of rebellion while they drifted apart from each other in their own sea of confusion and hurt.

Finally, during one of our talks together I worked up the courage to ask Herb to pray with me. We were at a restaurant and with a furtive glance at the surrounding tables he agreed to let me offer a prayer. Bolstered by this response,

I asked Herb if he would be willing to meet regularly just to pray. I let him decide where and when. That was the beginning of an extraordinary journey.

Herb and I met weekly for a number of months. At first our get-togethers didn't look much like prayer meetings, but the Lord was slowly beginning to work in the life of a man who had always prided himself in being independent and strong. Prayer had never been a resource or team member for him. He was discovering a whole new dimension as a parent and person.

In the beginning I kept a log of our meetings. It was simply a piece of paper with a line drawn down the middle. On the left side I would write down what Herb thought we should pray for. I never tried to change his mind in those requests. This was to be part of his growth. Too often I have been guilty of trying to manipulate the lessons the Lord should teach others. This time I wanted to allow God's Spirit to lead and change Herb where necessary. In the process He would also change me, I was quite certain.

I told Herb that on the right side of the page we would record God's answers to our prayers. I think at that point he was willing to humor me. But it wasn't too long before that right side began to fill up.

Sometimes we must look hard for those answers. We expect one response, and when we don't see it we can miss what God is doing. As prayer changes us, we gain a new perspective. We begin to see more from God's perspective and less from ours.

Herb's son, Kevin, did not become a scholar after the first prayer meeting, but he didn't get kicked out of school either. Herb needed to see God's provision in what God was doing, not in what Herb wanted Him to do.

After about eight months of meeting for prayer Herb and I evaluated our time. We had seen tremendous changes in Kevin. Sometimes Herb would come to our meetings with statements like, "I can't believe it; he's like a new kid!" He began to ask me if there were other things we could be praying for, and started praying for my family as much as his. *In the midst of all of the concern over Kevin, the most profound change was in Herb.*

God can change your kids. He will use prayer to ease the transitions of adolescence. But, if you are not willing to be changed in the process, you will have a difficult time sustaining your prayer life.

Adolescents will often disdain our advice simply because it is ours. If you are a parent of a teenager, you have probably been frustrated many times by the lack of response your suggestions get. But, let *them* come up with an idea, or worse yet, *one of their friends*, and it's golden. Let good old mom or dad offer an idea and it's, "Yea, *right*, Mom" (with the inflection making it negative).

At such times our most faithful team member, the one we keep coming back to, is prayer. Here we find strength and assurance. We are enlisting God's help—the most powerful force in the universe—to intercede on our behalf. Even in the midst of the storms of transition, when we are at a loss as to what to pray for, the Holy Spirit intercedes:

> In the same way, the Spirit helps us in our weakness. We do not know what we ought to pray for, but the Spirit himself intercedes for us with groans that words cannot express. And he who searches our hearts knows the mind of the Spirit, because the Spirit intercedes for the saints in accordance with God's will. (Romans 8:26-27)

THE KEY TO PRAYER IS SHOWING UP

I will never forget the words of Stephen Winward in his book *How to Talk to God.* "The whole of life should be a walk with God, and all times and all places should be sacred to Him."[1] Here we are given the admonition to pray our way through life. There is no magic place or circumstance for prayer. At any place and under any set of circumstances, we can and should bring our needs to the Father.

At the same time, we learn to live in communion with Christ by setting aside specific blocks of time for Him. A specific place or a special chair might help us, but prayer is interior. We must cultivate a quiet heart sensitive to the whispers of the Spirit.

The important point here is to do it. Prayer is something we must give ourselves to. We must open our hearts to the Lord and allow Him to speak back to us. Prayer must become a habit.

The habit of prayer doesn't happen by itself. It is in private moments of focus on Christ that we discover how to open our hearts and minds to Him. The skill of praying will be mastered by practice.

Paderewski, the famous Polish pianist, once said, "If I stop practicing the piano for a day, I notice the difference; if I stop for two days, my family notices the difference; if I stop for three days my friends notice the difference; and if I stop for a week the public notices the difference."[2] Certainly in our lives the lack of prayer is usually more obvious than we care to admit. During the turbulence caused by teenage transitions, we cannot afford to get "rusty" in our prayers. A consistent life of prayer keeps us focused and in touch with the Lord.

When I first asked Herb to pray, he was concerned about saying things right. He was under the impression that effective prayers should be offered in King James language with a lot of "Thees" and "Thous." He had been confused about *how* to approach God. Prayer to him was a formal ceremony done by serious and pious people, not by driven, rebellious folks as he had pictured himself.

I have often felt the same emotions Herb expressed. It was not hard for me to relate to his concerns. Often when I pray, my own fears and sense of failure inhibit my approach to God. I feel guilty asking Him for the same thing again or confessing the same misconduct I confessed the day before. At such times it is crucial that I remind myself that it is my problem and not God's. He is ready and anxious to hear my prayer. He is not shaking His finger at me like a stern schoolmaster. He is holding out His arms, a loving Father longing to embrace His child.

Our Lord told us about prayer in Matthew 7:7-8: "Ask and it will be given to you; seek and you will find; knock and the door will be opened to you. For everyone who asks receives; he who seeks finds; and to him who knocks, the door will be opened."

That is not the wishful thinking of some well-meaning person. It is a promise from Jesus Christ. If we seek Him we will find Him. He listens to our prayers and knows the longings of our heart.

He does not require us to address Him formally any more than we would require that of our own children.

When Herb discovered he could address the Lord with words from his heart, prayer became less formal and awkward. Prayer was still hard work, but Herb was beginning a journey that would lead him down a path of discovery and growth.

Brennan Manning recently shared with a group of our staff one of the most remarkable examples of this I have ever heard. Not too long ago he responded to a knock at his door. The woman standing in the doorway asked if he would please come and pray with her ailing father. Soon Brennan was sitting on the edge of a bed talking to a frail, elderly man about life, love, and eternity. The man shared that for years he was intimidated and confused about how to pray. He had asked others for help until someone finally told him he could talk to the Lord just like he would a friend standing right beside him. This had revolutionized his life.

He pointed an aged finger at an empty chair beside his bed and whispered to Brennan that now he simply pretended

Jesus was sitting in the chair, and they would talk. It was a secret he had been afraid to tell anyone else.

Brennan prayed with this dear saint and went home deeply touched and greatly encouraged.

Sometime later he heard from the woman again. This time it was to share the news of her father's passing. "The odd thing," she said to Brennan, "was that he had pulled himself over to the edge of his bed, and when I found him he had died with his head resting on the chair."

We may talk to the Lord as though He were right next to us, but in truth He is even closer than that.

As a parent you know that kids are always asking for something. It can be that constant need for more cash or the keys to the car. Requests for leniency and more freedom are frequent, too. But a relationship solely made up of asking is a tedious one. It has no depth and allows for only shallow perceptions of another's value.

Certainly we would not want to approach God the same way. Prayer that is exclusively asking becomes self-centered. When we ask from a posture of adoration, confession, and thanksgiving, our requests take on more of what God's will might be rather than ours.

Scripture tells us to ask in the name of Jesus: "Until now you have not asked for anything in my name. Ask and you will receive, and your joy will be complete" (John 16:24).

We are given that privilege in Christ to offer our cares and needs to the Father in His name because He has chosen to be our Advocate. Winward offers this further insight: "In the Bible 'the name' means nature; it stands for the person revealed in his character. To pray in Christ's name is to pray in accordance with His nature and character, in harmony with His revealed will and purpose."[3]

There is nothing so small that God is not interested in it or bigger than He is able to do it.

Too often we are tempted to give up. We just can't seem to get our message through. Don't give up. God has given you permission in Scripture to be persistent. You may have heard someone say that God's timing is not our timing. Rarely does God work within the time frame we create for Him. But He always works.

For over fifty years my grandmother faithfully prayed for my grandfather. I am sure that many times during those years she must have wondered if the Lord was listening. My grandfather was a wonderful man who, like so many others, shared a lifetime battle with alcohol. So for more than half a century Grandma prayed for him. And in the waning years of Grandad's life he opened his heart to Christ and went Home in peace.

I hope you are gaining a better understanding of the life of prayer. You see, if we will give ourselves consistently to adoration, confession, and thanksgiving, by the time we begin making our requests we will be changed. And when our hearts are united with Christ, we can approach the Father with confidence and joy.

COMMON BARRIERS TO PRAYER

I have often wondered why prayer is so difficult. If it is such a key transition team member, why do we hesitate to appropriate its power? Of the many possible reasons, I would like you to consider four.

GUILT

When I first began to pray with Herb, he wrestled with a familiar enemy: guilt. "I feel like I'm cheating," he would say. "I have never really prayed before, and to start now when things are such a mess doesn't seem right."

Many of us struggle with guilt because we recognize that we only pray when all else has failed. We resent being treated that way ourselves, and we know it must really irk God when we do it. The truth could not be more different. We have created a God in our image that says we must perform a certain way to have access to Him. That is not the God of my experience and certainly not the God of Scripture, who says,

> And call upon me in the day of trouble;
> I will deliver you, and you will honor me.
> (Psalm 50:15)

We have permission to call upon the Lord in times of trouble and distress. He will not hold our previous prayerlessness against us during those times. He loves us too much. If you have put off praying because you hadn't prayed in the good times, start now! Take your burdens of guilt and failure and lay them at the feet of your loving Father and watch Him take them away. Being a parent is a heavy burden. At times the transition periods in our kids' lives feel like they will crush us. Don't add an unnecessary burden to one already so heavy. Christ bids us in Matthew 11:28, "Come to me, all you who are weary and burdened, and I will give you rest."

FEAR OF THE COST

Another common block to prayer is fear. We fear what it might cost us to enter into a relationship of prayer with the Lord. Let's face it, we twentieth-century adults want a painless solution to our problems. We baby boomers want a quick and easy fix. We hesitate at the thought that something might infringe on our interests and lifestyle. We are afraid if we begin to pray we might be confronted with issues in our lives we are unprepared to deal with.

We have been amazed and at times shocked in our ministry to find a growing number of kids being checked into psychiatric hospitals because they are discipline problems and their parents want someone else to deal with them. Granted, there are times when the situation may warrant such action, but we are seeing a growing number simply put into these institutions because it's quicker and easier.

All of us have some fear of change. It is always difficult to be confronted with areas in our lives that require growth or correction.

We must gather the courage to risk such a confrontation. I don't know if Herb would have had I not pursued him. Perhaps it would be good to find a prayer partner to help you and hold you accountable.

DOUBT

Another reason some balk at prayer is doubt. What if I go to all this trouble, get my hopes up, and God doesn't come through? This is a desperate fear. Often our pain is so real, and on the surface there appears so little reason for hope, that we are not sure if even God can fix it.

The fact is, God may not "fix" our problem or problem child in the way we desire, but He has promised to hear our cries and meet us at our point of need. He has commanded us to "come to Me." Even in our moments of greatest doubt we can approach the Lord in obedience and He will meet us there.

Francois Fenelon, in her *Little Book of Prayers*, wrote, "Lord, I don't know what to ask of You; only You know what I need. I simply present myself to You; I open my heart to You. I have no other desire than to accomplish Your will. Teach me to pray. Amen."[4]

ADDICTION TO BUSYNESS

Lastly, a prayerless life may also result from an addiction to busyness. I find it deeply disturbing when people tell me they don't have time to pray. We have time to worry, we have time to complain, but we cannot seem to find the minutes in our day to go to our Lord in prayer.

Many of us are caught in the *need to produce*. Generally speaking, the busier we are, the better we feel. If we are living a hectic life, at least we appear successful and vital. To be still is to be alone with our thoughts and that may seem threatening. So we maintain the blur we call a life and look forward to the day we can retire and forget all of this.

But King David had a different idea. He wrote, "Be still before the Lord and wait patiently for him" (Psalm 37:7).

If your life is ruled by busyness, you need prayer on your team. When your teenager doesn't seem to respond to anything you do or say, prayer is the team member that offers quiet and peace. It has the potential to bring God's perspective to every situation. As you rally your transition team you will discover that prayer empowers every member.

The *heart* that seeks the Lord is always rewarded. We cannot substitute anything in its place, and a life of prayer will eventually leave its mark.

A *prayerful spirit* is a spirit to which God can speak. The more sensitive and responsive our hearts become to the voice of the Father, the more confident we are that He hears us.

Learning the *discipline of prayer* radically changed the direction of Herb's life. I want to encourage you to sit down and read Psalm 27 today. Make the words of the psalm your prayer. The last verse beautifully sums up this chapter.

> Wait for the LORD;
>> be strong and take heart
>> and wait for the LORD. (Psalm 27:14)

In conclusion, we join with John Baillie as he prays for vision, faith, and love. "Eternal God, you have been the hope and joy of many generations, and who in all ages has given men the power to seek you and in seeking you find you, grant me, I pray you, a clearer vision of your truth, a greater faith in your power, and a more confident assurance of your love. Amen."[5]

• • • • • • • • • • •

CHAPTER TEN

Team Member 6: Managing Time Factors

I went out Lord,
*   men were coming and going,*
*   walking and running.*
In spite of all their grand efforts,
*   they were still short of time.*
*   Lord, you must have made a mistake in your*
*   calculation.*
Lord, I have time.
*   I have plenty of time, all the time you give me,*
*   the years of my life,*
*   the days of my years,*
*   the hours of my days.*
Mine to fill quietly, calmly,
Up to the brim.

AUTHOR UNKNOWN

I first met Bill Piel when I was in eighth grade and he was in seventh. I certainly had no idea that our lives would be linked together from then on.

Bill and I played on our elementary school flag football team. None of us on the team understood the changes swirling through Bill's life. His mother was remarried that year and he suddenly became Bill Hamilton. Since becoming adults, Bill has shared with me the amazing events surrounding that experience. It became one of the turning points in his life. Up until then his reputation was less than desirable. His mother was overwhelmed with the task of raising five kids on her own. Bill and his older brother often found themselves without any supervision. Even though he was not a "bad kid," he had some minor brushes with the law and was on the verge of heading the wrong way for life.

For some reason, this change of name encouraged Bill to seek a change in his life. He thought with a new name a be he could become a new person. The marriage had put Bill in a different school where he was not known. He had a chance to be different.

Now Bill is a husband, father, and full-time minister. He is highly respected in his community and very effective in his work. We have been partners in reaching kids all our adult lives. But, he would be the first to tell you that it wasn't changing his name that rerouted his life. Bill's life-direction was still up for grabs until our Young Life leaders, Dr. Bob and Rillie Lee, got hold of him. It was through this remarkable couple that Bill found Christ. Still, all through high school Bill struggled with allowing the faith he held in his heart to manifest itself in his life. That's the part that took time. As a youngster he had experienced a name change, yet he still had to rely on the Lord to change and build his character.

Each of us "changed our name" when we came into the family of God. We call ourselves Christians and serve a new Master. Still, each day we face transitions as we allow our Father to change and mold us to the image of Christ.

I find there is a great deal of interest in shortcuts today. Too often we are consumed by a desire to move quickly past the challenges and changes in our lives. Many folks today want instant spirituality. They want to win the race without experiencing the agony of training for the event. If we push this on the adolescents in our home, we keep them from a healthy growth process.

In the next two chapters we will be looking at transitions from the vantage points of crisis, transformation, and change. To understand the scope of the transition your son or daughter is experiencing, you will want to view him or her from one of these vantage points.

When Bill changed his name and determined to change his lifestyle, he underwent a transition of transformation. He gained a feeling of newness and hope for the future. In this he reminds us of a valuable fact: transitions do not have to result in crisis. In fact, most transition is very normal and healthy.

A transition from crisis may be the result of the loss of a family member, a close friend's death or suicide, your own brush with death, or a divorce. Yet for teenagers without a support team and the correct coping tools, a serious crisis may emerge from what would be merely a simple transition for someone else.

TRANSITIONS OF GROWTH

As we discussed earlier, adolescence can be viewed in two broad time periods—early adolescence and late adolescence. We know that from approximately ages ten through fifteen kids go through tremendous physical and emotional change. Then from sixteen through about age twenty-two they go through late adolescence. During this time, you can expect greater intellectual development and need for independence.

Every child will face the basic transitions of growth and maturity differently. Some children reach puberty earlier than others. We can't do much about *when* puberty will strike, but there is a lot we can do when we see it approaching. Puberty is a major transition and the physical changes are very obvious, yet the greatest challenges are often not so visible. Many young people are plagued with feelings of insecurity and inferiority during this transition. They wiggle out of the warm cocoon of childhood and face competition and comparisons they have never felt before. Tall, gangly boys often look awkward and clumsy. Their voices are changing and nothing seems to fit anymore. Suddenly they become aware of how people see them. Many times they lack the social skills and confidence to relate to girls. They stumble through their first bout with love and panic at the potential for disaster.

As puberty approaches for your son or daughter, you can anticipate these challenges and provide coping resources.

For example, I have known parents who took their teen on a date. One dad took his daughter out to dinner and then to a movie. He opened the car door for her and made polite conversation all evening. He tried his hardest to help her relax and have fun, and he succeeded. Then at the end of the evening he asked her how she felt about the way he had treated her. "Daddy," she quietly replied, "now I think I know what I want dating to be for me. Thank you." When he received a positive response he left her with this challenge: "Never settle for less in your relationship with a boy." His daughter never forgot that invaluable lesson.

It may be helpful to call on one of your resource people to take your son or daughter on a date. Sometimes we need an outside voice in our child's life. A younger adult makes the date more comfortable for the teen. If you have thought through your team, you will likely know just who to call.

Physical attractiveness is one of the great threats to a young person's self-image today. We live in a society that places far too much emphasis on our body's appearance. We can point out all their good attributes, but most kids are simply going to go through a stage in early adolescence where they hate something about their physical appearance. They are too tall, too short, too heavy, too thin; they have pimples, or freckles, or "uncool hair."

Parents can have a positive influence on their adolescent kids in a variety of ways. If you are comfortable with the way you look, it will help. Also, be sensitive to styles and fashion. As much as you may hate to give in to the cost of fashion these days, allowing your son or daughter *some* current styles or even a brand name or two may give them some confidence in the face of drastic physical and emotional changes.

Our goal is not to speed up the transition process, but to help our children adapt to the various changes they are experiencing.

As parents we want to look for signs in our kids' ability to cope and integrate changes into their lives. We want to help them develop coping resources to move with as little strain as possible through the inevitable changes they will face.

Remember team member goals? We must remind ourselves to keep the end in mind during these crazy times. We must ask, what are we hoping the long-term results of this short-term discomfort will be? If you are firmly rooted in your goals, who you are, and how you will respond to your son or daughter, you won't panic during transition times. (A little panic is allowed in crisis, however!)

Our culture will continue to tell young people that they need to look a certain way, drive a certain car, and wear certain clothes to really have it together and be happy. We will not help the transition process by ignoring these messages or pretending they aren't there! Nor will we help them by giving in to every passing fancy. But, if we are thoughtful and take every opportunity to build up our children for *who* they are and not how they look or perform, we will give them an invaluable tool for adapting to change.

YOUR RESOURCE OF TIME

Here are three principles for managing time during transitions in an adolescent's life:

- Don't become a crisis manager.
- Make time for your children.
- Give your teenager time to grow up.

DON'T BECOME A CRISIS MANAGER

Most of us spend a good deal of our time managing crises. We are always putting out fires or trying to recover from the last major blaze. Time management means exactly what it says. We are to manage our time. Decide on what is important and then do those things. I remember Gordon McDonald saying that too many of us spend our lives doing good things when we need to focus on what's best.

If we can commit ourselves to pursuing what is "best," it can help us make good decisions.

Remember, choose your battles wisely. If your daughter wants to wear some clothes that you aren't sure about, ask yourself a couple of questions. Is this something that is truly inappropriate, or am I struggling with my own insecurity here? Check out the clothes she normally wears. Is this new outfit a fad or style that will be gone in a few months? Or does it represent some pattern I am concerned about? A "time manager" will carefully consider these and other questions before making a judgment.

Through part of my college career I chose to wear my hair pretty long. My parents were pastors and my shaggy looks must have caused them a fair amount of embarrassment. But they had a commitment to look beyond my hair and work hard to know the young man underneath. They saw me involved in ministry and working my way through college. So, aside from some good-natured kidding, they never made my hair a barrier in our relationship. They showed me a good deal of respect and didn't create an unnecessary need for me to flex my "independent" muscles. By the time I graduated from college my hair was a respectable length and my relationship with my parents as strong as ever.

If you focus on the strengths of your children and refuse to panic when you see something new, it helps create an environment where change can occur without as much trauma.

MAKE TIME FOR YOUR CHILDREN
If you have browsed through a bookstore lately, you will notice many books for the stressed, busy, and burned out. Life provides plenty of challenge and everyone's schedule feels out of control. When you add the time kids require, it is no wonder parents shake their heads and throw up their hands. But, no matter how busy you may feel there is still

some discretionary time in your schedule. We must choose to give time to our children. As important as once-a-year vacations are for your family, this is not what I have in mind.

All of us have time we cannot control. In the Los Angeles area where I live many people commute hours to and from work. Most of us feel our free time is greatly reduced by travel. Still, we have certain hours we must make choices about. Those need to be wise choices. Let me give you a couple of suggestions. Don't put off your personal relationship with Christ. Often if we don't wake up quite on time in the morning, we put the Lord off to the next day. This can become days, weeks, and years. The guilt and frustration we originally felt can become hardness and apathy. However, when we see such values modeled by our children, we know we have missed the mark. Unfortunately, even if we model a strong spiritual life—even a balanced, nonthreatening one—it's no guarantee our kids will, too. But if we don't, more often than not, our children won't, either.

The next priority is your discretionary time. You need to spend it with your primary relationships—spouse and children. I know many of you are thinking, *What about time for myself?* We often feel we are so busy caring for others that we have no time for ourselves. Please understand that time with Christ is the most powerful, positive, and healthy time you can give to yourself. If you think devotional time is duty and work, something you do "for God," think again. We spend time with Christ because in the hustle and stress of our everyday lives He is the only One who can take our ragged clothes of burden and care and exchange them for a fresh and clean garment of peace and rest.

Likewise, if we are giving time to our other primary relationships, we will have a great sense of freedom and release when we do spend time on ourselves.

And, of course, we must have some personal time. I love to exercise and read. That combination really helps me. The exercise is tough to get in regularly. I drive a lot (I live in L.A.!)

and other priorities often get in the way. I also try to read at least a little every day. I generally have three books going at once and almost always one is a novel or something fun. The point is, if we ignore our own personal time, and time with significant others, it will damage our own emotional life, as well as our children's.

GIVE YOUR KIDS TIME TO GROW UP
Transitions happen for different teens at different times. According to James Dobson, puberty "may occur as early as nine or ten years of age or as late as seventeen or eighteen, but each boy and each girl has his or her own timetable."[1]

Obviously, we can't orchestrate that change. We can, however, be prepared for the results and have our transition team in place. We should be especially aware of the following issues.

Many young people today are growing up too fast. Early dating is a concern in many affluent communities. Boys and girls, from age ten up, are begging their parents to allow them to date. "More affluent families want their children to be more socialized. They feel that social dealings, as well as academic programs, are somehow a race; the earlier you start, the better," says David Elkind, author of *The Hurried Child*. Elkind believes one cause of this trend is television and other "contemporary influences."[2]

On the other end of the spectrum we have the "boomerang" children. The term *boomerang* refers to young adults who have moved back into their parents' home for one reason or another. For many families this can be healthy and happy. But for others, parents *and* children, it can be embarrassing and frustrating.

The high cost of buying or renting a home these days is a key to this trend. Many of these young people are from more affluent communities. Often their income on their own would not allow them to live in the way they desire.

Parents must decide, based on the real needs of their

children, whether moving back in is an option. It is critical, though, to keep a few things in mind.

Family life with adult kids will not be the same as it was when they were children. Make up your mind immediately not to set your expectations at impossible levels. A young man or woman moving home should not be treated the way he or she was at sixteen. Don't become a maid or a butler. Make sure some guidelines are clearly stated and give the arrangement a timetable so you can regularly evaluate how it is going. Finally, if possible, charge them rent. To charge them what they would pay somewhere else may not be appropriate, but some kind of rent is critical for maintaining your peace of mind and their dignity.

The storms accompanying transition come in many sizes and levels of intensity. It is very difficult to judge when they will hit or how long they will last. The key to navigating the typical changes in a teenager's life is in the parents' ability to *adapt and integrate* these changes into the family's lives. A solid support base (your transition team), carefully nurtured values, forgiveness, and patience all help provide the stability necessary to keep the ship on course.

Managing the time trials of adolescent life will test both you and your teenager. Keep in mind the two basic categories of adolescent development—early adolescence and late adolescence. Remind yourself of the common characteristics of each stage. Then you can anticipate certain changes and be better prepared. If your daughter has suddenly become moody, you will be in a much better position to help her if you remember that teens commonly ride an emotional roller coaster when they reach puberty. On the other hand, if you react as though it is simply rebellion, it will likely end up that way. Further, stay committed to doing the "best" with the time you have. There are many "good" things and events that crowd out what we really value.

The challenge of mastering our time in today's culture is a formidable one. I don't think "mastery" is really the issue.

It is simply a matter of deciding what is important in your life and then making time for it.

One night in the course of writing this book, I played Boggle. As anxious as I am to make deadlines and keep everyone happy, I can seldom resist joining the rest of my family in playing a game. I want to make time to play with my three sons. These years of family life are over with so soon. So I reflect and make time for my three boys now, before I miss out on having any memories of them at all! Prayers like this one by Rev. Wilferd A. Peterson make me think:

Slow Me Down, Lord

Slow me down, Lord.

Ease the pounding of my heart by the quieting of my mind.

Steady my hurried pace with a vision of the eternal reach of time.

Give me, amid the confusion of the day, the calmness of the everlasting hills.

Break the tensions of my nerves and muscles with the soothing music of the singing streams that live in my memory.

Teach me the art of taking minute vacations—of slowing down to look at a flower, to chat with a friend, to pat a dog, to smile at a child, to read a few lines from a good book.

Slow me down, Lord, and inspire me to send my roots deep into the soil of life's enduring values, that I may grow toward my greater destiny.

Remind me each day that the race is not always to the swift; that there is more to life than increasing its speed.

Let me look upward to the towering oak and know that it grew great and strong because it grew slowly and well.[3]

• • • • • • • • • •

CHAPTER ELEVEN

Team Member 7: Laughter and Fun as Shelters from the Storm

A cheerful heart is good medicine,
but a crushed spirit dries up the bones.

PROVERBS 17:22

There is little in life that produces more good for body and soul than laughter. Laughing not only releases certain enzymes in your body that promote good health, but it also just feels good. To regain a healthy perspective on life we must cultivate our sense of humor. In the middle of the change and uncertainty of raising teenagers that may seem like a tall order.

Most of us have a few people in our lives who can make us laugh. If you stop to think about it, there may be quite a few. As we muster our resources we may forget to add the friend who can bring laughter back to our lips. When I was a child, my younger brother found in me the ideal audience. I always laughed at his silly antics and one-liners. These days my wife, Gina, and I laugh more with our kids than with anyone else. They seem to provide plenty of accidental *and* intentional comic relief.

Throughout this chapter I would like to share with you

a few stories and people who always make me laugh. I also want to share with you some thoughts on laughter and fun that may provide a framework for you during the otherwise dark hours of transition in your family. We will add laughter and fun to our arsenal for managing the trauma of transition in our lives and family.

High school can be a particularly awkward time. Young people stumble through the challenges of growing up. They are met with new experiences every day and are forced to gauge their success on how they fare among their peers.

While many of these experiences seem tough and humiliating when they're happening, often when we take a closer look we find some memories there to store away for the times we need to laugh.

"THE DATE FROM HELL"

Carl had dreamed of his prom for months. He couldn't wait for the night to actually arrive. Cindy, the girl he had always wanted to date, had said yes. Carl's feet had not touched the ground since. This was going to be the most romantic night on record. *Cindy will be so completely swept off her feet she'll be putty in my strong, manly hands,* thought Carl with a mental swagger. From now through eternity, when young people dreamed of true love and romance, the story of Carl and Cindy would be their example.

As he dressed for the big date, Carl rehearsed each moment of the evening. Every word he would say, each move he would make, were carefully and thoughtfully choreographed. Nothing was going to spoil this evening.

He pulled up in front of Cindy's house in his mom's newly washed and waxed car. As he approached her front door he frantically went over the mental notes he had made on how to react to her new dress and how to win over her parents with his maturity and charm.

Overall, Carl was pleased with how this first stage went

as he led Cindy to the car. He had endured the photo ses-
sion and had made polite and articulate conversation with
Cindy's folks.

He opened the car door for Cindy and his heart leaped
to his throat as he thought of driving alone to dinner. As he
scooted behind the wheel and turned the key in the ignition,
the nightmare began. The car wouldn't start. With Cindy
in the car and her entire family watching from the living
room window, Carl tried to be nonchalant. He turned the
key again. Nothing. Then he got out of the car and raised
the hood hoping that this act might create some self-healing
magic.

Still nothing.

As he got back into the car his eyes riveted on his mis-
take. In his excitement to pick up Cindy he had forgotten to
put the car in park. He coughed and tried to distract Cindy
as he quickly put the console gearshift back to P. When he
looked up Cindy was giggling and to his horror so was her
entire family.

Carl's heart began to sink as he drove away.

Dinner took forever. The service was slow and the waiter,
weary of high schoolers' tips, was not greatly helpful. Carl
kept wondering, *Why, when you are paying so much more,
does the service get progressively worse?* Conversation was
stiff, and Carl began to long for the crowded prom with its
noise and familiar faces. He barely had enough money for
dinner and for a fleeting second pondered what it would be
like to have to ask Cindy for help.

By the time they got to the dance it was just about over.
Still, it was an unmatched thrill for Carl to escort Cindy to
the dance floor. He felt every eye in the place on them as
he used the steps he had rehearsed for hours alone in his
bedroom.

After the dance came the party. A good friend of Carl's
was hosting the affair, and Carl was anxious to see his bud-
dies there. He picked up a plate of munchies for the two of

them and headed back to where Cindy was sitting with some friends.

He forget about the step. There was a step down into the next room and missing that step was disastrous. He went head first toward the floor and landed face down in the plate of food. Some of his friends thought "Crazy Carl" had done it on purpose, and his misstep actually turned out to be the highlight of the party.

All the way home Cindy assured her dejected suitor that she had had a wonderful time. As Carl walked her to the door he had one more chance for true love: a goodnight kiss. He stood shyly at the front door like a first grader meeting an adult for the first time. Just as they were about to embark on that epic kiss Cindy spoke up, "Carl, isn't that your mother's car rolling down the street?"

First in stunned amazement, then in panic, he saw the car rolling down the hill toward a truck. He sprinted into the street and quickly grabbed the door of his runaway vehicle.

It was locked.

The car continued to roll as Carl fished the keys from his pocket, unlocked the door, jumped in, and stopped it about one foot from the truck.

Carl was panting, sweating, and humiliated. He started the car and began to turn, hoping to go home and never be seen again, when he heard a tap on the window. Cindy was standing outside the car. He rolled down the window, red-faced and sweating, and looked into the eyes of the girl of his now-shattered dreams.

Then in an instant his world was turned back around. Cindy looked down at Carl, told him again that she had had a very nice time, leaned through the window, and gave him a kiss on the cheek.

Life *can* be beautiful.

Carl and his buddies have laughed many, many times about that evening. And each time I think of it I smile. Life has many funny moments.

ENJOYING LIFE REQUIRES PERSPECTIVE ON PAIN

For many teenagers and their parents life is full of deep pain, completely lacking in fun and laughter. As a result, it becomes almost impossible for these folks to embrace the idea that our lives need laughter. Yet life must not be completely boiled down to situations or surroundings. Our quality of life is not always determined by our circumstances, and even in the worst of situations joy can be an option.

Tim and Pam Hansel are two of my role models. Tim was an athlete and adventurer until a mountain-climbing accident left him in constant pain. Pam has worked alongside Tim through the darkest hours of his injuries. Through all of this both have maintained a remarkable perspective and sense of humor.

Tim has this to say about pain: "Pain is inevitable, but misery is optional. We cannot avoid pain, but we can avoid joy."[1] Indeed, we often avoid enjoying life because we only deal with pain externally.

In one of his books I found this poem, written by a young Jewish girl from a Nazi concentration camp.

> From tomorrow on
>   I shall be sad
> From tomorrow on —
>   not today.
> Today I will be glad,
>   and every day
> no matter how bitter it may be
>   I shall say
> From tomorrow on I shall be sad
>   not today.[2]

This poem and the status of its author should poignantly and appropriately startle us with the idea that joy is a choice. We don't have to like our surroundings and circumstances, yet in the midst of change and fear we can choose joy.

In Galatians 5:22-23, Paul lists for us the fruit of the Spirit. These products grow in the lives of those who are connected to the Vine that is Christ Jesus. It is not our job to produce this fruit; it is our challenge to stay rooted to the Vine. The fruit of the Spirit is a byproduct of our relationship to the Vine. One of the characteristics of the fruit is joy. It represents a happiness that the world cannot give and cannot take away.

Winning the lottery will not produce joy. It may create a sense of happiness for a time, but true joy cannot be won that way. It will only come as a result of carefully tending our relationship with Christ.

Joy is not a giddy response to tragedy. Nor is it an irresponsible approach to life. It is not to deny the pain and suffering we all experience. The fruit of joy comes from deep inside our souls, constantly assuring us that no matter how bad it gets or how hopeless life seems, there is life and hope and help in Christ alone. We live with the assurance that we are supremely loved and the very God of the Universe is aware of our plight.

The Apostle Paul underlines the fact that God is in control in his letter to the Romans.

> And we know that in all things God works for the good
> of those who love him, who have been called accord-
> ing to his purpose. . . . What, then, shall we say in
> response to this? If God is for us, who can be against
> us? He who did not spare his own Son, but gave him
> up for us all—how will he not also, along with him, gra-
> ciously give us all things? (Romans 8:28,31-32)

This is one of the reasons that we begin with adoration when we pray. Circumstances do not change who God is. We can be confident in Him and find joy in remembering His mighty works.

Shout with joy to God, all the earth!
Sing the glory of his name;
make his praise glorious!
Say to God, "How awesome are your deeds!
So great is your power
that your enemies cringe down before you."
(Psalm 66:1-3)

You may want to take a few moments right now to give God thanks and to accept the joy He offers.

In the midst of transition in our families we often find ourselves saddled with limited choices. Many times the choices we do have range from bad to worse. If we are dealing with change in our family or tough circumstances that require tough choices, we may still choose joy. Please don't confuse joy with happiness. Happiness can be derived from any number of sources. Joy only comes when we are drawing our strength from the Vine who is Christ.

Young Life staffer Bob Krulish asks the rest of us regularly if we are "enjoying" Christ. By this he means, are we more in love with Christ now than we were six months ago? Do we find ourselves more and more wanting to kneel in His presence and find ourselves in Him? Bob always finishes the conversation by saying, "He is enjoying you."

IDEAS FOR KEEPING TEENAGERS (AND THEIR PARENTS) LAUGHING

When I was in high school one of our club leaders was Jan Webb. As a fifteen-year-old girl she had contracted polio. A healthy, fun-loving teenager had been struck with a disease that seemed to trap her within her own body. She began a lifelong struggle and challenge both physically and emotionally. But though Jan felt keenly the restrictions of her body, she did not allow her disease to keep her spirit from soaring to new heights and impacting the lives of everyone she met.

I will never forget the many nights we cheered in anticipation as Jan made her way to the front of our Young Life club meetings on crutches. Her sense of humor not only made us laugh, but it amazed us. She was creative and at the same time in touch with what would appeal to kids. She could tease but would never go over the line by putting down or embarrassing anyone. There wasn't a kid in our school who had not heard of Jan. I don't know how many kids were won to Christ through Jan's humor, but many were attracted to the Savior by this winsome servant, and I know all of us grew to count on Jan. Her wit could always lift us no matter how we felt.

Today she has a new generation of fans, and I am deeply grateful that my three sons are among them. Whether it is making bird calls or pulling a dime out of their ear, Jan always creates a lot of laughs and fun. You see, along with her pain, in spite of her own physical challenge, Jan has learned to allow the joy of Christ to infect her own life and everyone around her.

You can't "make" people have fun. They must choose to have fun just as you do. Our responsibility is to find our joy in Christ and then to live that out in our family.

Here are some fun ideas you may want to try:

- *Take your teenager on a date.* Let the teen pick the restaurant; you decide on the activity afterward. Kids almost always enjoy plays and musicals more than they think they will. Try to think of something other than a movie to take them to.
- *Make your teen breakfast in bed.* Do you have a hard time getting your teen up in the morning? At least once, make getting up an event your teen will always remember.
- *Have a "welcome home" party after school.* Place your teen's favorite snack or dessert in some conspicuous place and put a few decorations around. If you

and your spouse both work, leave the treats out and attach a note.
- *Offer a dollar for the joke of the day.* Set certain standards for the kind of joke allowed, then at night or mealtime give everyone in the family a chance to share his or her funniest moment of the day or a joke.

Each family must work to discover fun. For me, as the father of three sons, almost any kind of sports is fun. We play, watch, and discuss sports. I have to work to make sure that sports is not the only way we have fun together, though. For many families, camping is a great way to enjoy each other and have fun. Still others work on cars, or play card or board games. Families must look for opportunities to have fun. But the secret is to let your joy in Christ "infect" everyone around you.

There are a number of resources available with fun things to do as a family. You may have tried them all. But, perhaps the key to adding fun to transition is your own attitude. Your kids may not be at an age where playing games or taking little trips will work, but you can still be a joyful person who is fun to be around.

We know we cannot "make" things fun if our teenager is determined not to participate. I am not always able to feel joyful either. When I experience those moments, it is usually because I have been focusing on my own feelings or circumstances and not on the truths of God's Word.

There is no denying the pain we all experience in life. Sometimes I feel so overwhelmed with my own emotions and pain that it is difficult to even focus on my kids. During those times I must turn to other members of my resource team like Scripture, prayer, and trusted Christian friends to gain the strength and perspective I need. I confront myself with the "facts" of the Christian faith—God loves me (John 3:16), He died for me (Romans 5:8), He is near (Philippians 4:4-5).

In the midst of life's transitions we can choose joy. We can find God's peace for our troubled souls, not in our ability to withstand pain or remedy every problem, but in our willingness to find Jesus each day and rely on Him for our strength and joy.

Finally, for those days when we need a little boost, here are a few one-liners I've gathered over the years from various sources. I hope they bring a smile to your face and lighten your heart.

- Middle age is always fifteen years older than I am.
- There is no safety in numbers, or in anything else.
- A verbal contract isn't worth the paper it's written on.
- Eat a live toad first thing in the morning and nothing worse will happen to you the rest of the day.
- The lion and the calf shall lie down together, but the calf won't get much sleep.
- Being in politics is much like being a football coach. You have to be smart enough to understand the game and dumb enough to think it's important.
- Nobody notices when things go right.
- An ugly carpet will last forever.
- When you're in it up to your nose, keep your mouth shut.
- You can lead a horse to water, but if you can get him to float on his back you've got something.

● ● ● ● ● ● ● ● ● ● ●

Chapter Twelve

Release in Transition

*Tears. You never know what may cause them.
The sight of the Atlantic Ocean can do it, or a
piece of music, or a face you've never seen before.
A pair of somebody's old shoes can do it. Almost
any movie made before the great sadness that
came over the world after the Second World War,
a horse cantering across a meadow, the high
school basketball team running out onto the gym
floor at the beginning of a game. You can never
be sure. But of this you can be sure. Whenever
you find tears in your eyes, especially unexpected
tears, it is well to pay close attention.*

*They are not only telling you something
about the secret of who you are, but more often
than not God is speaking to you through them of
the mystery of where you have come from and
is summoning you to where, if your soul is to be
saved, you should go to next.*

FROM *WHISTLING IN THE DARK* BY FREDERICK BUECHNER

S ometimes the trauma of adolescent transitions feels like a time bomb just a few seconds from detonation. Parents and teens, their stomachs in knots, become anxious and irritable and find it difficult to stand still. We know if we don't somehow escape this situation for a while, we may explode.

In the midst of such stress, we must know where to turn for support. We must learn how to handle stress and allow the pressure to slowly dissipate, thus avoiding those painful explosions.

UNDERSTANDING STRESS

The word *stress* is often misunderstood. Archibald Hart, author of the book *Adrenalin and Stress*, makes these very helpful comments:

It [stress] is a multifaceted response that includes changes in perception, emotions, behaviors, and physical functioning. Some think of it only as tension, others as anxiety. Some think of it as good, others as bad. The truth is that we all need a certain amount of stress to keep us alive, although too much of it becomes harmful to us. (When most of us use the term, stress, we usually are referring to this harmful aspect—overstress.)[1]

We all have a natural response to any emergency or demand. In these situations a "complex chain of responses is set in motion to prepare us for what has been described as a 'fight or flight' response."[2] When we are under stress our body is preparing itself to either fight or flee the situation.

Here are a few examples of stress:

- You are rushing around getting everyone ready on Monday morning and you notice your teenager is still in bed. You have gone over this a hundred times and he still can't or won't get himself out of bed on time. You can't afford to be late for work again and you begin feeling anxious and angry. You are under stress.
- You have a great deal of responsibility at work, at church, at the PTA, and at home. You love to serve and get very positive strokes for your effort. At the same time, you are gone almost every night and often too tired to really participate when you are at home. You feel guilty about all the time away, and yet you can't decide what to give up in order to be at home more. Something has to give and whether you are willing to face it or not, that something is probably you. You are under stress.
- As you stack the dishes in the dishwasher, you find your eyes brimming with tears. Your teenage daughter has dropped out of school and you can't seem to

control her anymore. Your husband wants to kick her out of the house, and several times your discussions with him have turned into shouting matches. You had so many dreams for your life and for your daughter's life. Now these have crumbled and been blown away by the winds of life. You are under stress.

Stress is an overexcitement of our body that can be caused as much by things we find pleasurable and rewarding as by things unpleasant or painful. The body does not distinguish between types of stress.

CAUSES OF STRESS

A variety of things cause stress. Anything that mobilizes your body for "fight or flight" is stress. It can be a painful experience or a pleasurable activity. The key is, too much stress without release or relief is unhealthy.

Stress can result from anything that:

- annoys you
- threatens you
- prods you
- excites you
- scares you
- worries you
- hurries you
- angers you
- frustrates you
- challenges you
- criticizes you
- reduces your self-esteem.[3]

DISCOVERING RELEASE FOR STRESS

The Apostle Paul offers sound advice about relieving stress. He writes, "Do not be anxious about anything, but in everything, by prayer and petition, with thanksgiving, present your requests to God" (Philippians 4:6).

When we know the God of Peace and have learned to take our burdens to Him, we can experience the peace that only He can give. It is a peace the world can't give—one that comes from deep within, rooted and solid, unshakable and strong.

Okay, we know this works. It is spiritual and mature. Yet, I often find that it is harder than it sounds to experience peace and release from my emotions when I face hard times. I have spent so many years being self-reliant that I don't always follow the prescribed remedy of prayer and focus on Christ immediately. While I certainly hope I am arriving at that place sooner now than in the past, I am still confounded by my own actions. It is during these times that I find I need a bridge from my emotions to my heart.

I don't cry very often. And when I do it is never for long. But tears are truly the rain of the soul. In California, where we now live, I have developed a special appreciation for the rain. After it rains I want to run out and look at everything. The mountains, stark against a clear sky, are always the most beautiful then. To our smog-choked area rain brings a few short hours when the earth and the sky look fresh and clean. There is something fresh and clean about the release from stress that can be produced by tears. Especially when we are baring our soul to our Father in Heaven.

If anyone ever appreciated this truth it was King David. He was one of the all-time great criers. We probably learn more about crying out to the Father from him than anyone except Christ.

> In my distress I called to the Lord;
>   I cried to my God for help.
> From his temple he heard my voice;
>   my cry came before him, into his ears.
>   (Psalm 18:6)

Out of the depths I cry to you, O LORD;
    O Lord, hear my voice.
Let your ears be attentive
    to my cry for mercy.
        (Psalm 130:1-2)

Then David himself gives us the next step to releasing stress.

I wait for the LORD, my soul waits,
    and in his word I put my hope.
My soul waits for the Lord
    more than watchmen wait for the morning.
        (Psalm 130:5-6)

When men and women cry out to the Lord, they should wait for an answer. The discipline of waiting is crucial. For when we have cleared our mind with tears, we must wait for the Lord to fill the void with His peace and assurance. We will not find it if we, embarrassed by our outburst, rush off to find the shelter of busyness and activity to hide us from our feelings.

Wait for the LORD;
    be strong and take heart
    and wait for the LORD.
        (Psalm 27:14)

I waited patiently for the LORD;
    he turned to me and heard my cry.
He lifted me out of the slimy pit,
    out of the mud and mire;
he set my feet on a rock
    and gave me a firm place to stand.
He put a new song in my mouth,
    a hymn of praise to our God.

Many will see and fear
and put their trust in the LORD.
(Psalm 40:1-3)

From the mud and mire of our distress, the Lord desires to set our feet on solid rock. When we feel like our lives are stuck in a swamp of pain, our Father hears our cry and rewards our waiting with sure footing and a new song in our hearts.

Sometimes I wait on my knees. But on days when waiting comes hard you may find me walking somewhere. It may just be around the block or even around the house. When possible, I walk on the beach or along a path in the hills. Walking helps me clear my mind. It allows me to be more receptive to the voice of the Lord. I know others who find jogging accomplishes the same thing for them. Exercise can relieve just enough tension in our bodies to get us refocused, or at least calmed down.

CONNIE'S STORY

Connie was a driver. She put a tremendous amount of effort into everything she did. Even though she did not hold down a full-time "paying" job, I have rarely met anyone more busy. When schoolkids were scheduled to go on a field trip, Connie was the first mom called and then she arranged the rest of the transportation. She was always the team mom for soccer or Little League and was an aide in the classroom. On top of this, she was the caretaker for her aging parents and just as involved in church as she was at the kids' school.

Sometimes all the activity and busyness would get her down. Fred, her husband, would put his foot down and they would try calmness for a while. But it simply couldn't last. One of the children would have trouble with a teacher and in she would go. The cycle had begun again.

Connie was obsessed with the need to be a great mom.

As the children grew older life began to change for

Connie. She had a difficult time adjusting to her diminished control in her teenagers' lives and was genuinely hurt by their demands for autonomy and privacy. Before she knew it, Connie had made the transition from obsessed to distressed. She felt rejected by her kids and at a loss for how to find meaning in her life. She began to manipulate her family by constantly letting them know how much she had done for them and how hurt and lonely she was. This only caused more alienation and resentment within the family. Connie's carefully constructed world was beginning to crumble. She thought maybe she was going crazy.

Little did she know that a group of women who met weekly had begun to pray for her. They had seen her distress and began taking their friend before the Father. Then they invited Connie to join them and she jumped at the chance.

During the early weeks of Connie's involvement, she dominated the time. She would bring the group up to date on the hurt in her life from an unappreciative family. The other women would listen and then pray with her. Slowly a change began to take place in Connie. A transition team began to emerge. She discovered resources she hadn't known before. Friends and confidantes to share with. Through these loving sisters she learned that venting her hurt was not enough. She must give it over to God. Gradually she embraced the peace that comes from waiting on the Lord. Her feet landed on solid rock and the changes in her family couldn't shake her. Most important, Connie got the log out of her own eye.

As Connie rediscovered life she met Joy and Laughter. Her children would come home and hear the joyful sounds of praise songs as they came through the door. Home was no longer a prison for them, and each one began to quiz mom about what had transpired in her life. Connie was no longer obsessed about being a great mom. She was one.

Connie found a release from the mire of transition. She discovered grace and truth through some friends, then she appropriated it in her life.

If you have not discovered an outlet for your own stress yet, let me offer some steps.

1. *Find a person or small group to share with.* There are three rules to follow here.

    a. If you cannot choose your spouse or a couples group, then choose a person or persons of the same sex.

    b. Use this as an opportunity to express feelings and hurts, not to gripe about your family and friends.

    c. Make prayer the central focus of your time together.

2. *Learn to wait on the Lord.* Waiting may include walking, crying, or singing hymns, but commit to developing a listening ear to the Father.

3. *Choose joy.* You are a child of the King. His greatest desire is that you experience His joy and peace. The choice is yours.

HELP FOR YOUR TEEN

Teenagers also have the need to release the stress from transitions in their life. They are going through changes so rapidly that their mood swings are often very difficult to read. A stable Christian home is the first line of defense. You create an environment of love for Christ and family, and no matter how much they buck it, at least they will always know that home is a safe harbor in a storm.

You may not be able to choose your kids' friends for them, but you can recruit caring adults who will help you keep in touch with your son or daughter.

I would like to encourage you with six things you *can* do to help your teen learn to release tension during times of change.

1. *Be a careful and thoughtful listener.* When teens express anger or explosively react to transition, listen to understand, not simply to respond. Empathize with your kids. Listen for what is in their heart as well as what is coming from their mouth. Many young people are living with fragile egos. They need to know that someone really cares enough about them to listen.

2. *Don't become the judge.* Too often parents simply want to solve problems and then get on with life. Or, they over-react to what their teenager just said. Take a deep breath before you respond to something said. Make sure the statement requires a response before you speak. Your kids need your acceptance. Often they are simply trying out new ideas and exploring foreign concepts or reacting to stress they're not sure how to articulate.

Isn't it better they do that *with you* than a peer? If we are quick to pass judgment on what they are saying, they will eventually stop talking to us.

3. *Model what you want them to be.* If you want your children to have a vital relationship with Christ, work on yours. If you want them to experience joy, then choose joy in your life. Don't manufacture something you think they need to see, but rejoice because you have taken your burdens to your Father and left them at His feet.

4. *Encourage teens to get exercise.* You would be surprised how many young people today are out of shape. Exercise is a great stress breaker. Set a goal to run a 10K together, or go on a bike trip. There are lots of options. Be creative.

5. *Learn to know when they need "space" and privacy.* Respect their right to some time alone. When, with the best intentions, we don't allow our kids some space, we will force them to find that space outside the home. As we have said before, it is a natural part of adolescent life to need some privacy and space away from mom and dad. We can't let our own transition crisis interfere with their need at that point.

6. *Know when to ask for help.* If you notice behavior in your teen that concerns you, ask a professional for advice and counsel. For example, if your teenager suddenly stops hanging out with his or her friends and just sits in the bed-room listening to music, ask the teen how he or she feels. If you can't get a response, begin looking for other symptoms of stress. Have his or her eating habits changed? Does the teen look well? If you see too many things you don't have answers for, ask for help. Decide right now who you would call first. Keep your resource team handy and up to date.

In the first chapter of this book I shared a painful story about Kit. He did not have the coping resources to manage the transitions in becoming an adult and no one noticed. In retrospect, I believe he was avoiding many of us who knew him well. Then when the hole he had dug for himself was too deep to go unnoticed any longer, he buried himself in it.

Almost every kid in the world thinks about suicide some-time during adolescence. We won't be able to stop that. But we can create an environment of hope in our homes. It begins with us. Our growth in Christ and the coping resources we deploy in the midst of change in our lives will be the first step in creating that "safe place" for our kids.

My friend Tim Hansel is fond of saying, "Until further notice, celebrate life!" And to this my dad would add, "If you have the joy of the Lord in your heart, don't forget to inform your face."

Can the Lord relieve the stress in your life?

Maybe you should wait and see.

• • • • • • • • • • •

CHAPTER THIRTEEN

Closing the Book
on Transition

There is a legend about the Apostle Peter in which it is said he was fleeing Jerusalem after hearing he was being sought for execution. As Peter fled down the dusty highway he saw Jesus walking toward him.

"Where are You going, Master?" Peter is supposed to have asked as he came to a halt in front of the Lord.

"I go to die for you a second time," was the Savior's reply.

With those words Peter is said to have turned on his heels and headed back to Jerusalem and certain death.

As we live through the trauma of transition with our teenagers, the temptation to run is a common one. We feel the changes in life smothering us under the dark quilt of the unknown. We long to escape the pace and pressure of our hectic lives and find a place of peace and rest.

WE HAVE FOUND THE PLACE AND IT IS YOU

We now call upon our team members of prayer and Scripture. Through these two gifts we are able to find a quiet place in our hearts, regardless of the storms raging in our lives. There is help for our distress and it begins and ends with knowing Christ. This is not wishful or unrealistic thinking. These disciplines take our focus off our circumstances and place our attention on the Lord.

Find a quiet place and you will discover a quiet heart.

He who had the power to calm the storm when the disciples feared they would perish is the same God who can still the tempest of our souls. In Mark 6:45-51, Jesus "makes" His disciples get in a boat while He dismissed the crowd that had been with them all day.

I don't know what the disciples were thinking as they began their journey across the lake. Perhaps they spoke in quiet reverence of the miracles they had witnessed that day. Maybe they discussed the unusual and haunting parables that Jesus had spoken in their presence. Whatever the topic, their conversation was suddenly broken by panic.

A great wind came against them and their muscles bulged as they pulled the oars through angry waters.

These men had done nothing in particular to deserve this plight. They were merely obeying orders. In fact, had they time to think, they may have considered their situation unfair.

Many of us won't go so far as to blame God for the storms of transition in our life. But we often harbor notions that somehow the whole thing is unfair. After all, we have been trying our best in a difficult situation we never asked for, and now we find ourselves in the middle of a storm.

Our only hope is to raise our heads and look out into the storm. Somewhere on the horizon we will see Jesus. He walks on the waters of our storms. He is not overwhelmed by our troubles. He has authority over the crashing waves of change.

As we work toward seeing the Lord, other team members begin to emerge. Our perspective on time gains clarity and we understand more of the nature of change among kids. Where we may once have been confused by the seemingly slow march of days and hours, now we look resolutely forward to the adults God is building in our sons and daughters.

When resources are marshaled and key people put in place, we can approach each change in our teen's life with new hope and confidence. We worry less because those who have surrounded our family encourage us and step into the gap when needed.

WHEN WE'RE NOT AFRAID TO PICK UP THE PHONE

Adolescence can be a very difficult time for young people and their parents, but it doesn't need to be impossible. Help is available if we know who to call and aren't afraid to pick up the phone.

Laughter is available to jump start us toward joy. Brennan Manning offers this thought:

> Here is the root of Christian joy and mirth. It is why theologian Robert Hotchkins at the University of Chicago can insist: "Christians ought to be celebrating constantly. We ought to be preoccupied with parties, banquets, feasts, and merriment. We ought to give ourselves over to veritable orgies of joy because we have been liberated from the fear of life and the fear of death. We ought to attract people to the church quite literally by the fun there is in being a Christian."[1]

Joy becomes a byproduct of those who find their life in Christ. It is a happiness the world can't give and the world can't take away. Too many people today work at *creating* joy or happiness. They work and plan and dream about the day when they will have nothing else to do but be "happy." Yet true happiness cannot be manufactured. The kind of joy God offers us grows out of a life that is focused on Him. Like a carefully groomed tree that bears fruit in season, so shall we bear fruit as we are connected to the vine which is Christ and are pruned by the Father (see John 15).

Even in her nineties, my Granny Pierce never lost her joy. A wisp of a woman with an unquenchable fire for Christ in her soul, Granny bubbled with zeal for the Savior. She had the ability to enjoy Him even in old age and declining health. From her bed when she grew too old and frail to get about, we could hear her singing and praying at the top of her lungs, never lamenting her failed health, but with her focus on Christ clear and unwavering. Anyone who came to visit her was struck by her love for the Savior and a joy that seemed to fill the room.

If joy is a byproduct of our walk with Christ, then tears are His gift to clean the room in our heart for joy to fill.

Tears. They may come as a result of the untimely death of one too young and vulnerable. They may spring from the frustration of watching sons and daughters make bad choices and risk their future for insignificant pleasures. Or, they may simply fill the little creases in the corners of our eyes as we watch the relentless march of time.

Whatever the reason, tears will flush out the pain and sorrow and give us the opportunity to fill our hearts with something else. It is our choice.

To choose joy requires one major ingredient: trust. We must believe that God will fill our hearts with His peace. We must believe Him capable of fulfilling His promises to us. Trust begins when we acknowledge that we are accepted by God regardless of our ability as parents. His love is unconditional and never-ending.

As our children begin to emerge from childhood into adolescence and we are faced with separation from them and their quest for independence, we must have the freedom to let them grow. Our perception of ourselves is not dependent on how responsive they are, or if the folks at church applaud us as "Christian Parents of the Year." We are saved by grace;

our joy is not a result of success, but acceptance. We were accepted by our loving Father when we didn't deserve it, and we will always be accepted by Him regardless of our performance or failure.

Brennan Manning puts it this way: "You may be insecure, inadequate, mistaken, or potbellied. Death, panic, depression, and disillusionment may be near you. But you are not that. You are accepted. Never confuse your perception of yourself with the mystery that you are really accepted."[2]

DANIEL'S STORY:
THE FINAL KEY TO MANAGING TRANSITION

I don't exactly remember when Daniel first came to our Young Life club. He was just there and we were glad. Daniel had muscular dystrophy and other complications. He walked awkwardly on his toes and often lost his balance. He had none of the social skills of his peers and as a result had virtually no friends at school.

He loved coming to our group every Monday night to sing and laugh and be one of the gang. He began to feel accepted, and when some of the kids he met at the meetings recognized him at school, he felt like he was in Heaven.

As an outlet his parents let him take voice lessons, and we would often let him help us lead songs. Monday nights were the highlight of his week and a window to a world he had never known.

As an elementary student and even in high school, he had been brutally teased. His tormenters would say cruel things, mark his face with magic markers, or knock his books out of his hands as he walked to class. With no recourse, Daniel would endure the humiliation while a great hate and rage boiled in his heart. At home he would tear up his room at the end of the day.

When we became friends he was on medications for his illness and his anger.

Late in the fall when Daniel expressed a desire to go on a weekend retreat, we were all thrilled. He had never been away from home alone, except for being in the hospital. I still remember vividly heading up to camp early to make preparations and thinking about the responsibility of having Daniel with us for the weekend.

In the mystery of God's providence, all of Daniel's medication was somehow lost on the trip up. I called his dad to share the bad news and asked if Daniel could stay anyway. I promised that at the first sign of trouble I would drive him home myself.

Daniel had the time of his life. And there were two primary reasons. First, two popular, dedicated guys in our cabin decided on their own that the terrain around the camp might be too difficult for Daniel by himself. So they positioned themselves on either side of him and stayed there all weekend, making sure he didn't fall. There is no doubt Daniel walked straighter and taller than ever in his life that weekend, and I can't even write about it without feeling some tears of gratitude for those two young men. Daniel had never really experienced friends outside his family, and suddenly he had two sticking with him.

Second, Daniel heard about the love of Christ while he was seeing it on either side of him. The combination was too powerful, and he committed his heart to Christ.

He knew he had been accepted. For the first time in his life he understood that fitting in and being accepted were activities that had been done for him. He had been accepted by Christ and he belonged to that family.

The impact of that experience pierced my heart when I saw Daniel at a track meet several months later. In his dreams he had scored winning touchdowns and won gold medals, but in his real life he would never know the feeling of competing and wearing a team uniform. Yet Daniel had something infinitely better.

I watched him during a distance race. He had positioned himself in the middle of the infield and was screaming encouragement to one of the runners.

Can you guess which one?

He was cheering for a little guy who was in last place and about to be lapped by the leaders. Daniel yelled for this boy like an Olympic gold medal was at stake. He empathized with anyone running last and wanted to help that runner.

It was a picture I'll remember the rest of my life. This physically challenged young man scooting around in a little circle yelling, "Come on, Ross! You can do it!" While everyone else at the meet was focusing on the strong, the successful, the winners, he was giving all he had to the one who needed him the most.

I watched in utter amazement as Daniel cheered Ross to the very end. Even as others were preparing for the next race, he matched each step with a word of encouragement.

I was very proud of him and walked over to tell him after the race. As we talked he shared with me another event in his day. Just before coming to the meet he had stuck his head in to watch the pom-pom girls' practice session. One of them spotted him and asked him if he wanted to dance with them. They all laughed as Daniel left and made his way onto the track.

As he was telling me this story my blood pressure was reaching dangerous heights. I was thinking about how to punish those girls, I mean, really make them pay, when Daniel recaptured my attention. He looked me in the eyes and, somehow sensing my anger, shrugged his shoulders and said, "It's okay, because I like myself now."

Suddenly my anger was replaced by wonder. Here was someone who with all his physical problems seemed healthier than me. I realized that humiliation was nothing new to him. He had experienced it before. Rejection by a few kids was not going to kill him. He had survived it many times. Two of the things I feared most were almost daily occurrences for this dear young man. And he could say, "I like myself."

He had been accepted for who he was by the One who made him, and he was happy with the results. Daniel's story illustrates for us the key to handling teen transitions: As the changes in our children and our own lives threaten the image we have of ourselves, *we need the courage that comes from knowing we are accepted.* If we have experienced grace, we can dispense grace.

THE GREAT TRANSITION

If the humiliation of looking like a failure as a parent causes us to rush toward hasty solutions, we only need to look at the humiliation Christ experienced on the cross to stop us in our tracks.

As we try to run from the fear of rejection, whether from our teenagers or anyone else, we must hear the voice of Christ say, "I go to die for you a second time." And only when we will turn on our heels and face life's dangers will we know the great transition of becoming like Christ.

Your transition team awaits. Your teen's future is at stake. Sound the alarm and let them join you in the battle.

Notes

CHAPTER TWO — TEEN PASSAGES

1. Diane E. Papalia and Sally Wendkos Olds, *A Child's World*, 4th ed. (New York: McGraw-Hill, 1987), page 466.
2. John W. Santrock, *Life-Span Development*, rev. ed. (Dubuque, IA: William C. Brown Publishers, 1986), page 356.
3. As quoted by Papalia and Wendkos Olds, pages 496-497.
4. David Elkind, *All Grown Up & No Place to Go* (Reading, MA: Addison-Wesley, 1984), pages 93-94.
5. Santrock, page 369.
6. Santrock.
7. General Douglas MacArthur, as quoted in Brennan Manning, *The Ragamuffin Gospel* (Portland, OR: Multnomah, 1990), page 193.
8. Papalia and Wendkos Olds, page 500.

9. Santrock, page 360.
10. Elizabeth B. Hurlock, *Adolescent Development* (New York: McGraw-Hill, 1955), page 5.
11. Kevin Huggins, *Parenting Adolescents* (Colorado Springs, CO: NavPress, 1989), page 237.
12. Manning, pages 205-206.

CHAPTER THREE—MANAGING EXPECTATIONS

1. Bruce Newman, "Classroom Coaches," *Sports Illustrated*, November 19, 1990, page 63.
2. Tim Kimmel, *The Legacy of Love: A Plan for Parenting on Purpose* (Portland, OR: Multnomah, 1989), page 35.
3. Kimmel.
4. *Youthworker Update: The Newsletter for Christian Youth Workers*, vol. 4, no. 7, March 1990, page 1.
5. *Youthworker Update.*
6. *Youthworker Update*, vol. 5, no. 1, September 1990, page 2.
7. John Baillie, *A Diary of Private Prayer* (New York: Charles Scribner's Sons, 1949), page 61.

CHAPTER FOUR—MAKING TRANSITION YOUR ALLY

1. *Youthworker Update: The Newsletter of Christian Youth Workers*, vol. 5, no. 1, September 1990, page 1.
2. *Youthworker Update*, page 1.
3. *Youthworker Update*, page 1.
4. Cited in "Young Adults: the Foundation of Tomorrow's Families," *Implications: Taking Research Beyond Information to Application*, Spring 1990, vol. 3, issue 1, pages 2-3.

CHAPTER FIVE—TEAM MEMBER 1: KNOWING GOD

1. Max Lucado, *God Came Near: The Chronicles of the Christ* (Portland, OR: Multnomah, 1987), page 85.

CHAPTER SIX—TEAM MEMBER 2: REALISTIC GOALS FOR TRAUMATIZED PARENTS AND TEENS

1. Robert Fulghum, *All I Really Need to Know I Learned in Kindergarten* (New York: Ivy Books, 1986), pages 4-5.
2. Tim Kimmel, *Legacy of Love* (Portland, OR: Multnomah, 1989), page 67.
3. Tim Hansel, *When I Relax I Feel Guilty* (Elgin, IL: David C. Cook, 1979), pages 29-30.

CHAPTER SEVEN—TEAM MEMBER 3: MAXIMIZING RESOURCES

1. Ezra Taft Benson, as quoted in Stephen R. Covey, *The Seven Habits of Highly Effective People* (New York: Simon and Schuster, 1989), page 309.

CHAPTER EIGHT—TEAM MEMBER 4: MAINTAINING INTIMACY IN THE MIDST OF TRANSITION

1. Gary Smalley and John Trent, *The Language of Love* (Pomona, CA: Focus on the Family, 1988), page 33.

CHAPTER NINE—TEAM MEMBER 5: PRAYER—HEALING STRENGTH FOR THE STRESSED

1. Stephen Winward, *How to Talk to God: The Dynamics of Prayer* (Wheaton, IL: Harold Shaw Publishers, 1961), page 23.
2. Winward, pages 17-18.
3. Winward, page 78.
4. Francois Fenelon, as quoted by Bob Benson and Michael Benson, *Disciplines for the Inner Life* (Waco, TX: Word Publishers, 1985), page 28.
5. John Baillie, *A Diary of Private Prayer* (New York: Charles Scribner's Sons, 1949), page 115.

CHAPTER TEN—TEAM MEMBER 6: MANAGING
TIME FACTORS

1. James Dobson, *Preparing for Adolescence*, rev. ed. (Ventura, CA: Regal Books, 1989), page 73.
2. David Elkind, as quoted in *Youthworker Update: The Newsletter for Christian Youth Workers*, vol. 4, no. 10, June 1990, page 2.
3. Quoted in Tim Hansel, *When I Relax I Feel Guilty* (Elgin, IL: David C. Cook Publishing Co., 1979), page 9. Used by permission.

CHAPTER ELEVEN—TEAM MEMBER 7: LAUGHTER
AND FUN AS SHELTERS FROM THE STORM

1. Tim Hansel, *Ya Gotta Keep Dancin'* (Elgin, IL: David C. Cook Publishing Co., 1985), page 55.
2. Quoted in Tim Hansel, *When I Relax I Feel Guilty* (Elgin, IL: David C. Cook Publishing Co., 1979), pages 61-62. Used by permission.

CHAPTER TWELVE—RELEASE IN TRANSITION

1. Archibald Hart, *Adrenalin and Stress*, rev. ed. (Waco, TX: Word Books, 1988), page 20.
2. Hart, page 22.
3. Hart, page 30.

CHAPTER THIRTEEN—CLOSING THE BOOK
ON TRANSITION

1. Brennan Manning, *The Ragamuffin Gospel* (Portland, OR: Multnomah, 1990), page 149.
2. Manning, page 25.

Bibliography

A Dad Named Bill [pseud.]. *Daddy, I'm Pregnant.* Portland, OR: Multnomah, 1988.

Arterburn, Stephen, and Jim Burns. *Drug-Proof Your Kids.* Pomona, CA: Focus on the Family, 1989.

Clark, Chap. *Next Time I Fall in Love.* Grand Rapids, MI: Zondervan, 1987.

Dobson, James. *Preparing for Adolescence.* Ventura, CA: Regal Books, 1978.

Huggins, Kevin. *Parenting Adolescents.* Colorado Springs, CO: NavPress, 1989.

Melton, Tom. *Sex From Inside Out.* Englewood, CO: JTM Press, 1989.

Sizemore, Finley H. *Suicide: The Signs and Solutions.* Wheaton, IL: Victor Books, 1988.

Smalley, Gary, and John Trent. *The Language of Love.* Pomona, CA: Focus on the Family, 1988.

Swindoll, Charles. *Growing Wise in Family Life.* Portland, OR: Multnomah, 1988.

Author

Larry Anderson is the Regional Director for Young Life in greater Los Angeles. He has been on the staff of Young Life for more than fifteen years, during which time he has served as Area Director for Phoenix/Scottsdale and Regional Director for Arizona.

Larry holds an M.Div. from Fuller Theological Seminary and is an ordained Assembly of God minister. He has written numerous leadership training materials for Young Life. He is married and has three children.

Other Books from Vision Forum

Jonathan Park
A New Beginning

By Pat & Sandy Roy

Adapted by John J. Horn

Adapted from the Exciting Radio Drama
The Adventure Begins

2

Vision Forum Ministries
4719 Blanco Rd.
San Antonio, TX 78212
www.visionforum.org

ISBN 978-1-937460-60-0

Photography and Cover Design by Daniel Prislovsky
Typography by Justin Turley

Printed in the United States of America

Table of Contents

Introduction

Since 1998 the Jonathan Park radio drama series has delighted thousands of children (and adults) with exciting family stories that honor God as the Creator of this world and leave listeners waiting breathless for the next adventure.

Now, all the drama of Jonathan Park rests in your own two hands.

In *Jonathan Park: The Adventure Begins Part 2* you will read the novel version of radio episodes five through eight, in which you join the Park and Brenan families to tackle obstacles in the path to building their creation museum, including unstable cliffs, a scheming millionaire, and an alien cult.

Read and re-read your favorite parts, find new scenes not included in the radio drama episodes, and immerse yourself in the world of Jonathan Park as you live life through his and other characters' eyes. Each episode teaches fascinating proofs for creation and ways to refute evolution—not because the Bible needs to be proved, but because as Christians, it's our job to be "ready always to give an answer" for the hope within us.

This is our Father's world. God created it. We can explore it. So, live the adventure!

Disaster at Brenan Bluff

For many months, a small team of diggers had been looking for a dinosaur graveyard at Brenan Ranch in Abiquiu, fifty miles north of Santa Fe, New Mexico. On a cool Monday morning, paleontologist Dr. Kendall Park and Jim Brenan sped toward the dig site in a red 4x4 truck.

Kendall was wearing a Fedora and grinned as he swung the truck around the worst ruts and bounced over the shallower ones.

"Kendall, what are we doing?" Jim asked. He was smiling too, but in a confused sort of way.

"Jim, have I got something to show you."

"This is something good, isn't it?"

Kendall roared into the temporary dig site and killed the engine. "Remember when we first discovered that dinosaur fossil in the Hidden Cave? I couldn't help but think we might find more somewhere else on your ranch."

Jim nodded slowly. "Yes, that's why we hired people to help you excavate. So, what is it?"

Kendall threw his door open. "Get out and take a look for yourself!"

About a dozen workers in hardhats and orange safety vests were scattered at the base of the cliffs, most wielding shovels and pickaxes. A Bobcat beeped as it backed away from a pile of dirt.

One of the workers waved at Kendall as he and Jim approached. "Sir, we've found another one over here!"

Jim looked at Kendall. "What's going on?"

"We've found a dinosaur graveyard!" Kendall wanted to fling his hat into the air, but it didn't seem very professional. He grabbed Jim's shoulders instead. "A few days ago we moved closer to the cliffs, and since then we've found many more *Coelophysis* fossils."

"Thank God!" Jim exclaimed. "We've got our dream!"

"Not only will we be able to build our museum, but we'll be able to provide the public with a view of a real dinosaur graveyard, as it's being excavated!"

Something rumbled high above them. Kendall jerked to look up at the cliff. He gasped. A load of rocks was tumbling down the cliff-face.

"Run!" one of the workers yelled. "Get away from the cliffs!"

The workers dropped their tools and raced for the open, their hands clamped over their hard hats. Kendall and Jim sprinted for the cars. Kendall thought about his Fedora—it wouldn't stop a rock very well.

They reached the cars breathless, but safe. The rumbling had stopped, and the landslide seemed to be over, but the cliffs still looked unsteady. A pile of boulders lay near the dig site. Several of the rocks had bounced into the work area.

"Is everyone all right?" Kendall asked.

Joe, the foreman, counted the men off on his fingers. "Yes, sir, we're all okay."

"Those cliffs look badly eroded," Jim said.

The spot where most of the rockslide had come from was a darker red than the rest of the cliff, as it hadn't been baked by the sun. The rock-layers surrounding the new cleft looked unstable.

"It's probably from that terrible storm we had last year," Joe said. "Do you guys remember? This whole area was flooded."

Jim coughed. "Oh, I seem to remember something about a flood, how about you, Kendall?"

Kendall shrugged. "I was in the dark over the whole thing—like a cave." He grew more serious as he studied the cliff-face. "If those cliffs collapse, we may lose the whole graveyard."

Jonathan Park dashed into his classroom with a group of boys.

"King of four-square—Jonathan Park!" he announced. He sat down, panting. Four-square under a middle-of-the-day New Mexico sun was draining.

The science teacher, Mr. Benefucio, walked between the desks, calming kids and making sure that everyone settled back into their correct seats. "Okay, okay, I hope everyone had a very fulfilling recess."

Eddie stuck his hand up. "Mr. Benefucio, I personally think that recess provides us with an excellent chance for socialization and the opportunity to rehearse our future roles in society."

The class tittered at his mock solemnity. He sounded like Calvin from the Calvin and Hobbes comic strip on one of the days he was trying to act good.

Mr. Benefucio smiled. "Thank you for that insightful editorial, Edward. We will now proceed with the learning phase of your education." He reached his desk and turned around. "I've cleverly devised a project that combines a history assignment with our science lesson. What I'd like all of you to do is write a report on a great scientist of the past."

Thad raised his hand. "Like Isaac Newton?"

"Yes, Thad."

"I could do the report on my dad!" Jonathan said.

Somebody at the back of the room guffawed. It was Rusty, the class bully, who had fiery red hair, a long nose, big fists, and a nasty personality.

"That certainly fits the assignment," Rusty said. "After all, your dad really is a scientist of the past."

Jonathan clenched the edge of his desk. "What do you mean by that?"

"I heard your dad got fired from a museum in Montana."

Jonathan scowled. "My dad is the best scientist that has walked the face of the earth! And that's where I got my brains—too bad for you."

Mr. Benefucio rapped his desk. "Okay, that's enough."

But Rusty wasn't done. "You always think you're so much better than everyone else." He glared at Jonathan.

Mr. Benefucio's voice hardened into punishment mode. Everyone in class knew that tone. "Okay, Rusty, I'll see you after class tomorrow for detention. And Jonathan, you're one step away, my friend. Got it?"

Jonathan sighed. "Yes, sir."

Kendall parked his truck and walked into his home slowly, twirling his Fedora in his hand. Angela greeted him at the door.

"How was your day?" she asked.

Kendall tried to smile. "Angela, we found a dinosaur graveyard!"

"Well—congratulations!" Angela's eyebrows narrowed. "So, why the long face?"

Kendall tossed his Fedora onto the couch and sat down next to it. He steepled his fingers for a moment, thinking about the problem at the dig site. "The cliffs above the site are unstable, and we're afraid they may collapse on the graveyard."

Kendall's phone rang. "Wait a minute, Honey, I'll be right back." He dug his cellphone out of his jeans pocket and walked into the next room. "Hello, this is Dr. Kendall Park."

A man was on the other end. "Hello, Dr. Park, my name is Sherman Bott. I'm a creationist here in Santa Fe."

Sherman Bott. The name wasn't familiar.

"So what can I do for you, Mr. Bott?" Kendall asked.

"Actually, I was hoping that you would help me make the case for creation. You see, last week I was on a local talk show. It was horrible. The host made the claim that there aren't any real scientists who believe in creation. He was so confident that he challenged me to come back on this Wednesday at three-thirty to prove him wrong. Dr. Park, I heard you're a Ph.D. vertebrate paleontologist. Would you be willing to go on the program with me?"

Kendall scratched his chin. It sounded like a good opportunity to present the creation message. Three-thirty on Wednesday? He should be able to make it. "Sure, I'll do it, Sherman. Would you mind if I brought my son with me?"

"That would be fine. Maybe we can even let him sit in with you."

Jonathan, Jessie, and the rest of the Eagle's Nest gang sat in the Parks' living room with Grandpa Benjamin. A plate of chocolate chip cookies and a pitcher of milk were on the table.

"Grandpa, thanks for taking the time to help us with our report," Jonathan said.

"Yeah, thank you, Mr. Park," Thad echoed.

Eddie performed a sitting bow with clasped hands. "Mr. Park, you're great. Without you, this would be impossible!"

Grandpa Benjamin chuckled. "My pleasure, Thad and Eddie."

Mike groaned from one of the armchairs. "I can't believe I'm here. I'm not even doing a report."

"Me too," piped Timmy.

Jessie shrugged. "Just because we're not in Mr. Benefucio's class doesn't mean we can't learn something."

Mike rolled his eyes. "You're just saying that because you homeschoolers love pain."

"Mike," Grandpa Benjamin said, "Jessie just enjoys learning new things. But back to our subject. Did you guys know that some of the best scientists in all of history believed in the Creator?"

"Like who?" Timmy asked.

"Well, possibly one of the most famous was Isaac Newton. He was an astronomer who lived from—what was it—I think 1642 to 1727. One of his great accomplishments was to develop the type of math known as calculus."

"Oh." Eddie snapped his fingers. "So he's the one to blame."

"He was also the inventor of the first reflecting telescope, and studied the motions of our solar system. But he's most famous for the discovery of gravity."

Thad cocked an eyebrow. "You mean they didn't know that things always fall down before Newton?"

Grandpa Benjamin laughed. "No, they knew things fell, they just didn't have a theory to explain why. Newton was a genius. He also believed that God created this world. He once said, 'this most beautiful system of the sun, planets, and comets could only proceed from the counsel and dominion of an intelligent and powerful Being.'"

Eddie tapped his milk glass with his fingernail. "Hey, what about the guy who invented milk?"

Mike snorted. "Eddie, it comes out of cows—no one invented it."

"But the guy's name is on every carton," Eddie said.

Grandpa Benjamin smiled. "That's Louie Pasteur. He's the one who invented the process we call 'pasteurization.'"

"What's that?" Timmy asked.

"It's the process that takes harmful bacteria out of milk." Grandpa Benjamin poured himself a glass and held it out for inspection. "The milk we buy at the store, like this milk, is not straight from a cow's udder. You see, Louis Pasteur was the one who identified several harmful bacteria, and made vaccines to cure them—harmful diseases like rabies, diphtheria, and anthrax." Grandpa Benjamin sipped his milk. "Thousands of people owe their lives to the work done by Pasteur."

"So what exactly did he do?" Thad asked.

"Before Pasteur was born, people believed that if you left meat out to rot, maggots would form—or if you left out dirty rags that it would make mice. They thought this because they always found maggots in rotten meat, and mice in places they kept dirty rags. Then, during Pasteur's time, evolutionists liked the idea that life came from non-living objects, because it meant that life could form without God."

"But that's not true—is it?" Timmy asked.

"No, and Pasteur proved it. He did a series of experiments that proved the scientific law that says that life can only come from life."

"That seems pretty simple," Thad said. "I thought everybody knew that."

"Well, they do now." Grandpa Benjamin set down his glass. "That scientific law has never been broken—no one has ever seen life come from anything but another living creature. Pasteur's experiments dealt a serious blow to evolution."

Eddie dipped another chocolate chip cookie in his milk and took a big bite. "I never thought of milk as a proof for creation. Maybe Mom will let me drink more, now. How does all of this hurt evolution?"

"Well, evolutionists say the universe started with a Big Bang that formed planet Earth, and then somehow a single-celled organism came to life in the ocean. But that's just as silly as saying that mice come from dirty rags. It violates this law of science—that life can only come from life."

"So Louis Pasteur must have believed in a Creator?" Jonathan said.

"Absolutely. He once said, 'the more I study nature, the more I stand amazed at the work of the Creator.'"

Jessie spoke. "My dad also told me about Robert Boyle."

Grandpa Benjamin nodded. "Ah, yes. He was the founder of modern chemistry, and well-known for speaking about the Bible."

Dr. and Mrs. Park came into the living room and smiled at the group.

"Quite the party in here," Dr. Park said.

Jonathan leaned back in his seat and propped his feet on the coffee table. Some days it just felt good to be alive, and today, he felt super proud of how important his dad was.

"Dad, you're going to go down in history as one of the best paleontologists ever. We'll be famous!"

"Jonathan—"

"It's so neat to have a special family," Jonathan said.

Timmy frowned. "Well—my dad is a state police officer."

Jonathan waved his hand. "That's nice, Timmy, but that's nothing like having a world-famous paleontologist for a dad."

"Jonathan!" his mom exclaimed.

Jonathan looked up quickly. Neither of his parents looked happy. Was something wrong? "But, Mom, that's why the radio station wants us to be on the air."

"All right, young man, that's enough," Dr. Park said.

Jonathan gulped. Now what had he done?

Grandpa Benjamin looked at Dr. Park. "Son, what's all this about?"

Dr. Park sighed. "There's a talk show host claiming that real scientists can't believe in creation."

"Well, I was just pointing out to the kids that many of the founding fathers of science believed in the Creator."

Eddie frowned. "It's too bad you couldn't bring a few of them back to life so they could go on the radio with you. And, I'd interview them for my report."

"Hey! That's an idea!" Dr. Park said.

Eddie jumped up. "You know how to bring them back to life?"

"Hmm? Oh, no, I didn't mean that, but why not invite some *living* creation scientists to be on the radio with me?"

"That's an excellent idea," Grandpa Benjamin said.

The excitement fell away from Dr. Park's face. "Unfortunately, I don't know any. Ever since I became a creationist, I've been the Lone Ranger."

Mrs. Park patted his shoulder. "Well, maybe this is your chance to get plugged in!"

"I think you're right. Let me talk to Sherman and see if he has any other contacts. Oh, and Angela, I think you need to have a talk with Jonathan."

Jonathan followed his mom to his room. He found himself counting the rows of flowers on the wallpaper as they walked down the hall. Judging by his mom's face and his dad's tone, this conversation wasn't going to be comfortable.

Mrs. Park sat Jonathan on his bed and stood by the door, her arms crossed. "Jonathan, I heard the way you were bragging about going on the talk show."

Jonathan gulped. "I was just excited Dad and I get to be on the radio in front of everyone."

"In front of everyone?" Mrs. Park frowned. "Jonathan, what are your motives? Are you going just so you can be a star, or are you interested in why the Lord has given you this opportunity?"

Jonathan wound a loose thread from his blanket around his right index finger. "I didn't mean anything bad. . . ."

"Yes, but Jonathan, God says He hates our pride. And sadly, our pride can oftentimes hurt others. Think about how the other boys felt when you said your dad is better than theirs."

Jonathan hadn't thought about that possibility. Come to think of it, Timmy had looked a little offended. And Mike.

"In Proverbs 16:18 it says: 'Pride goeth before destruction, and an haughty spirit before a fall.' Jonathan, the Bible says that if you are prideful, you will fall."

"I guess talking big makes me feel like I'm okay," Jonathan said.

"Jonathan, you're already someone special—you're the child of the Creator. But when we build ourselves up, our attention is on us, not on Him."

"I know."

"Whenever you feel prideful, stop and remember to focus on Him."

Jonathan nodded. "I'll try." He wished it was as easy as it sounded.

His mom unfolded her arms. "For now, we better tell Grandpa that it's time to break up the study session. If your father is going to show you and the gang the dinosaur graveyard tomorrow, we all need a good night's sleep."

Kendall double-checked the number on his cellphone's LCD screen with the number on the paper in front of him. They matched. He punched 'call' and held the phone to his ear.

"Hello?" answered a deep voice.

"Hi, I'm looking for Dr. Humphreys."

"Russ Humphreys speaking."

"Hello, Dr. Humphreys, my name is Dr. Kendall Park. I'm a Ph.D. vertebrate paleontologist here in Santa Fe and I got your number from Sherman Bott. You're a physicist, from what I understand?"

"Yes, that's right."

"Would you mind telling me what areas you specialize in?"

Dr. Humphreys coughed slightly. "Well, I'm a physicist at Sandia National Laboratories, and I've done nuclear physics, geophysics, pulse-power research, theoretical atomic and nuclear physics, and I've been on the particle-beam fusion project."

Dr. Park raised his eyebrows. This was definitely one of the men he was looking for. "Wow, I'm impressed," he said. "Dr. Humphreys, I've recently been invited to be on a talk show. The host has been claiming that no real scientists believe in creation. Would you consider calling in during the program?"

Dr. Humphreys hesitated for a moment. "Sure, Kendall, I'll be happy to call in, but I've never done radio before."

"Don't worry. All I'm asking for is a brief call, to give your name and areas of scientific expertise. Lord willing, we'll have a number of creation scientists from different fields doing the same."

The next day, the Parks, Brenans, and Eagle's Nest gang drove to the dig site on Brenan Ranch. The construction workers had all been given a couple days off until an engineer could look at the cliff and give a recommendation.

The group converged near the Bobcat, where two fossils were halfway through the excavation process.

"Look at all these!" Thad said.

"This graveyard is so neat!" Timmy craned his neck back to look up at the cliff.

Mrs. Brenan was also looking up at the cliff, but she didn't look impressed. "Okay everyone, let's stay back from the cliffs."

"You're right, Martha," Mr. Brenan agreed. "They're still very dangerous."

Shadow, the Brenans' dog, eyed the dinosaur bones expectantly. Mr. Brenan rubbed his ears. "Sorry boy, those bones are a little too valuable for you."

Thad spoke. "Dr. Park, studying fossils seems pretty neat—do you like it?"

"I love it. I get to see first hand the evidence that the Creator has left behind. Ever since before I could pronounce the word I've wanted to be a paleontologist, but now that I'm a Christian, it's more fulfilling than I had ever dreamed."

"Dad, are you the only creation paleontologist?" Jonathan asked.

His dad laughed. "Sometimes it feels that way, but did you know, one of the first paleontologists was a creationist? His name was John Woodward. He lived in the late 1600s and died around 1728. He was the man who started the science of looking for fossils and trying to understand what creatures left them behind."

"You said he believed in creation?" Mr. Brenan asked.

"Yes, and listen to this—he believed the reason for so many fossils in the ground was a direct result of Noah's Flood. Just like our dinosaur graveyard—it shows evidence of a great flood."

Shadow started barking furiously and dashed toward the cliff.

"Look, it's a rabbit!" Mike said.

Jessie called Shadow to come back, but he was too intent on his quarry to notice, so she ran after him. They were both running straight for the cliff.

Mr. Brenan cupped his hands. "Jessie, don't go any closer!"

"I'll get her," Jonathan said. He started running after her. Something rumbled.

Eddie put his hand to his ear. "Uh, guys, something is grumbling, and that's *not* my stomach."

"Rocks!" Mike yelled. Jonathan looked up. There was a gash in the cliff where the first rock slide had come from, its red coloring less faded than the surrounding rocks. The rocks at the bottom of the fresh cleft were crumbling. Shadow's barking was causing another slide.

"Get out of there!" Dr. Park yelled.

Jonathan was already too close to the cliffs to escape the slide. Jessie turned, her face twisted with horror.

"Jonathan!"

"Jessie!"

There was a narrow trench in the dirt, parallel to the cliff, from one of the excavations. Jonathan grabbed Jessie and pulled her into it. He was still face up, looking into a sky full of falling debris, but the trench was too narrow for him to turn quickly, so he squeezed his eyes shut, covered his face with his hands, and prayed.

There was a grinding, and crashing, and enormous thuds all around, while the ground trembled like mattress springs under a jumping kid. The little bit of light he sensed from under his closed eyelids was blotted out. Then everything was quiet.

Jonathan opened his eyes. A huge chunk of rock straddled the trench four inches above his nose. He tried to blink the settling dust away from his eyes and cautiously breathed in. Dirt particles clung to his throat and set him coughing violently. Little bits of light sneaked under the edges of the rock.

"Jessie?" he whispered, trying to keep his lips as narrow as possible to stop the dirt from getting in. "Jessie?"

"I'm—over here." Her voice was weak. It came from the other side of the boulder.

Jonathan tried to move his legs, but they wouldn't. *Broken?* No, they didn't hurt. They were trapped under the rock.

"Are you okay?" Jonathan whispered.

"It's hard—to breathe. It's really—tight—on my chest."

"Jessie! Jonathan!"

Somebody was scrambling over the rocks. Many people, judging by all the scraping stones.

"Dad! Mr. Brenan! Down here!" Jonathan yelled.

Something blocked even more of the light that was seeping through. "They're under this boulder," Dr. Park said. His voice was close, but deadened by the stone. "Let's rock it to the left so we can get Jessie out, then we'll move it back the other way for Jonathan. On three! One—"

"We're coming, Jessie!" Mr. Brenan yelled.

"Two—"

Both men grunted. "Three!"

Jonathan yelped. The rock was squeezing his right shinbone like a nut in a nutcracker.

"Stop!" Dr. Park yelled. The rock dropped back into place, and the worst of the pressure was relieved. "Jonathan, what's wrong?"

"My leg—when you moved the rock." Jonathan squeezed his eyes shut, trying to stop the tears. He was trapped. It was like being buried alive. The skin on his back tingled.

"Okay," Mr. Brenan said, "then let's rock it to the right so we can get Jonathan, and then back the other way for Jessie."

The pressure lightened—another few inches and Jonathan could move his leg.

Jessie gasped. "Dad—I can't breathe!"

"The rock is pushing against her chest!" Mr. Brenan said.

The rock dropped back into place and a little ridge jabbed into the thin layer of skin on Jonathan's shinbone.

"Now what are we going to do?" Dr. Park said. His voice was loaded with tension. "If we rock it one way, we'll break Jonathan's leg—if we go the other way, we'll crush Jessie."

Jessie was breathing in crisp gasps. That rock needed to come off *now*.

Jonathan gulped. There were only two ways out of this, and one of them was over his leg. It had to be done.

"Break my leg."

"What?" Jonathan's dad got down so that his mouth was close to the cracks where the light came in. "Son?"

"Push the rock on my leg. We need to get Jessie out *now*."

"Son—I can't do this to you."

"Dad, it's the only way to save Jessie."

Mr. Brenan's voice was shaky. "Kendall, I could never ask you to hurt your own son."

Jessie's gasps were quicker and shorter.

Jonathan clenched his hands. "Dad, there's no other way. You've got to do it!"

Dr. Park's voice was husky. "I love you, Son! Okay, Jim—on three. One—" the boulder started rocking. "Two—" the weight jammed into Jonathan's right shinbone like a corkscrew. One more push—

"Wait!" Dr. Park said. "What am I thinking? Boys, I have some two-by-fours in the back of the truck. Run and get them, quick!"

The dads were propping the rock now, so that Jessie could breathe a little easier. If it slipped down any farther on Jonathan's leg—he shivered at the thought.

Jonathan counted every second that the Eagle's Nest was gone. It was nineteen—only nineteen?

"We found six boards," Mike called.

Dr. Park's voice was still close to the crack. "Quick everyone, wedge an end under the rock. We don't have the strength to lift it, but if we use these two-by-fours as a lever, we'll be able to topple the rock down this pile of rubble."

The boards scraped against the rock as they were wedged into nooks and crannies.

"Push!"

Jonathan opened his eyes. For a moment, nothing happened, then slowly, very slowly, the light increased. The boulder was lifting. It kept rising, and soon Jonathan saw a glimpse of the sky above. The rock teetered on the edge. Another push—

The boulder rolled down, gouging a deep furrow in the pile of debris. Jonathan and Jessie were free.

Jonathan lay, dazed, now that the danger was gone. Hands grabbed his shoulders and pulled him out of the trench. He blinked in the sunlight. Jessie was already out and sitting on a rock with her parents kneeling next to her.

"I'm okay," Jessie said, "I'm okay. My chest is just a little sore."

Jonathan wiped his face. A little cloud of dust settled over the gravel. He smiled vaguely. "My leg is good." He looked up at everyone. "Thanks."

"Hello, this is Dr. John Baumgardner."

"Hello Dr. Baumgardner, this is Dr. Kendall Park—I'm a creationist here in New Mexico." Kendall switched his cellphone to his left hand and grabbed a pen. "I got your name from Dr. Humphreys. He says you accept the literal account in Genesis?"

"That is correct."

Kendall leaned back in his office chair and crossed his legs. "Can you tell me a little bit about yourself?"

"Well, for the last twenty-five years I've been very interested in the mechanism responsible for the Genesis flood. I got a Ph.D. in geophysics to be able to work on this problem at a professional level. I've been a scientist in the theoretical division of Los Alamos National Laboratory. And I've been able to do a great deal of work in modeling, using some of the super computers open to me to model this catastrophe—a large tectonic catastrophe that I'm persuaded completely resurfaced the planet Earth in a very short period of time."

"I feel the same way," Kendall said. "Dr. Baumgardner, tomorrow I'm going to be on a nation-wide talk show. The host has been claiming that there are no scientists who believe in a literal creation. Would you be willing to call in?"

"Sure, I'd be pleased to do that."

Kendall checked Dr. Baumgardner's name off on the list in his notebook. That was check number ten. Lord willing, Kendall was going to be with a very surprised talk show host tomorrow.

Jonathan stood facing the rest of his class, three pages of double-spaced paper in his hands. He was on the last paragraph and still flub-free.

"I just want to finish by explaining why I chose Wernher von Braun for my report. Although I thought it was really neat that he designed the rocket that put man on the moon, it really meant a lot to me that he believed in the Creator. Although most people know him for his achievements during his time as the director of NASA's Marshall Space Flight Center, few know about his faith in God."

Somebody in the back of the class tittered. Jonathan cleared his throat loudly and continued.

"Wernher von Braun once said, 'I find it as difficult to understand a scientist who does not acknowledge the presence of a superior rationality behind the existence of the universe as it is to comprehend a theologian who would deny the advances of science.' The world experienced a great loss when Dr. von Braun died in 1977." Jonathan folded his papers. "And that's my report. Thank you."

Mr. Benefucio led the class in a round of applause. "Good work, Jonathan," he said warmly.

Jonathan smiled. "Thanks. Since I come from a scientific family, I had a natural grip on the subject—that's why it really came together so well."

Mr. Benefucio coughed slightly. "Jonathan, remember, one should practice humility."

Jonathan thought of his talk with his mom. His chest deflated a little. "Yes, sir, I'm sorry."

One of the girls, Elizabeth, raised her hand. "I have a question. It's not exactly about your report, Jonathan, but about creation. The Bible says that God has always been around, but how can that be scientifically true?"

"Well, Elizabeth—" Jonathan paused. How could you prove God scientifically? He gulped, and he felt his cheeks getting hot. "Um—well—Elizabeth, I'm not really sure."

"Hey," Rusty said, "you stumped the know-it-all!"

The recess bell rang.

Mr. Benefucio smiled. "Saved by the bell. After recess we'll hear Edward's report. Eddie, who is your report about?"

"Samuel Morse, the creationist who invented the telegraph."

"All right, everyone be back in fifteen minutes."

Rusty and another one of the tough kids, Spike, came out of class together and headed for the playground.

"Hey Rusty," Spike said, "you gonna pound that kid Jonathan at recess?"

"Naw." Rusty smirked. "I've got a better plan. You know how Jonathan has been bragging how he and his 'scientist' dad are gonna be on a talk show tomorrow? I'm going to call in and make him look like a fool."

"How you gonna do that?"

"Did you see how Elizabeth stumped him? He had no clue how to answer her." Rusty winked. "What would happen if he got asked the same question on *national* radio? He'd start babbling like a monkey. He'd look like a fool."

It was Wednesday. Kendall Park stood in the Brenans' kitchen, finishing a few details before heading to the radio station. Martha Brenan came into the kitchen with a load of grocery bags.

"Hey, Kendall. I sure hope your wife didn't mind watching Jessie while I was running errands in Los Alamos."

"Are you kidding?" Kendall grinned. "They probably went to the mall, or something. Besides, now Jessie can ride over to the radio station with Jonathan."

The home phone rang.

"Hello?" Martha looked at Kendall. "Yes, actually, he is here. I'll get him." She clapped her hand over the receiver. "It's for you."

"Interesting." Kendall took the phone. "Hello, Dr. Park speaking."

"This is Dr. Danny Faulkner," a man said. "I was just talking to Russ Humphreys, and he told me you were looking for some creation scientists to help you out on some sort of radio program?"

"Wow, your timing is perfect. Did you just try over at my house?"

"Yes, and your daughter gave me this number."

"Perfect." Kendall looked at his watch. He could probably squeeze a couple minutes in before he had to scram. "I was about to head out the door to get over to the radio studio. Can you briefly tell me about yourself?" he asked.

"Sure," Dr. Faulkner said. "I'm an astronomer—I have a Ph.D. in astronomy. And I'm a professor at the University of South Carolina, Lancaster, where I teach astronomy and physics. And I'm one of just a small number of creation astronomers today in the world."

"So, you're a Young Earth creationist?"

"Yes I am."

"The program starts at three-thirty. If I gave you the number, would you be willing to call in some time after that?"

"Three-thirty? Sure thing."

The door burst open and slammed against the wall, revealing Jim Brenan framed in the doorway.

"Jim!" Martha said.

"Kendall! The cliffs are starting to collapse!"

"What?" Dr. Park stared. "Oh, uh, Dr. Faulkner, I need to go." He dropped the receiver.

"Just as I was leaving, the cliffs started to go." Jim motioned outside. The sound of his truck motor came faintly through the open front door.

"But the talk show!" Kendall pointed to the clock. "I can't miss it."

"We've got to get out there to help the other men!"

Kendall picked the phone back up and dialed Jonathan's number. "Son, it looks like I'm not going to make it for the radio show."

There was a moment of stunned silence. "What?"

"The cliffs are collapsing at the graveyard. Jonathan, I've already made arrangements for several scientists to call in. It wouldn't be fair to cancel the show because of me. I want you to go ahead with our plan. Have your mom drive you and Jessie to the studio."

"But, Dad—"

"It will be okay, Sherman will be there. Son, just remember, Neal West is very smart. I would say as little as possible and let the scientists speak. I'll be praying for you."

A little click came over the phone, as if Jonathan was gulping. "I'll be praying for you too, Dad."

Kendall hung up and dashed for the door. "Okay, Jim, let's go!"

Jonathan rubbed the insides of his knees together. He was sitting in the studio with Mr. Bott and Neal West, the show's host. Mr. Bott didn't look comfortable. Mr. West looked very comfortable. He wore a black sports coat and his hair was combed straight back from his forehead and cemented with gel. He was fussing with a stack of papers under the microphone, which hung from the ceiling and was wrapped in a fluffy windbreak.

Mr. West had been watching a big digital clock near the door, and now he held up his hand. "Here we go. Three. Two. One." A bare bulb in the wall flashed red.

"Good afternoon from beautiful Santa Fe, New Mexico. You're tuned to talk radio's best, *Chat Line America*! I'm Neal West, your host, heard for two hours from coast to coast. Well, those of you who tuned in last week will remember our guest Sherman Bott, the director of Genesis Foundations." Mr. West waved his hand at Mr. Bott to cue him up. "Sherman, welcome back to the broadcast."

"Thanks, Neal," Mr. Bott said.

"Last week I challenged Sherman to try and find out the names of real scientists who believe in creation and then come back on the show." Mr. West turned toward Jonathan. "Now, folks, I wish you could see this—I have here in the studio with me a *boy*. No offense, but you look a little young to be a scientist."

Jonathan licked his lips. "I'm eleven."

"Sherman, do you want to introduce your guest?"

"This is Jonathan Park," Mr. Bott said. "He's the son of a vertebrate paleontologist that I was going to bring with me today—but he couldn't make it."

Mr. West smiled patronizingly. "Now Jonathan, do you consider yourself an expert on creation science?"

Jonathan shrugged. "Pretty much—yeah." He moved closer to the microphone in response to Mr. West's hand motions. "Why don't you give me a try?"

Mr. West scanned the call-list. "Better yet, we've got a call from twelve-year-old Rusty. Rusty, welcome to the program."

"Hello? Am I on?"

Jonathan's leg-muscles tensed. He knew that voice.

"Um, I have a question for Jonathan," Rusty said. "You believe in God, right?"

"Yes." Jonathan scraped his fingernails together, waiting for the punch line. He knew that Rusty must have a trick planned.

"How could God have existed forever? Everything has a beginning and an end."

Mr. West laughed. "I like this kid."

"What a dirty trick," Jonathan muttered.

"I'm sorry, Jonathan, were you saying something? You need to speak up." Mr. West nodded smoothly toward the microphone.

Jonathan glared at the microphone. *Nice one, Rusty*. He felt like a fool. "I don't know," he said. "The Bible just says that God has always existed."

"Jonathan, you don't have an answer for my question, do you?" Rusty chuckled.

Outside in the station's lobby, Mrs. Park and Jessie sat listening to the interview, which was piped through on speakers.

Jessie whispered to Mrs. Park over the droning voices. "Mrs. Park, Jonathan isn't doing very well, is he?"

Mrs. Park shook her head. "I'm afraid not. Jessie, I think his pride led him into a trap. I'm afraid this is the fall we've been warning him about."

Jessie twisted her fingers together. She wanted to do something. If Jonathan hadn't started out sounding so cocky, he would have had an easier time answering Rusty's question, or at least explaining why he wasn't the best person to do so. Now, he was being made fun of on national radio.

Rusty's voice came over the speakers. "Well, Jonathan, I guess you don't know *everything* after all!" He laughed and hung up.

"Regardless, Rusty," Mr. West said, "you've made an excellent point, thanks for being on the show."

Jessie groaned. This was going to be a long two hours.

"Kendall, look! We're too late!"

Kendall and Jim stared through the windshield. The dinosaur graveyard was completely covered by masses of red stone. The cliff had collapsed.

Kendall flung his door open. "Was anyone hurt?" he called.

"No, sir, everyone is okay." Joe, the foreman, ran up. "There was nothing we could do. They just collapsed right in front of us. This could take years for a crew our size to dig out."

Kendall raked his fingers through his hair. "Our dream— it's gone. Why?"

Jim laughed bitterly. "I guess we can forget about an on-going fossil dig for the public."

"Why did the Lord allow this?"

Jim sighed. "Well, partner, maybe it's to test our faith. I'm sure He has a plan, but I don't think we can do anything for now."

Kendall smacked his forehead. "No! I forgot about the talk show! I'll bet we can still make it for the last hour."

Back at the radio station, Neal West was enjoying himself. "Well, Sherman, you've been pretty quiet. Do you have anything to add?"

Mr. Bott cleared his throat. "Neal, you're making a huge mistake. When it comes to explaining the universe, we're in the same boat."

"You mean, Noah's Ark?" Mr. West laughed. "Really, what *do* you mean?"

"As creationists, we believe in an eternal God, but evolutionists have to believe in eternal matter. The Big Bang doesn't solve anything because it said that all the matter in the universe already existed. Either you have to believe that matter is eternal, or that God is. And to be honest, when we see all of the design in the universe, it seems that the Creator made the matter—that is the most logical explanation."

Mr. West shuffled his papers. "Well, I disagree, but it's time for a break anyway. We'll be right back after this."

The red bulb on the wall turned off and Mr. West grabbed a glass of water. The door opened.

"Dad!" Jonathan said.

"Hi, Jonathan." Dr. Park stepped inside. "Hello, Mr. West, I apologize for being so late, but I had an emergency at a dig-site I'm involved with."

"Dr. Park?" Mr. West shook hands. "I was beginning to wonder if you existed. Thanks for coming."

Jonathan settled back in his chair. Things would be

okay now that his dad was here. His dad could handle these questions.

Now that he could relax, Jonathan looked around the room, noticing things for the first time. The walls were decorated with framed awards and posters. The pictures usually showed Mr. West's head close to a microphone, but the strange thing was that he never smiled with his mouth open. His lips were always shut. Jonathan looked at the talk show host as he gulped some more water, and realized that his front teeth were slanted, as if somebody had punched him in the mouth a long time ago. Maybe that was why he was on radio, not television.

The break ended, and Mr. West blinked at his computer screen. "I see that another scientist is waiting on the phone. The question is, does he believe in the literal account of Genesis? Let's find out."

It was one of the scientists Dr. Park had lined up, a Dr. Otto Berg who had been in astrophysics since before NASA started, using German V-2 rockets, and had been in the field for over fifty years.

Mr. West looked surprised. "You're kidding. You really worked for NASA?"

"Yes, I was an original employee."

Dr. Park winked at Jonathan. Mr. West was going to have a few more surprises.

The calls kept coming in. Men like Dr. John Morris, the president of the Institute for Creation Research, and Dr. DeYoung, who argued that there was abundant evidence for creation in all fields of science, from physics to chemistry to biology.

At 5:28, Mr. West answered his last call.

"Who is this?" Mr. West said.

"My name is Dr. John Morris, and I am a geology professor, and president of the Institute for Creation Research."

"And what is the Institute for Creation Research?"

"Neal, the Institute is a group of scientists, all of us with Ph.D.'s in various fields of science. In geology, biology, physics, science education, all of us are thoroughly trained in our fields, all of us have been professors at major universities, but we're also Bible-believing Christians who believe the Word of God."

"Thanks for the call, Dr. Morris." Mr. West looked at the clock. "Well, I am Neal West and this has been another edition of *Chat Line America*. We are out of time for today, and what a day. Sherman, although I'm usually right, I must admit that you proved me wrong."

"And Neal," Mr. Bott said, "we've only heard from about twenty scientists today. I want to remind you that there are thousands more all around the world who claim the truth of creation."

"Including Dr. Kendall Park. Thanks for being on the program."

Jonathan's dad nodded. "It has been great!"

"And Jonathan, I think you've been my youngest guest ever. Thanks."

Jonathan was glad to get away from the fluffy microphone and stretch his legs, which were aching from his having kept them tensed for the past two hours. Out in the lobby, Mrs. Park, Jessie, and Mr. Brenan formed a 'welcome back' committee.

"Kendall, that was great!" Mrs. Park hugged them both.

"Boy, did you see how many scientists called in?" Dr. Park grinned.

"Dr. Park, thank you so much," Mr. Bott said. He looked far more comfortable now that the show was over.

"Sherman, thank *you*. It was wonderful to see that there are so many others who have rejected evolution like myself. A couple days ago I said that I felt like the Lone Ranger, but now I feel like Tonto with a whole regiment of Lone Rangers. Most of the scientists who called in were better qualified than me to be on that show."

Jessie grinned at Jonathan. "How is the radio star?"

Jonathan grunted. "I sure learned a lesson. I needed it."

Dr. Park sighed. "You know, all I could think about during the whole program was losing the dinosaur graveyard."

"Dr. Park?" The *Chat Line America* producer was holding a phone. "I have someone who is looking for you."

"This must be my day for receiving calls at other people's places. Okay, I'll take it."

"He has been on the phone in there for a long time." Mrs. Park tried to peer through the frosted glass on the office door.

"Do you know who was on the phone?" Mr. Brenan asked.

The door opened and Dr. Park came out with a huge grin. "You'll never believe what happened!"

"Then you'd better tell us, partner," Mr. Brenan said. "What's going on?"

"That was Dave Phillips, who was calling to be on the show, but was too late. He's a creationist who is currently working on his Ph.D. in paleontology, and knows several creationists who have been on dinosaur excavations. I guess there is a group of people from around the nation who have been on several digs together."

The graveyard, Jonathan thought. It has to be something about the graveyard. "Can he help you, Dad?"

"When he heard about our dinosaur graveyard, he said he could have a huge team of diggers ready to help us in just a couple of weeks!"

Mr. Brenan held his hands up. "Kendall, you're kidding—right?"

"He thought we'd have that graveyard uncovered in just a couple of months! Jim, we've got our dream back! We'll be able to open the dig site up to the public after all."

"And begin construction on the museum!" Mr. Brenan said.

Dr. Park removed his glasses and rubbed his sleeve over his eyes. "Jim, not only has God allowed us to have our dream, but now we've found others to help us live it!"

Jessie clapped her hands. "It's like we've become part of a huge team of friends reaching the world with the creation message!"

Jonathan grinned. He felt great. The show had turned out to be a huge success, God had taught him a much-needed lesson in humility, and now the dig-site would soon be back in operation. He took a big breath.

"We've got an awesome adventure ahead of us!"

African Safari

A blue helicopter slowly descended to the African plain. The draft from the rotors leveled the thick savannah grass and blew wispy bushes far away from the landing site. The skids sank into the shifty soil and the engine quieted. A man jumped from the driver's side and hurriedly attached a portable stairway below the cabin door.

A second man stomped down the stairs and growled at the surroundings.

"What I don't appreciate, Edward, is being dragged out from under air conditioned splendor, out into this—this wilderness."

The passenger's voice was almost as sharp as his profile. His jaw made a ridge on each side of his face and poked out into an irrepressible chin. The only softening aspect was a slender mustache which shaded a pair of thin lips.

"Dr. Cassat, please. I don't want to spoil the surprise." Edward seemed undisturbed by his employer's sharp tones. He was obviously used to them. Both men spoke with English accents.

"All right," Dr. Cassat grumbled. "I've allowed the charade to go on *this* far. Just tell me one thing."

"Yes, sir?"

"Why must Africa be so hot?"

Edward coughed. "Well, we are near the Equator, sir."

"Be quiet. It was a rhetorical question. This heat I have no control over—yet. But you saw all those mangy beasts we flew over?"

The men were now trudging up a slight incline. Sweat-beads streaked both men's faces.

"Yes, sir, they're called 'endangered species,'" Edward said.

"Pests, Edward, pests. Fouling up all that perfectly good real estate. I detest these wide open spaces. The jungle is what I like—an asphalt jungle."

The two men reached the top of the incline and looked back on the plain behind. It was covered in coarse brown grass, with here and there a clump of spindly trees. Edward took a handkerchief from his pocket, folded it neatly in half, and dabbed at the sweat on his forehead.

"This so-called 'wide open space' is the Lake Turkana Wildlife Reserve," Edward said. "All of this, as far as the eye can see. One hundred square miles dedicated to the preservation of vanishing African species—and you own it."

Dr. Cassat grunted. "Must you remind me? What's the going rate in Africa to bulldoze and pave over one hundred miles?"

Edward smiled. "May I remind you, sir, that this is tribal land you're leasing, and our local Kikuyu chief is firmly committed to conservation. And that includes mineral rights."

Dr. Cassat looked at his man sharply. "Mineral rights, Edward? So, that's your game."

"Edward! Edward!" A husky African ran up the other side of the slope shouting Edward's name.

Dr. Cassat growled. "What's wrong with the fellow? Did he swallow a bullhorn? Who is that?"

"His name is Kamoya," Edward said.

"Edward! Edward! Over here!" Kamoya called.

Dr. Cassat stalked down the incline. "Calm down, Kamoya. What's gotten you so excited?"

The dirt was pockmarked by shovels. Two yellow hazmat suits and a pile of equipment lay nearby. Kamoya was pointing at a pile of dirt, his teeth gashing his face in a wide grin.

"Here, sir, look! It's beautiful! You see, Dr. Cassat?"

"A pile of dirt. Yes, charming. What is it, an endangered ant mound?"

Edward lifted a small box from the ground.

"What's that device?" Dr. Cassat demanded.

"It's a Geiger counter, sir. It measures radiation."

"I know what a Geiger counter does. Hand it over."

"Place it next to the dirt, sir."

Slowly, a smile stretched over the rich man's face. He unhooked an attachment from the box and held it toward the dirt. The box began beeping.

"Don't be shy, sir." Edward was grinning. "Closer."

The beeping grew louder and louder, until it blocked out all the other sounds of the African wilderness.

"By the sound," Dr. Cassat shouted, "I take it that this dirt is radioactive!" He pulled the box away and the beeping died down.

"Uranium-235," Edward said. "Top quality. Reactor and weapons grade. We happen to be standing near what appears to be an enormous deposit of it." He lowered his voice. "It's worth millions."

"Really?" Dr. Cassat fingered his mustache. "You're speaking my language, I must say."

"But we do have that problem with the Kikuyu chief."

"Ah, yes, mineral rights." Dr. Cassat pointed at Kamoya. "Perhaps we could have Kamoya here talk to them."

Kamoya shook his head vigorously. "No, sir. The Kikuyu no trust Kamoya. They know me too well."

"Regardless, I have the will." Dr. Cassat folded his arms. "All I need to do now is find the way."

It was a lovely spring Saturday at Brenan Ranch, and full-scale picnic preparations were in progress. The Parks were over, and both families had driven to a quiet spot on the ranch where they set up a portable grill. The dads fired this up while the ladies spread a blanket on the grass and distributed plastic plates and utensils.

Jonathan sprawled on the blanket next to Ryan and smiled as he watched the dads grilling. They were bent over the charred racks as if they were performing surgery. When the operation was finally over, they had two plates of chicken legs and burgers and another plate of charred *something*. Jonathan couldn't quite tell what it was.

"Anything I can do?" Jonathan asked.

"No, I think we're ready to eat," Mrs. Park said.

Grandpa Benjamin asked the blessing. "Our Father in heaven, we ask that You would bless this glorious picnic lunch and the skilled hands of the ones who prepared it. We ask it in the name of Jesus, amen."

"All right, everybody," Mrs. Brenan said. "Dig in!"

Jonathan speared a chicken leg with his fork. The outer layer was a little burnt, but the inside was nearly perfect. He heaped the remaining space on his plate with potato salad and chips.

"Mom, can I have a cookie?" Ryan asked.

"I think you need a sandwich first."

"What a day for a picnic!" Dr. Park exclaimed. "A warm sun, green grass, red cliffs, and delicious food."

"And ants," Jonathan said. He flicked at a small parade forming on the blanket's edge.

Dr. Park turned to Jessie. "So, I hear you're making a creation presentation for your homeschool group?"

Jessie nodded. "Ever since we got trapped in the cave I've really become excited about creation science."

"Well, now that we've found a dinosaur graveyard here on the ranch, you can tell the kids about the fossil evidence for a worldwide flood."

"Doesn't the fossil record tell the history of fossils since the very beginning of time?" Mrs. Brenan asked.

Dr. Park nodded. "Close. You see, evolutionists believe it's a record of billions of years of evolution. They say it tells about the order in which evolution happened. However, creationists say that most of the fossils came from Noah's Flood. The Bible says that all of the land-dwelling animals that weren't on the Ark were drowned. All of that water and mud from the flood would have made millions of fossils."

Mrs. Brenan frowned over her glass of lemonade. "So, if the fossil record is used by both evolutionists and creation scientists, how can we prove which one is right?"

Dr. Park reached for another burger. "If evolution were true, that would mean that millions of animals evolved into millions of other types of animals over millions of years." He pointed to a pair of birds which were chasing each other nearby. "If dinosaurs actually changed into birds, then there would have to be hundreds of thousands of part-dinosaur, part-bird animals as the change was happening. These changing animals are called 'transitional forms.' When they died, they should have left some fossil evidence."

"But there isn't any!" Jessie said.

"You're right—and that is a huge problem for evolution. Just think about it—there should be hundreds and hundreds of thousands of transitional fossils in the fossil record."

"So what does the fossil record really look like?" Jessie asked.

"That's the exciting part!" Dr. Park said. "We see fossils that match extinct animal groups, like the dinosaurs in our graveyard, and we see fossils for animals still alive today, like those birds, but we don't see in-between 'transitional forms.' And that is what we should expect to find if creation is true—because God said He made all of the animals distinct from the beginning."

"Thanks for steering me in the right direction for my report."

"Speaking of directions—" Dr. Park turned to Mr. Brenan. "Jim, can you reach into that bag and hand me those blueprints?"

Mr. Brenan looked at his greasy hands, then at the leather bag. "I'm going to get fried chicken all over them. Is that okay?"

Dr. Park laughed. "They're only copies."

He took the blueprints from Mr. Brenan and spread them out in the middle of the blanket. Jonathan squinted at the lines, trying to make sense of the building's outline. Whatever it was, it was big.

Dr. Park cleared his throat. "As you all know, Jim and I have been planning to open a creation museum, Hidden Cave, and our dinosaur graveyard to the public." He paused, letting the suspense build. "These here are the preliminary drawings for the main building."

Everyone gathered around eagerly. Jonathan was impressed at the plan's detail. It looked tangible—it was more than a dream.

"Have you found a good piece of land on the ranch to build on?" Mrs. Park asked.

Dr. Park motioned to Mr. Brenan. "Jim, will you do the honors?"

Mr. Brenan grinned. "Well—you're sitting on it!"

Jonathan nearly jumped. No wonder the dads had chosen this spot for the picnic.

"Hidden Cave is less than a hundred yards to the south," Mr. Brenan explained, "and Brenan Bluff where we found our dinosaur graveyard is right over there within easy walking distance."

"The idea," Dr. Park said, "is to have a continuous working dig as an exhibit, with our museum visitors joining in on the fun."

Mrs. Park grinned. "You're just trying to get someone else do your digging for you."

Everyone laughed but Dr. Park. He looked at Mr. Brenan.

"I wish it were as easy as that. Unfortunately, we've hit a snag."

"It's money," Mr. Brenan said. "We're not going to take government money, and even if we were, they probably wouldn't give it for a creation museum. So we need private funding—but we've been having a really hard time getting people interested in giving money for a creation museum."

Dr. Park nodded. "Even if we do get funding, we'll probably have to scale back to a tenth of what we planned." He folded the blueprints. "If we're able to build at all."

Grandpa Benjamin spoke. "I'm sorry to hear that, Son. It sounds pretty grim, but remember, God is in control." He rubbed his chin with his index finger. "Philippians 4:6-7: 'Be careful for nothing; but in every thing by prayer and supplication with thanksgiving let your requests be made known unto God. And the peace of God, which passeth all understanding, shall keep your hearts and minds through Christ Jesus.'"

"Thanks, Dad."

"Everything that happens in our lives happens because the Lord allows it. Why? To draw us closer to Him. To make us more like the Savior."

Jonathan reached for a third cookie. When he listened to Grandpa Benjamin, he knew where his dad got his personality and his easy-to-understand way of speaking.

"Just trust God," Grandpa Benjamin finished. "Sometimes He says 'yes,' sometimes He says 'no,' and sometimes He says 'wait.'"

When his grandfather stopped talking, Jonathan realized that something had been buzzing for awhile, and was growing quite loud. A mosquito attack? He looked up.

"A helicopter!"

The buzzing became a roar as a low-flying chopper approached. It looked like a four-seater and had thick blue stripes wrapping round the fuselage.

"I think it's going to land here!" Jonathan said.

Everyone scrambled to their feet. The helicopter hovered over them for a moment, then swung down toward a level spot.

"Everyone stay *away* from the blades!" Mr. Brenan shouted.

Mrs. Brenan grabbed Ryan and held him close. Jonathan was glad that he was old enough to stand by himself, but he also edged away from the chopper. The grass under the helicopter was blown flat until the skids grounded and the rotors finally slowed. Three men got out.

Dr. Park gasped. "Angela, look—isn't that Zach?"

"Wow. He got old!"

"You can't be twenty-two for ever."

"Who is Zach, Dad?" Katie asked.

Mrs. Park answered. "The one in the middle is Zach Benson, your father's old college roommate."

Jonathan remembered stories about Zach Benson, who was just a few days younger than his dad. The two had gone to college together, and both had graduated as vertebrate paleontologists in the same class. Since then, though, Dr. Benson hadn't been around very much. Jonathan had only seen pictures in an old photo album.

The man on Dr. Benson's left was dressed in a tailored black suit, and walked a step behind the other men. The third man wore wrinkled khakis, a Hawaiian shirt, and sunglasses. His face was lean.

"Zach! What are you doing here?" Dr. Park called.

Dr. Benson strode toward them, a big grin on his face. "It's a bit dramatic, I know, but wait until you find out why we're here! No, I'm afraid a handshake isn't going to cut it, Kendall."

He wrapped Dr. Park in a bear hug and almost lifted him off the ground. The man in the Hawaiian shirt grunted.

"Well, am I going to get any introductions?" Dr. Benson asked, after he had released Dr. Park and let him recover his breath.

"Angela, you know."

"Pretty as ever, you haven't changed."

Mrs. Park blushed. "Thanks, Zach."

"My daughter Katie, son Jonathan, and father Benjamin." Dr. Park pointed to each in turn. "And these are our friends, Jim and Martha Brenan, and their children, Jessie and Ryan."

"It's a pleasure to meet you all," Dr. Benson said. "Here with me is Dr. Cassat and his assistant, Edward."

Edward nodded. "A pleasure."

"Dr. Park, I'm a man of few words, so I'll get to them." Dr. Cassat's voice was harsh, but it sounded to Jonathan like this was normal, not that he was extra grumpy at the moment. "You're a vertebrate paleontologist and I need you for a fossil recovery effort on my game reserve at Lake Turkana, in Kenya."

Jonathan blinked. *Africa? Wow!* The last time a stranger tracked them down and asked them to go somewhere, they went to Florida. That seemed pretty neat at the time, but Africa? That would be incredible.

Dr. Park stroked his chin. "This is rather sudden, Dr. Cassat. Could I ask what kind of fossil it is?"

Dr. Benson answered. "*Australopithecus afarensis.*"

"Really?" Dr. Park looked impressed.

"I don't know *that* one," Jonathan said.

"Jonathan, one of the most famous *Australopithecus afarensis* is Lucy. It's a partial female skeleton discovered by Donald Johanson in 1974, not too far from Lake Turkana."

Dr. Benson nodded. "Our Lucy came up near Tanapoi, at the southern end of the lake."

Jonathan remembered his dad going over that area's geography with him. It was in Africa's Great Rift Valley, where lots of primate fossils had been found. Evolutionists were using them to try to link man to his so-called 'ape ancestors.'

Dr. Cassat snapped his fingers impatiently. "So far we have found what—teeth? A partial jaw?"

"And a hamate, which of course is a wrist bone, and a hip joint." Dr. Benson looked enthusiastic. "It really is an exciting find."

"Excuse me for interrupting," Dr. Park said, "but Dr. Benson here is a very good vertebrate paleontologist. Why do you need me?"

Dr. Cassat growled. "You see, the chief of the Kikuyu—the indigenous tribe on the land—has the final say when it comes to these matters. He is one of you. They all are, actually."

"Vertebrate paleontologists?"

Dr. Benson smiled. "No, born-again Christians."

Dr. Cassat continued. "The only way he is going to let us continue the dig is if we include a scientist with a Christian creationist's worldview. Someone such as yourself. Dr. Benson recommended you, so here I am. Of course, you'll be well paid." He smiled, a sort of tight, wry smile.

Dr. Park hesitated. "I just don't like the idea of flying off to Africa on a whim and leaving my family and commitments behind."

"Is that all?" Dr. Cassat shrugged. "Then bring them. Your family—my treat."

"I don't know. Jim and I have an awful lot of work to do here."

Dr. Cassat turned to Mr. Brenan. "Ah, yes, you're his partner in that museum venture. Oh, don't look surprised, I know all about it. Very well, you can come too, and I'll pay you." He glanced at his watch. "I want you all to be happy. Because if you're happy, Dr. Park can turn his thoughts to the task at hand. Our Kikuyu chief is happy. And that makes Dr. Benson happy. And that makes *me* happy. I like happiness."

Jonathan didn't think he looked like a very happy man, but he didn't say anything. He wanted to go to Africa.

The parents moved a few yards away to talk about the opportunity. Dr. Cassat put his hands in his pockets and whistled to himself. Edward handed him a handkerchief and picked it up off the ground after his employer threw it there. Finally, the parents returned.

"Dr. Cassat," Dr. Park said, "we feel that this may be the Lord's way of providing some of the funding for our museum. We'll do it!"

The air throbbed with drum-beats and strange animal noises. The ground was brown and dusty, with waist-high savannah grass on each side of the dirt road. There were no clouds, and the sun was intense.

Jonathan was jittery. *A real African village!* The Jeeps stopped in the middle of the village, where a crowd of dusky Kikuyu surrounded them.

"The Kikuyu tribe believes in a warm welcome," Edward said. He waved back. "A beautiful people with a beautiful culture. I hope you all are able to get to know them as I have."

"We will," Mrs. Brenan said. "We've decided to make this a teaching expedition for the children. The timing is perfect. My daughter was just preparing a report for her homeschool group about human fossils."

Everyone climbed out of the Jeeps and stretched their legs after the bumpy ride from the airstrip.

Dr. Benson nodded approvingly at Jessie. "Studying fossils has been a life-long study for me. I'm glad to see such a young lady finding an interest in the subject."

Jessie grimaced a little at being called *such* a young lady, but responded cheerfully. "I like to learn new things, and I think fossils are neat."

Dr. Benson turned to Dr. Park. "Speaking of fossils, Kendall, I've wondered how you reconcile the ape-man fossils now that you're a Christian."

"Zach, I used to believe the evolutionary story, but now that I'm a Christian, I've been able to look at the facts from a different perspective."

Dr. Benson laughed. "I'll bet."

"Zach, think of all the fossils claimed to be in the human evolutionary line. They fall into two categories: either they're within the range for modern humans, or they have traits similar to apes or chimps. There haven't been any half man, half ape fossils."

"What do you mean, Dad?" Jonathan asked.

"A good example of this is the Neanderthals. For the most part, the Neanderthal skulls we've found have had slightly bigger cranial capacity than the *average* person—but no different from some people alive today."

Jonathan nodded. Basically, his dad meant that Neanderthals had big heads, but no bigger than some people today.

"Although evolutionary scientists are claiming that Neanderthals were an evolutionary breakaway from human ancestry, many other scientists now agree that Neanderthals were fully human. And we've found evidence that Neanderthals made musical instruments, buried their dead, and had religious traditions just like modern humans. Yet, most of the public has seen pictures of the Neanderthal people as ape-like brutes."

Dr. Benson looked slightly uncomfortable, but said nothing.

"What about the others?" Jessie asked.

"Another great example is *Ramapithecus*. When people found a few teeth and a part of the jaw, artists drew pictures that looked half ape and half man. Later, some more fossils were found, and it became evident that *Ramapithecus* was almost identical to modern orangutans. And that's what often happens—when they find ape fossils they make them look more human-like, and when they find human fossils, they try to make them look more ape-like."

Dr. Benson frowned. "I agree with you that the media will often hype things up a bit, but I disagree with your total rejection of evolutionary interpretation."

"How interesting," Dr. Cassat said, sounding very uninterested. "Two men who started down the same path but have arrived at two totally different destinations. Well, shall we get you all settled in?"

By now, everybody was out of the Jeeps and standing in the middle of the village. The houses were all round, with one rectangular doorway, and a thatched roof that overshot the walls and provided a little bit of shade, depending where the sun was. Jonathan was surprised to see most of the Kikuyu wearing T-shirts and cutoff jeans. They didn't look like the wild tribesmen he had imagined.

"Uh, Dr. Cassat," Mrs. Brenan said, "there are several men going through our things in the backs of the Jeeps."

Dr. Cassat waved his hand. "Not to worry, Mrs. Brenan. It's just more of the Kikuyu's five-star service. They should have you unpacked and settled into your huts in no time."

Another Jeep pulled up next to them and the driver waved to the rich man. "Dr. Cassat!"

Dr. Cassat scowled. "Well, I certainly am popular today. Yes, Kamoya, what is it?"

Kamoya leaned over and swung the passenger door open. "Sir, we're having a—problem—at site twelve. We need you, sir."

Dr. Cassat shrugged. "Ladies and gentlemen, children, unfortunately, duty calls. I'm confident you'll be able to entertain yourselves."

"Why don't you drop us off at the dig?" Dr. Benson said. "I'm sure Kendall and Jim would like to get a first look."

As the Jeep drove away, Jessie turned to her mom. "Mom, can we go exploring too?"

"Yeah!" Jonathan and Katie said.

Mrs. Brenan looked around. "I don't see any harm. What do you think, Angela?"

"I think it's okay. As long as you stay close."

Jessie hooted. Jonathan was a little less expressive, but just as excited. Who needs Indiana Jones when you can explore Africa for yourself?

Edward added a note of caution. "You have free reign here at the compound and the surrounding bush. The only place *off* limits is the northeast quadrant of the park. We have—sensitive research going on out there. If you do venture out, I do ask that you all exercise caution. There are many wild animals about. Some are quite dangerous."

Jonathan trudged through waist-high grass. Jessie came behind, followed by Katie. It was like walking through a *National Geographic* picture. The plain was mostly flat, though there were a few hills and depressions, as well as some clumps of trees.

Katie lagged behind. "Guys, I think we're getting too far away from the compound."

Jonathan shaded his eyes. They were rather far away. Actually, the huts were little dots and the people were indistinguishable. He hadn't realized how far they had gone. He was about to suggest that they head back when Jessie interrupted.

"Wait a minute. Look at this." Jessie pointed to two parallel lines of beaten-down grass. "Tire tracks? What is a car doing way out here in the middle of nowhere? There aren't any roads."

The tracks were easy to follow through the grass, and it looked like they led into a ravine ahead, which was fringed with trees.

"Come on," Jonathan said. "Let's go check it out!"

Katie grabbed his arm. "Wait, guys, you remember what Edward said."

Jonathan pulled away and started for the ravine with Jessie.

"This is Africa, guys," Katie called after them. "You never know what could be hiding in a ravine. Jonathan—Jessie—don't!" She waited a moment, but they kept going. "Oh fine, wait for me."

The ravine's slopes were covered by trees and rocks. The tire tracks led straight down the level bottom. Jonathan wanted to explore, but Katie did have a point. Anything could be hiding on the slopes. *I'd better stay alert*, he thought.

The tracks led to some type of work site full of trash and equipment. There were a couple of temporary buildings, like storage sheds, but no buildings to live in.

"What is this doing way out here in the middle of nowhere?" Katie asked.

Jonathan rattled an empty can with his foot. "I don't think the Kikuyu use this place. I mean, look at all this modern technology."

"Look at these." Katie pointed to a pile of yellow suits.

"Rain coats?" Jessie wrinkled her nose. "Does it even rain here?"

"Look, they have some kind of symbol on them." Jonathan leaned closer. Each suit was printed with a black circle from which three shapes, almost like propeller blades, radiated. "Doesn't that stand for radiation?"

Jessie gasped. "These aren't rain jackets—they're radiation suits!"

Jonathan was immediately suspicious. Why would a game reserve have radiation suits? They wouldn't stop a wild animal attack.

"Remember what Edward said?" Katie reminded. "Don't go into the northeast corner of the park. There was some kind of research going on there."

Something roared in the bushes. Jessie screamed. Jonathan's chest tightened as he grabbed the girls and backed slowly toward the ravine's mouth. He'd heard that sound in the zoo many times—but this wasn't a zoo. There was a real, live, wild lion in the bushes.

"Right there!" Katie screamed. "A lion, a lion!"

A head and mane poked out of the bushes, followed by a chest, stomach, and pair of powerful hind legs.

Jonathan gulped. "Yeah, that's a lion." He tensed his muscles, waiting for the spring. It was his job to stop the lion long enough for the girls to get to safety.

But the lion didn't spring. And it didn't roar again. It lay down on its side and began growling. It looked like a huge house-cat purring in the sun.

"What is he *doing*?" Jonathan said.

"You want to go over to him and ask?" Katie's voice was high.

"He's just laying there," Jessie said. "If I didn't know better, I'd say he was—smiling."

"Well, why doesn't he eat us or something?" Katie shook her fist at the beast. "Get it over with, lion."

"You really don't have to taunt him, Katie." Jonathan tugged on the girls' shoulders. If they could back up without disturbing the lion—

"Leo!"

Jonathan jumped. Someone was coming down the ravine.

"Oh, Leo! You bad lion. Scaring these children like that." It was Edward, and he walked fearlessly toward the lion. "You ought to be ashamed of yourself. Go on. Go home!"

The lion slowly got up and whimpered. Only now did Jonathan notice the skin-colored collar around the lion's neck. It was half-buried in the bushy mane.

"Go home!" Edward repeated.

Leo whimpered again and padded back into the bushes, his shoulders drooped and his tail tucked between his legs.

Edward chuckled. "I'm sorry, children, I neglected to warn you about Leo. He is our resident—er, watch lion, you could say. We found Leo when he was a cub, raised him as a village pet. As you can see, he's quite harmless. He's very protective of the Kikuyu children—even gone up against other animals to save a life. Unfortunately for you, he does like a good practical joke."

"Well, Kendall, what do you think of our dig site?"

Kendall scanned the piles of dirt and tools and the dozens of workers. "It's—big."

Zach smiled. "Dr. Cassat has deep pockets, and his hands haven't gotten stuck yet. Something strike your fancy, Jim?"

Jim looked puzzled. "Zach, how did they find the original fossils?"

"Actually, Dr. Cassat's assistant, Kamoya, spotted them."

"You mean, they were just laying in the dirt? Just like that?" Kendall raised his eyebrows. Fossils were usually like buried treasure, only more fragile.

"Just like that. But since then, we haven't found anything."

Jim spoke. "So why did Dr. Cassat hire so many men to dig over there if there haven't been any indications of more fossils?"

Zach shrugged. "That's the million dollar question. After the initial find, nothing turned up. So now we're digging out the recovery site."

In the park's northeast quadrant, a group of men in yellow hazmat suits grunted and sang terse native chants as they dug in the dirt. Kamoya led Dr. Cassat toward the site.

"Well here we are, gallivanting all over East Africa. Kamoya, you're starting to remind me of Edward."

Kamoya's face was stolid. "It was Edward who asked that I bring you here. He has called the emergency."

Edward approached, his usually placid face twisted into a worried frown. "Thank you for coming so quickly, sir. There is something here you need to see right away."

Dr. Cassat growled. "I don't see anything wrong, Edward."

Edward pointed to a long low building on a little rise above the dig site. Moaning was coming from its windows.

"Dr. Cassat, sir, the workers—they're starting to get sick now. It's exposure, radiation sickness. We have ten more men out just today."

"We've given them radiation suits. What more do they need?"

"It's not enough. They need proper equipment. Modern equipment to limit their exposure to this ore. Sir, lives are at stake."

Dr. Cassat folded his arms. "We don't have time to get them, Edward, you know that. Our time is running out. Besides, it would make people ask questions. Curiosity kills more than cats." He leaned closer to Edward, his eyes narrow. "Developing a conscience at this late hour, are we, Edward?"

Edward straightened. "Sir, it brings me no pleasure to say this. In the past your business practices were—unethical. Certainly, immoral. But they've never been murderous—until now."

"Edward, there have never been so many millions at stake."

The two men locked eyes. They stayed thus for many seconds, their bodies motionless. Then, slowly, Edward turned away.

"You're not dismissed," his employer snapped. "Where are you going? Edward!"

"I don't know." The valet's voice was unsteady. "I've never had a conscience before."

"If we tell the truth we lose the mine, the money, and I really do not relish the idea of spending the rest of my life in some rotting prison cell. You too, Edward! We continue as planned! Edward!"

Kamoya coughed respectfully. "There is something else."

"There always is, Kamoya."

"The American children were out hiking and found one of our sites. It is not too hard to put two and two together. In my opinion, they pose a serious security risk to this operation."

Dr. Cassat sighed. "Then I guess you'll have to remedy that."

Kamoya grinned. "Yes, sir. Kamoya will take care of the children."

Jonathan, Jessie, and Katie were nearing the compound after their adventure in the ravine when Kamoya drove up in a Jeep.

"Hello, children!" he called, stopping the Jeep. "You look hot."

Jonathan wiped his forehead on his sleeve. "No kidding. And I thought New Mexico's summers were bad."

"Are you too hot for some adventure?" Kamoya asked.

Jessie perked immediately. "Adventure? Where?"

"I was just talking with your parents. Dr. Cassat has asked me to ask them if it was okay to take you all out to our new research site in the northeast corner of the park. Want to go?"

"Did our parents say yes?" Katie asked.

"Of course! There is no danger with Kamoya nearby. What do you say?"

Jonathan looked at Katie. "Sounds good to me."

"Okay," Katie said. "As long as there aren't any more lions."

Kamoya grinned. "Hop in, children."

"This is the fossil, isn't it? The one that got us all the way to Africa?" Jim pointed to a neat row of bones at the dig site.

"That's it," Zach said. "Our initial discovery here represents—oh, probably about fifteen percent of a complete skeleton."

"Is this the famous Lucy?" Jim asked.

"Actually, no, Lucy was found a hundred miles to the north. But strangely enough, these fossils look identical to the Lucy fossils." Zach frowned. "It's really weird."

"Has she been named yet?" Kendall asked.

"Well—" Zach grinned sheepishly. "I was thinking of the name 'Ethel.'"

"Lucy and Ethel? As in, *I Love Lucy*?"

"Together again!"

Kendall laughed. "That's cute, Zach, real cute."

"Sorry to break into your American TV cultural

references," Jim said, "but what can you tell about this creature from these partial fossils?"

"It's a hominid, an early ancestor to humans."

Kendall raised his hand. "I hope you don't mind if I disagree with you, Zach."

"Oh, I'm used to it. What's your story?"

"Think about it, Zach. You're assuming it's a hominid because you believe that hominids existed millions of years ago."

Zach nodded. "I will grant you that the evidence is somewhat circumstantial, but I believe that human beings evolved from lesser forms."

Kendall squatted next to the bones. "Look at the jawbone for a moment." He lifted it carefully and ran his finger around the edge. "This jaw is 'U' shaped. That's typical of gorillas." He set the bone down and pointed at the others. "And look at these toes. They're curved. So are the fingers here. What does that tell you?"

"That this hominid clearly spent much of its life in the trees, not on the ground. I grant you that. But this hip indicates an animal capable of walking upright like a human. That's really the key reason for describing this fossil as a human ancestor."

"I agree," Kendall said, "but I would add that they can walk *somewhat* upright. Not like humans. More hunched over, like this."

Kendall let his arms fall, rounded his shoulders, and shuffled around the fossils with his back bent forward. The diggers stopped their work and stared.

"Not everything has changed since college," Zach said.

Kendall straightened. "Oh. Right. Well, anyway, that's an idea of how they could walk. Pygmy chimps walk just like that. When I look at this skeleton, I see an extinct created ape-like animal. Not an evolved form."

"What's this one right here?" Jim pointed to one of the fossils.

Kendall picked it up. "It's a hamate, a part of the wrist. You see this here? This is a hook that the tendons grab on to. It's much larger than a human's. That gives it much stronger hands." He set it back down. "This fossil supports my hypothesis as well, that this skeleton is from an extinct, predominately tree-dwelling primate."

Zach shook his head. "I think we can agree to disagree, Kendall. By the way, you appear to have a fan club."

"Hmm?"

The workers had stopped digging again and were watching Kendall eagerly. They probably expected another exhibition.

"Oh." Kendall grimaced. "Today's show is over. But back to the point—if evolution is right, then there should be thousands of non-disputable ape-man fossils in the fossil record. However, the truth of the matter is that evolution can only offer a very few, questionable, so-called ape-man fossils. To me that settles it—the fossil record can't support evolution."

"I have a different interpretation."

"Zach, remember what David Pilbeam said?"

Zach nodded. "We took that class together, remember?"

"Well, I didn't," Jim said.

"David is a well-respected evolutionary paleoanthropologist," Zach said. "He said that 'paleoanthropology reveals more about how humans view themselves than it does about how humans came about.'"

Jim looked at Kendall. "Translation?"

"He said that the study of fossils can sometimes be more about our beliefs than in finding out the truth about our beginnings."

A helicopter approached, heading for the landing pad. It was Dr. Cassat's big blue chopper.

"I suppose he's come to check on the site," Kendall said. "He's a strange man. He doesn't seem very keen on paleontology."

"No, I think money is more his area of expertise." Jim shaded his eyes. "I see Edward and Dr. Cassat, but who are those uniformed men with them?"

"They're Kenyan State Police!" Zach said. "They're waving us over. Come on!"

Jonathan stuck his head out the window and let the breeze whip through his hair. They had been driving for a while, much longer than he had expected, but the landscape was so similar that it was hard to determine how far they had traveled. For all he could tell, they might have been driving in circles. But he wasn't worried. Life was good. A Jeep to ride in, an African country to explore, a big dinner back at the compound to look forward to—

Sput. Sput.

The engine seemed to be having trouble. Kamoya pressed the gas pedal, trying to rev the engine. Instead, it spluttered again, then died completely.

"What's wrong?" Jonathan asked.

"I don't know." Kamoya turned the key, but the starter simply clicked. He tapped the gas gauge. "I think we are out of gas. Yes, I think we are out of gas."

"Out of gas?" Jessie said. "But we're out in the middle of nowhere. There can't be a gas station for miles."

"We have the radio," Katie said. "We should call for a tow truck or something."

Kamoya opened his door. "I don't think the radio is going to work. The battery is dead now, too. Well, site number twelve is about five miles down this road. If I start now, I *could* be back in a couple of hours."

"And leave us out here all by ourselves?" Katie opened her own door. "Are you crazy?"

Kamoya shut Katie's door. "Trust me, children, with all the wild animals about, you are much safer here in the Jeep."

Back at the fossil dig site, two tight-faced Kenyan policemen were explaining the situation to Kendall, Jim, and Zach. Dr. Cassat's hands were handcuffed behind his back, and his mustache drooped.

"So," Jim said, "you're telling us this whole fossil dig was a distraction to keep the Kikuyu from finding out about this ore-mining operation?"

It was Edward who had turned Dr. Cassat in. His face was sad, but settled. "The fossils were stolen from a legitimate dig at the northern end of Lake Turkana. Dr. Benson was brought out to verify the find. When the Kikuyu wanted a creation scientist, yours was the first name."

Kendall faced Dr. Cassat. "So bringing us all the way out to Africa was what—an elaborate deception?"

Dr. Cassat only glared back, but Edward answered. "We needed the Kikuyu away from the mine long enough to remove the ore. The Kikuyu wanted you. Dr. Cassat gave them what they wanted."

"And I would have gotten away with it," the rich man said. "It took this *traitor* to bring it all down."

Edward sighed. "Well, sir, it looks as if we'll both have plenty of time to discuss this—behind bars."

One of the dig site radios crackled. "Kendall! Kendall, are you there? Kendall!"

Kendall grabbed the transmitter. "Go ahead, Angela. Is something wrong?"

Angela's voice was near panic. "Jonathan, Katie, and Jessie are gone!"

"Gone?" Kendall said. "Where?"

"We don't know. One of the villagers said they saw them get in a Jeep with Kamoya and head for the northeast corner of the park. I didn't give Kamoya permission to do that. It's been a couple of hours and they haven't checked in."

Edward turned on his former employer. "What have you done with them?"

Dr. Cassat twined his fingers, the links on the handcuffs chain clinking together. "Oh, why, why me? If that fool has done anything—" he broke off and pointed to the helicopter. "We'd best look for them with that. I don't need any more charges against me than I already have."

"Coats, boots, shovels, umbrellas—wait. Umbrellas?" Jonathan shrugged. "I guess Kamoya is an optimist." He tossed the umbrellas over his shoulder and kept digging through the rubbish in the back of the Jeep.

Katie poked her head out. "What are you doing back there?"

"I'm looking for something useful in this flea market. I don't think Kamoya cleans his Jeep very often."

Katie joined him. "I don't like this," she said. "Kamoya knows the area. He's smart. How could he just run out of gas?"

"Maybe—aha!" Jonathan spotted a dusty red jerrycan. "We *didn't* run out of gas." He lugged the can to the side of the Jeep, twisted the cap off the gas tank, and started pouring.

"We can't drive this," Jessie said, hanging through the window. "We're not old enough. We'll get a ticket."

"I know *that*," Jonathan said, "but if we start the motor it will charge the battery so we can use the radio."

Katie frowned. "Why didn't Kamoya think of that?"

"I don't know, but I'm having serious doubts about Kamoya. Anyway, once we contact help, we'll be out of here in no time."

Katie shaded her eyes with her hands and wandered to the other side of the Jeep.

"Hey, Jessie, look over there. Is that Leo?"

Jonathan couldn't see, because he was bent over the tank, but he heard Jessie take a sharp breath.

"If it is, he's brought company. Guys, you'd better get back in here."

Jonathan tilted the jerrycan higher and emptied the last few glugs. "That's done." He dropped the can and jumped on the running board to see over the roof. There, no more than forty yards away, was a pride of lions.

Jonathan gulped. "Eight, nine—eleven lions. This is *not* good, guys."

"They look hungry!" Katie said.

The lions formed a semicircle and walked forward slowly, their tails twitching. They looked like huge house-cats stalking a bug. Only, this time, Jonathan was the bug.

"We better get out of here," Jonathan said. "We're going to drive after all. Katie, get behind the wheel."

"Me? Why me?"

"Because you're the only one tall enough to reach the pedals!" Jonathan tiptoed around the hood, afraid that the lions would charge if he showed signs of running. He eased the passenger door open, climbed in, and eased it shut. Katie was in the driver's seat.

"Okay, Katie, the keys are in the ignition. Start her up and let's get out of here."

"This better not go on my driving record when I grow up."

Katie clicked the seat belt, gripped the top of the steering wheel with both hands, and jammed on the gas pedal. Nothing happened. She pumped it up and down, but the car was silent. The lions were thirty yards away.

"Katie, keys!" Jonathan grabbed the key and turned it in

the ignition. The starter clicked. Nothing.

Jessie leaned forward from the back seat, her eyes wide. "Dad says that if you pump the accelerator before starting the car, it'll flood the engine."

Katie threw her hands up. "Now what?"

A single lion charged from the left side of the car, which had been clear of lions a minute ago.

"He probably wants to be first in line," Katie said, her voice hoarse. She shook her fist at him. "No cuts, lion! If you're going to eat me, I want it done with a little order and dignity! You got that?"

There was something strange around the lion's neck. Jonathan squinted. "Wait a minute, he has a collar. It's Leo!"

With a roar, Leo ran past the Jeep and sent the closest lion sprawling on its back. The others crouched in the grass and watched the fight. Roars punctured the air and clumps of fur flew from the two beasts, but the wild lion was no match for Leo's well-fed strength. It quickly rolled away from the fight and ran for cover with a big patch of fur missing from between its shoulder blades.

"Get 'em, Leo!" Katie screamed.

"Go, Leo, go!"

"I don't believe it!" Jonathan said. "He's doing it! He's chasing the others away!"

Lion after lion slunk away from Leo and burrowed into the grass, probably to look for an easier dinner somewhere else.

As the roars faded out, a buzzing above faded in. It was a helicopter.

The Parks, Brenans, and Zach Benson stood in a Kenyan airport waiting for their boarding call. People from a dozen different nations were strolling the aisles, while here and there a belated passenger dashed toward his gate. A muffled roar came from the snack court nearby.

"What a week," Martha said. "Praise the Lord the kids aren't hurt from yesterday's adventure."

"It will be good to be home," Angela agreed.

"Jessie," Jim said, "I'll bet you have some pretty interesting information for your presentation to the homeschool group."

Jessie grinned. "I've learned so much about human fossils! I'm so glad we came to Africa, even though it was really a hoax. There couldn't have been a better way to learn."

Zach's flight was first, but they were all lingering together at the Parks' and Brenans' gate, making the most of their last few minutes.

Zach slapped Kendall on the back. "I feel like we're just starting to get reacquainted, and now I'm flying back to Chicago, and you to New Mexico."

"Zach, we'll always stay in touch."

"I wish you guys well with the creation museum." Zach shook his head. "I've got to admit, it would be interesting to see a fossil dig run by creation scientists."

"You should fly out and see it sometime," Jim said. "We've found hundreds of *Coelophysis* fossils."

"Can I ask, why is a *creation* museum so important to you? There are plenty of good fossil museums."

Kendall answered. "We believe that it's important to teach people that there is a Creator. Think about it, Zach. If you believe in evolution, you have to believe that you're no more than molecules that came together by random chance. But *we* want to teach people that there is a loving God who made us and has given us meaning and purpose. Think of how that change in perspective can change a life."

Zach's left eye twitched. "I must admit, you're a changed man."

"Zach, it's not me. The Bible says in 2 Corinthians 5:17: 'Therefore if any man be in Christ, he is a new creature: old things are passed away; behold, all things are become new.' Zach, Christ can change your heart, too."

Zach held up his hands. "Hold on, friend, I'm not ready for this yet."

"Well, when you are, I'm only a phone call away."

Jonathan raced toward the adults from the food court, his camera bag flapping against his hip.

"Jessie, you've got to get over here. There's an Egyptian Cobra loose in the snack bar! And there's this big, scary looking guy trying to catch it."

"Oh, wow!"

"Hold on, guys, I'm coming too!" Katie called.

"Flight 1723 for Chicago is now boarding," a woman announced on the loudspeaker.

"Well, Zach, I guess this is goodbye." Kendall held out his hand.

Zach paused. He reached for something in his bag and stopped, his hand still inside.

"Kendall, I know you were counting on Dr. Cassat's funding to help you build your museum. It's a shame you're going back empty handed."

Kendall waved at the little group around them. "Take a look, Zach. You see this family? My friends? This is what really matters. If the Lord wants that museum built, He'll open the doors."

Zach coughed. "Here, take this." He took a package from his bag. "It's the proceeds from the sale of a small piece of ore from that uranium mine. The Kikuyu own the mine now, and they're going to develop it—without harming the workers or environment. They wanted to reward us for putting a stop to Dr. Cassat. It's not a lot, and it won't last, but it'll get you started on that museum of yours back in New Mexico."

Kendall fingered the package. Could this be the Lord's provision? Could this be why they came to Africa?

"But, Zach," Kendall said, "your name is on this package too."

Zach shrugged. "Yeah, it is. Take it. It's a gift, I insist." He paused again. "You know, Kendall Park, you and your family, and your friends—you *almost* make me believe in God."

Kendall grinned. "And you, Zach Benson, confirm my belief in miracles."

Escape from Utopia

A man maneuvered the steep stairs in the stands behind home plate at a minor league baseball game in Santa Fe, New Mexico. He balanced a cup-carrier with three drinks in his right hand and carried three bags of popcorn in his left. It was a night game, and the bright lights that ringed the stadium dimmed the otherwise brilliant stars in the black dome above.

The man sank into an empty seat next to a woman and a young boy. "I've got enough to feed a truckload of firefighters," he said, handing the food out.

"It's so good to have you home, Myles." The woman wrapped her arm around his shoulders.

"Thanks for bringing us, Dad," the boy said.

"Kirk, when I was your age, my parents took me to ballgames all the time."

The crowd shouted as the home team's biggest slugger walked to home plate. He swung his bat twice in slow-motion, then took his stance next to the plate and waited.

The ball came in fast and low, but the slugger dug for it and sent it hurtling toward the back fence. The Morgans jumped to their feet, watching as it neared the boundary.

"It's going, it's going—gone!" the announcer said. "Home run! What an amazing hit for . . . What is *that*?"

Gasps hissed from the crowd.

"Dad, what is it?" Kirk said.

Something was rising in the sky behind the scoreboard. Something big. Something with flashing lights and a green glow.

The stadium was hushed. The *thing* climbed higher, and higher, and the farther it got from the stadium lights, the brighter it seemed. A faint swooshing, and bell-tingling noise replaced the usual stadium buzz.

Myles grabbed his son's arm.

"I think—I think it's a UFO!"

Late the next night, the Park and Brenan families were driving south on Highway 285, a hundred and fifty miles south of Santa Fe, New Mexico. Both families were crammed into the Brenans' van along with all of their luggage. Kendall had a local radio station on, which was playing a special broadcast about an unusual sight at a ballpark the night before.

"The batter had just hit a home run," an eyewitness said. "We were all watching when we saw these bright lights, and something that looked like a UFO shooting across the sky!"

Martha flicked the power button and shivered. "This is why I hate going to Roswell—especially at night."

Jim, who was driving, laughed. "Everything's going to be just fine."

"Jim's right," Kendall said. "Besides, this trip is important. Now that we're going to open our own museum, we really need to see the Robert Goddard display at the Roswell museum. It should give us some great ideas."

"Speaking of this whole UFO thing, haven't people been looking for aliens for a long time?" Jessie asked.

Kendall nodded. "You could say that mankind has always wondered about the possibility. But the modern search for extra-terrestrials began in the fall of 1960, when a man named Frank Drake began 'listening' to the sky on a radio telescope."

"I've heard about that," Jonathan said. "It's called Serti, or something like that."

"Actually, it's SETI," Jim said. "The Search for Extra-Terrestrial Intelligence."

Kendall nodded. "That project is now being carried on as Project Phoenix by non-governmental agencies."

Jim changed to the left lane to pass a slow white van. There were few cars on the road this late—it was nearly 1:00 A.M.

"Dad," Katie said, "what are they looking for?"

"Project Phoenix? They believe that if there's intelligent life out there, they probably have the ability to make radio or TV signals, like we do. They're listening for anything that sounds like an intelligent signal from space."

"The funny thing is, they haven't found anything yet," Angela said.

"That's right." Kendall twisted in his seat, trying to find more space to stick his legs. "It's been over forty years, and they haven't heard a single non-natural signal from any place other than Earth."

Martha grinned. "Anyone monitoring *Earth's* TV broadcasts would have a hard time receiving intelligent signals as well."

Through the window, Kendall saw the brilliant array of stars over the desert. They were magnificent tonight—a thousand shining pinpoints slashed onto a black canvas. Kendall had always found astronomy fascinating. Before he was a Christian he loved to stand outside on a dark night and fantasize about alien worlds up there.

Katie interrupted Kendall's thoughts. "Wouldn't some people say that even if we haven't picked up radio signals, there's other proof for aliens?"

"They've looked for aliens in many other ways as well. It was in the 70s—" Kendall ticked numbers on his fingers. "1976, I think. NASA launched two probes which mapped the surface of Mars and searched for life. Ever since then, billions of dollars have been spent on the search for life throughout the galaxy."

"That's part of what they're trying to do with all the latest probes to Mars," Angela said.

"So, Jessie, to answer your original question—people do believe in aliens, but scientifically speaking, there hasn't been any confirmed evidence, not even a clue, for intelligent life except for here on Earth."

Jim pointed to a sign. "Just a few miles from Roswell." He winked at the rear-view mirror. "Maybe we'll find something here."

"I have a funny feeling about this," Martha said.

Jessie waved her hand. "Mom, this is going to be great!"

"What, are you kidding?" Kendall slapped his armrest. "The Park and Brenan families on a road trip? What could possibly go wrong?"

Ka-lump. The van began vibrating, and the needle on the RPM gauge soared into the red zone. Jim swung into the road's shoulder and turned off the engine. The van slowed, then gradually stopped.

"Honey, what's wrong?" Martha asked.

Jim shook his head.

"It sounds like your transmission," Kendall said.

Martha groaned. "If we're going to keep taking these road trips, one of us is going to *have* to get a decent van."

Headlights beamed through the back windows. A car— actually, a van—was stopping behind them.

Kendall eyed it warily. "I wonder what this guy wants."

The two dads got out and walked slowly toward the other van. A ditch was next to the road, and there was a cross with a wreath around its shoulders stuck in the bank. Someone must have died in a car accident here.

"Are you guys okay?" the driver of the other van called. His shoes clicked on the pavement as he walked closer.

"I think it's our transmission," Jim said. "Is there an auto shop nearby?"

"The closest one is in Roswell, about five miles down the road." The man glanced through the back windows of the Brenans' van. "Look, this is an awful time of night for your families to be stranded by the side of the road. I'm in charge of a retreat center just over that hill." He pointed to a hill slightly ahead of them. A road wound down the hill and intersected with the highway. "We could call a tow truck, and you and your families could be our guests tonight."

Jim extended his hand. "Thanks for your generous offer, Mr. . . ."

"I'm sorry, my name's Andy."

Kendall also shook hands. "I'm Dr. Kendall Park. I'm sure glad you came along when you did."

"Yes." Andy smiled. "I think it was meant to be."

The retreat center was dark when the Parks and Brenans arrived. The main building looked like a small conference center, and the sleeping-rooms were in two wings which jutted straight out from the main rectangle.

Andy took the Parks and Brenans to two rooms in the right wing, then led Kendall and Jim to the lobby, where he said he had the number of a tow truck driver.

"I know the driver personally," Andy said, unlocking the door. "He's probably the only one who would come out at this time of night. He'll tow it into town for you."

Andy flipped a switch next to the door and the overhead fluorescents flickered to life.

Kendall stared. Strings of little crystals hung from the ceiling, and bigger crystals dotted the floor in thick glass cases. Framed newspapers and brightly-colored murals covered the walls. The floor was black marble, flecked with little dots of white, like stars.

Kendall was instantly suspicious. Andy seemed nice, but Kendall didn't actually know anything about him. And this building did *not* look normal.

"What exactly is the purpose of this center?" Kendall asked.

Before Andy answered, a door in the left wall opened and a man clattered toward them over the marble. He didn't seem to notice Kendall and Jim, but ran straight for Andy.

"Andromedus!" he called.

"Andromedus?" Jim said.

Andy nodded. "That's my full name, but I go by Andy."

"Andromedus, the chosen time has come!"

Andy frowned. "Orion, where are your manners?" He waved at Kendall and Jim. "These are two visitors from the outside."

When Andy said 'Orion,' Kendall at first thought that it was an Irish name, like O'Malley, or O'Connell. But then he remembered that Orion was a constellation. And with Andy's full name being Andromedus . . . something was weird.

Orion held up his hand. "Universal peace to you."

Kendall blinked. "Uh, right back at you."

Orion grabbed Andy's arm and started leading him toward the door. "We're late," he said.

"Sorry, Kendall, Jim, I've got to go to a—well, a meeting. The phone is right over there, and the driver's number is on the list on the wall. Just pull the door shut after you leave. Breakfast is at ten o'clock."

The door banged behind the two men. Kendall and Jim looked at each other.

"I wonder where they're going at two o'clock in the morning?" Jim said.

Kendall slowly scanned the walls. At first, it looked like a room with an astronomy motif, since most of the pictures had stars, and planets, and space ships. Then he looked closer. Those space ships weren't like anything from NASA. Most of them glowed green, and one had little pointy things sitting in chairs inside a glass cockpit.

Kendall gritted his teeth. "Something is telling me that this isn't a nice little family camp."

Jonathan eased the heavy door open and tiptoed into the hallway. He wasn't sure if there were people staying in the other rooms, and he didn't want to wake anybody up. Dim light came from round globes embedded in the ceiling. There was a small window in the right wall, but it simply mirrored his face, showing his hair sticking up in a forest of tangles. He yawned.

Something moved at the end of the hallway.

Jonathan tensed. Who could it be? He felt jittery with all these strange pictures on the walls. He slunk against the wall and something jabbed his back. He spun and found a three foot by two foot picture-frame. At first, he thought it was abstract art, but then he realized that the artist had *meant* to draw a goggle-eyed, five-legged creature. Jonathan shivered.

Whatever was at the end of the hallway came closer.

"H-hello?" Jonathan said.

The other person gasped. "Jonathan?"

"Jessie! Whew." Jonathan smiled in relief. "What are you doing?"

Jessie came into the light. Her loose hair fell around her shoulders. She looked tired. "Ryan is using the restroom, so Mom said I could use the bathroom out here. What about you?"

"Katie's not feeling well, so Mom woke me up and asked me to get her a ginger ale from the vending machine." Jonathan pointed to the picture. "I hope there aren't any of *those* wandering around."

"This place gives me the creeps." Jessie paused. "Do you hear something?"

"The lights buzz."

"No." Jessie cocked her head. "It's coming from this window."

Jonathan couldn't see through the glass because of the glare, but he was able to lift it. The distant hum, or chanting, grew stronger, and a cold wind raked through the tangles in Jonathan's hair. Jessie stuck her head next to his and they looked out together.

Little pinpoints of light moved in a huge circle on what looked like a field. Jonathan squinted. It looked like hundreds of people were walking around with candles.

Jonathan looked at Jessie. "What are hundreds of people doing out in a field at two-thirty in the morning?"

Jessie backed away. "We'd better tell our moms."

"Yeah." Jonathan shut the window. "I think this trip is going to be interesting. See you at breakfast."

Breakfast was served in a little room off the lobby. The breakfast bar was pretty similar to a regular hotel's, with bacon strips, scrambled eggs, little plastic cups of yogurt, stale Danish, and a fruit bowl with seedless grapes and slices of pineapple, apple, and orange. An older lady with inch-long earrings was taking orders for omelets.

Since no one else was eating, the Parks and Brenans pulled three tables together and piled them high with plates, bowls, and cups of orange juice. The kids ate quickly and excused themselves to go outside. Kendall gave strict instructions to not go far from the building. He wasn't sure about this whole place, and he didn't want the kids wandering off into who knows what.

Jim speared his last slab of bacon with his fork. "This food isn't half bad," he said.

Kendall washed a biscuit down with a gulp of orange juice. "You might say it's 'out of this world.'"

"You never know!" Martha said.

Angela winked. "I don't like the way my egg jiggles."

"It's alive!" Jim said.

Kendall dug into his last yogurt cup and spooned himself a delicious mouthful of the blueberry-flavored mixture. It wasn't exactly gourmet, but in Kendall's mind, no continental breakfast was complete without at least one pre-packaged cup of yogurt.

Martha glanced at the lady behind the breakfast bar, then leaned closer. "I'm really concerned about what Jonathan and Jessie saw last night."

The others scooted their chairs closer to the table.

"What kind of a place do you think this is?" Jim said.

Kendall shook his head. "I don't know, but if one more person says 'universal peace to you,' I'm going to scream."

Andy entered the breakfast room from the lobby. He was followed by Orion and a young woman, probably about twenty-five, with a pony tail. Andy smiled when he saw the Parks and Brenans.

"Do you mind if we join you?" Andy asked.

Kendall gestured to the empty seats.

"You remember Orion, and this is Ursula."

The man and woman raised their hands. "Universal peace to you."

Kendall tried to turn his scream into a coughing fit, and Angela played along by thumping his back. The newcomers sat down and didn't seem to notice.

After several gulps of water, Kendall regained his composure. "Andy, in all the busyness of last night, I never had the chance to find out what this retreat center is all about."

"We're the Utopians," Orion said.

"Utopians?"

Andy nodded. "It's an acronym for Universal Teachings Of Peaceful Interplanetary Alien Nations."

Martha's cup clattered against the table top and coffee splashed over the brim. "You're an alien cult?"

"We are not!" Ursula said.

Andy put a hand on Ursula's shoulder and spoke calmly. "Ursula, it is true that some from the outside view us that way. But really, we are seekers of the truth. We think it somewhat arrogant to believe that we are the only inhabitants in this universe." He handed Martha a napkin to blot up the coffee. "What about you? Do you seek knowledge from our universal brotherhood?"

Jim grunted. "To be honest, I'm just trying to figure out things down here on Earth."

Orion leaned forward, obviously eager to discuss their beliefs. "We believe that the universe is teeming with life. With thousands of planets similar to planet Earth, the chances for evolution to produce life elsewhere are overwhelming."

Kendall saw his first loophole. "Actually, mathematically, the odds are completely *against* evolution," he said.

"You sound pretty confident."

Angela cleared her throat. "Kendall is a scientist."

Kendall shrugged. "Well, I have a Ph.D. in vertebrate paleontology, but I've studied quite a bit of astronomy, and my brother Nathan is a Ph.D. astronomer who works for NASA."

Orion rolled his eyes. "Uh-huh. A cover-up artist."

Andy motioned him to be silent. "Very interesting, Kendall." He rubbed the sides of his thumbs together. "As a scientist, how can you *not* believe in evolution?"

"As a Christian, the Bible is the basis for my belief. And, unlike what the media tries to paint, there are actually many scientific reasons."

"Really?" Andy held up a finger to pause Kendall and waved to the lady making the omelets. "Delphius, I'll take one with potatoes, broccoli, cheese, parsley, and a dash of cayenne." He turned back to Kendall. "You were saying?"

"If you want an example, think of how complex our bodies are. The human body is made up of building blocks known as amino acids that string together to form proteins. And these strings have to be in exactly the right order."

Orion raised his eyebrows. "So?"

"Let's compare a chain of amino acids to people standing in a line. Let's say that we have eighteen people. Do you know how many possible ways they could line up?"

Orion shook his head.

"Believe it or not, eighteen people can be arranged in a line in more than six quadrillion, four hundred trillion different ways."

"I can't even imagine a number that high!" Jim said.

"Now here's the amazing part. If those people could switch places in line once every minute it would take them over twelve billion years to stand in every possible order in line. Andy, how old do you say the universe is?"

Andy coughed. "I believe some scientists now say the universe began with a big bang about twelve billion years ago."

Kendall laughed. "I don't believe the universe is anywhere near that old, but even using your number—do you realize that eighteen people moving every minute through the entire course of evolutionary history wouldn't have time to stand in all the different line-orders that are possible?"

Andy shrugged. "What's your point?"

"It takes an average of four hundred amino acids to make up one protein in our body—they have to be in perfect order. Then it takes sixty thousand proteins to make up a single cell. Even worse, our body is made up of trillions of cells." Kendall leaned forward. "Andy, if random chance can't even line up eighteen people in all of the possible ways in twelve billion years, I certainly know that random evolution couldn't have made our super complex human bodies."

Delphius interrupted with Andy's omelet. It looked amazing, with little green bits of broccoli and parsley peeking between gooey egg and cheese and chunks of crispy potato. If Kendall was planning to be here for breakfast tomorrow, he would order one of those omelets for himself, but he was definitely *not* planning to be here tomorrow.

Andy waved for Kendall to continue.

"Andy, if evolution is impossible, there can't be other life forms out there that have evolved."

Orion tapped the table. "You're forgetting one very important point. There have been many UFO sitings recently in this area."

Kendall shrugged. "I don't know what people are seeing, but I doubt it's alien in nature."

The Utopians looked like they wanted to continue the conversation, but Jim steered them into less controversial waters.

"Andy, I called the auto shop before breakfast. They said my van just needs a new clutch, and that it would be done by noon. Is there any way that we could get a ride into Roswell?"

Andy grimaced. "I'd love to help, but unfortunately I can't today—it is the continuation of the Parley of Light."

"The 'Parley of Light?'" Martha said.

Ursula nodded. "It's an annual festival for the Utopians—a ritual celebration of our universal brotherhood. We rehearse our future meeting with the Cosmutons." She smiled. "You're welcome to join us."

"No offense, but, we'll pass," Kendall said.

Andy glanced outside. "Of course, that's your choice, but you may want to reconsider." He nodded at the windows. "As you can see, your kids seem to be getting along famously with mine."

There were very few trees on the property, and the grass was the brown, spindly stuff that comes up when there isn't enough rain. After leaving the breakfast room, the Park and Brenan kids strolled to a basketball court they had seen from the window. It was a concrete court, with only one hoop.

A boy, probably sixteen, was practicing his free throws. Four girls sat talking on a bench just off the concrete pad.

Jessie went straight for the girls. "Hi! I'm Jessie. This is my little brother Ryan, and my friends, Jonathan, and his sister Katie."

The girls grinned and stood up. The oldest was probably seventeen, with bracelets on both arms and a necklace that fell over her blouse. She was the one who spoke.

"My name is Venus, and this is Luna, Star, and Pleiades." She pointed to the boy at the free throw line. "That's Apollo."

Apollo tucked the ball under his arm and came over. "Universal peace!" he said.

Jonathan grunted. "I feel like we just met the whole Milky Way Galaxy."

Ryan looked at the other children with wide eyes. "You guys believe in aliens?"

"Of course," Venus said. "There are probably tons of other civilizations that have evolved out there. So, you don't believe?"

Jonathan hesitated. He'd never met anyone who actually believed in aliens. What do you say?

Katie cleared her throat. "Well, I've always been told they don't exist, but I've never—"

Jonathan cut her off. "Like my dad always says, the possibility of any life evolving is impossible."

"What if life evolved somewhere else, and then was brought to planet Earth?" Venus asked.

Jonathan shrugged. "You're just transferring the problem somewhere else."

"What?" Apollo tossed the basketball away and propped his right foot on the bench. Jonathan thought that he looked interested.

"Life is too complex," Jonathan said. "There's no way to explain it but by a Creator."

Venus looked confused. "I don't know. Maybe. But what if our creator was a cosmic brother?"

"So, who made him?"

She nodded. "I see your point."

Jonathan wondered if he should talk about God. They obviously didn't believe in God—at least, not the God of the Bible. He squared his shoulders. He knew he should always share his faith with unbelievers, and he was happy to do so, but that didn't stop him from feeling nervous.

"The Bible talks about the Creator who has always existed. He's the One who planted life here on Earth, and He told us how. And, He made humans in His image."

That sparked lots of conversation, so much that Jonathan didn't realize how long they'd been talking until his parents and Mr. and Mrs. Brenan came out of the building.

"I see you're all getting along," Mrs. Brenan called. She sounded uncomfortable to Jonathan.

"Mom, these are our new friends!" Jessie introduced the galaxy and somehow managed to get all of their names right.

Jonathan's dad shook hands, then tapped Jonathan's shoulder. "We'd better get back to our rooms."

Katie frowned. "But we're just getting to know these guys! I'm not ready to go yet."

"Katie, we're *all* heading back to our rooms."

Katie hung her head. "Yes, sir."

By four o'clock that afternoon, Jonathan was getting tired of sitting in their room. His mom and Katie were laying on one of the beds, reading, and his dad was out looking for someone to take them into Roswell. He wandered to the desk and started opening drawers. A phone book? Not interesting. An old black comb with red hairs stuck to the bristles? Gross, but not interesting. He found another book in the back and pulled it out.

"Don't regular hotels have Bibles in their drawers?" Jonathan asked his mom.

"Most of them."

"Well, this place has their own kind of Bible." He held the book up. "It's called *Bollo: A Speculative Guide to Extra-Terrestrial Cultures*."

Dr. Park came in, shaking his head. "That was weird. All day long I've been trying to find a ride into town so we can get out of here, but no one will take us."

Someone knocked on the door. Mr. Brenan came in.

"Anything?" Dr. Park asked.

"Nothing. I even met our tow truck driver this morning, and he said he couldn't give us a ride because he didn't want to be late to tonight's 'Parley of Light' celebration."

Mrs. Park groaned. "I feel like they're keeping us here for a reason."

"That does it." Dr. Park slapped his knee. "Pack your stuff—I've got a plan."

Jonathan blinked. The asphalt shimmered and grew sticky. The heat baking through Jonathan's shoes made him think about the hot tubs he occasionally soaked his feet in at hotels. He rolled his shoulders, trying to ease the pressure from the duffel bag's straps. At first, carrying the bag like a backpack with his arms through the straps sounded like a great idea. Now, not so much.

Mr. Brenan called a halt and set his suitcases down. He rubbed his red hands and nudged one of the suitcases with his foot. "What's in here?"

Mrs. Brenan shrugged. "You know—moon rocks, crystals, a phaser—just the essentials for around here."

Katie had been lagging in the rear, but she now caught up with them. Her lips were tight, so tight that she looked like she was pouting. "I don't see why we had to leave all of a sudden, anyway."

Jessie tossed her suitcase into the air and caught it. "I think this is kind of an adventure!"

Jonathan glared at his own luggage. *I'd find it much more adventurous if my suitcase was as light as her's.*

A car sped by in the left lane. Jonathan wondered what they thought of eight people walking with all of their luggage along the highway toward Roswell.

"Kendall, do you think we'll really be able to reach Roswell before dark?" Mrs. Park asked.

"Yes, Honey, we'll make it long before dark."

Crickets chirped. The asphalt was still warm, but it no longer shimmered. It was a dull black, faintly lit by the moon, and occasionally washed by the headlights of a passing car.

Mrs. Park coughed. "Kendall, we didn't make it to Roswell by dark."

"Look, everyone," Dr. Park said. "I'm sorry I dragged you all out here."

"It's okay, you were just doing your best to protect everyone." Mrs. Park looked to the others for encouragement. "Right, guys?"

The chorus was weak.

"Dad, isn't there *any* possibility there are real UFOs?" Katie asked.

Mrs. Brenan groaned. "You guys have been talking about that for the last two miles. Can't we play twenty questions, or something?"

"I think they're playing forty questions," Jonathan said.

Dr. Park considered his words for a minute before responding. "Katie, remember that UFO stands for 'Unidentified Flying Object.' Sometimes they're just that, something that hasn't been identified. I'm sure most of the cases are people seeing a natural phenomenon, or what they *want* to see. Sometimes, it's intentional trickery. Some people have even speculated that there's spiritual deception going on."

"Speaking of aliens," Mrs. Park said, "have you guys noticed that all the pictures look the same?"

Mrs. Brenan laughed. "Like Casper the Friendly Ghost on one of those starvation diets."

Jonathan looked up at the sky, thinking about man's fascination with aliens. He could understand how someone without a biblical understanding could look at all those planets and stars and think there might be life. He noticed one star in particular. It was very bright, and it was moving across the sky.

"Look, a shooting star!" Jonathan said.

It grew larger, and brighter. It was coming toward them.

"That's no shooting star!"

The crickets' chirping faded under a swooshing, bell-tingling noise as the bright *thing* came closer.

"Dad, it's a UFO!" Katie yelled.

Jonathan dropped to the pavement and hugged his duffel bag to his chest. He was afraid to look up, but even more afraid to close his eyes. The sound buzzed in his ears like hornets, and the light grew brighter and brighter. Everyone, even his dad, was crouching on the ground, waiting for they didn't know what.

For a moment, the asphalt glittered in a green glow, then the object whooshed overhead and sped away.

Bright light lit the road again, this time from a van coming toward the Parks and Brenans. It slowed, then stopped in the opposite shoulder. The driver's window rolled down and a man's head stuck out.

"What are you guys doing out here at this time of night?"

Dr. Park stood up. "We're trying to get into town." He sounded shaken.

"Can I give you a lift?"

"Please."

Jonathan's muscles were still shaking when he climbed into the back of the van. He squeezed into the right corner and pulled the chest strap on his seat belt as tight as he could. He felt a little less vulnerable inside the car, and it seemed that whatever the *thing* was had gone, but he was still tingly from the whole experience.

Up in the front seats, Dr. Park was thanking the driver again for the ride.

"My pleasure," the man said. He flicked his direction signal on and turned onto an exit ramp. "By the way, I'm Lucius. Universal peace to *you*, my brothers."

Andy sat in a ten by ten office deep inside the retreat center. The overhead light was dim, but still enough to reflect off the line of crystals on Andy's desk.

Someone knocked twice gently, then once hard.

"Come in, Orion," Andy called. "Have a seat."

Orion plopped into the chair on the other side of the desk. "Andromedus, our lease is running out. Unless we find a new retreat center, we won't have a place for our annual Parley of Light."

Andy slid one of the crystals out of line and stroked it with his index finger. His eyes were hid in shadow, but a slight smile clung to his lips.

"Orion, what do you think of our new outsiders?"

"You mean the Parks and Brenans?"

"Did you know that they own a very large piece of property in Abiquiu? They're trying to build some sort of religious center on the property—a museum, or something." Andy slid the crystal back into line. "It would be the perfect place for our new retreat center."

"But they're not followers of the Utopian way. They were even caught trying to get away from here last night."

"I know. Fortunately, Lucius was coming back from town when he saw them alongside the road." Andy winked.

"Unfortunately, he was in too big of a hurry to take them into town, so he had to bring them back here."

"But Andromedus, they would never give us their land!"

Andy shook his head. He leaned forward until the light conquered the shadows under his eyebrows and shone on his cold, piercing eyes. "My children tell me that Dr. Park's daughter, Katie, is already beginning to question her beliefs. Then to see a real UFO last night—she may begin to investigate the Utopian way. It's possible the others may follow."

Dr. Park groaned. "I can't believe we're back here in—in Utopia!"

Jonathan agreed. Last night, he had thought their problems were over when the van driver offered them a ride. Then he said he didn't have time to take them to Roswell—and, it turned out, he was a Utopian headed right back to where they had come from. It was déjà vu, only this time Jonathan had blisters on his feet.

The Parks and Brenans were crowded into the Parks' room, trying to figure a way out of this alien-lover's nest. No one would take them, there were no cars they were allowed to drive, and now walking didn't work.

Jonathan snapped his fingers. "Why don't we call a taxi?"

Dr. Park shook his head. "I tried, but there isn't any cellphone coverage. It turns out the only land line is the one we used to call the tow truck driver. For some reason the door is locked, and no one can find Andy to ask to let us in."

"They haven't *forced* us to stay here," Katie said. "And can't they believe what they want?" She sounded defensive. She had been that way recently, and she kept talking about UFOs and aliens. Jonathan wondered. . . .

Dr. Park set his coffee cup down and leaned closer, looking Katie in the eyes. "Katie, we need to be thankful for the help the Utopians have given to us, and to treat them with respect because they're also made in God's image, but we don't have to agree with their beliefs."

Jessie nodded. "Especially because they don't believe in the Bible."

"They never *said* that," Katie said. "Dad, can't people believe in the Bible, and still believe in aliens?"

"They can, Katie, but remember, the main reason that people believe in aliens is because they believe in evolution."

"Yeah, but—what if God created people on other planets? The Bible doesn't say He didn't, does it?"

Dr. Park hesitated. "While the Bible doesn't say specifically that there aren't other people out there, there would be some serious problems if there were."

"Like what?" Mr. Brenan asked.

"One problem is when man rebelled against God. In Romans 8:22 the Bible says: 'For we know that the whole creation groaneth and travaileth in pain together until now.' The Bible tells us that *all* of creation was cursed as a result of man's sin. If there are other people on other planets, were they cursed because of what *we* did on Earth?"

Katie half-shrugged. "I've never thought about that."

"That doesn't sound like a just and loving God to punish innocent beings for *our* sin. The only other possibility is that all alien civilizations sinned at exactly the same moment throughout the entire universe. But that seems pretty far-fetched."

"What about Jesus?" Mr. Brenan said. "The Bible says that He came to die for our sins. If there were all kinds of other worlds with other people, did Jesus have to go from planet to planet, dying for each one?"

Mrs. Park shook her head. "No, that can't be. Remember what it says in Hebrews 10:10? 'We are sanctified through the offering of the body of Jesus Christ *once for all*.' And in verse twelve it says: 'But this man, after he had offered *one sacrifice* for sins for ever, sat down on the right hand of God.'" She put her hand on Katie's knee. "So if Christ died once, He couldn't have died other times for people on other planets."

Katie pulled her fingers until the joints popped. She definitely wasn't convinced, but it looked like she was having a hard time figuring out a good counter-argument. Her eyebrows raised. "So why did God make the universe so big, if there isn't anyone else living there?"

"Katie," Mrs. Park said, "I think God is the divine Artist who created this big universe simply because He likes to create—like a painter, who hides things in his paintings he knows no one else will see. He does it just for His own good pleasure."

Mrs. Brenan changed the subject. "For now, we better come up with a way to get out of this place."

Jessie bounced out of her chair. "While you plan, do you mind if we go outside and look around?"

Jonathan almost wished they would say 'no.' His blisters were enjoying some rest and relaxation. But they didn't say 'no,' so Jessie dragged him out of his chair and led the way downstairs. Katie came with them, but Ryan stayed with his parents.

Outside, they saw Andy's kids on the path toward the main building. Venus waved.

"We were just on our way to get some soda. You guys want to come?"

"Sure!" Katie said.

Jonathan glanced sideways as they walked, trying to remember their names. He knew Venus, the older one, and Apollo, the boy, but the other ones were a bit hazy.

Apollo grinned at him. "So, now that you've seen a *real* UFO, are you a believer?"

"Not really."

News must travel fast, Jonathan thought. They hadn't said anything to people about seeing a UFO. Lucius must have said something.

"Did they seek to contact you?" one of the girls asked.

"Who?"

"The inhabitants of the UFO."

"Oh." Jonathan shook his head. "Not exactly. By the way, your name was—Moon?"

"Luna."

"Luna. Right, sorry."

The vending machine was in a little room right next to the front doors. The Utopians began inserting quarters and cranking out cans of soda.

"You know," Jonathan said, "ever since we came here, everyone has been talking about all of the inhabited planets. The only problem is that Earth is the only one that can support life."

"What do you mean?" Luna asked.

"Earth is special. It's designed perfectly for us to live here."

Jessie knelt to pick up a dropped quarter. "I heard that if we were just a tiny bit closer to the sun, we'd be fried. If we were any farther away, we'd freeze to death."

Apollo handed a drink to Jonathan.

"Thanks!" Jonathan punched the lid open with the cap and watched the carbon dioxide steam out of the can. "You've heard of ozone? That's another way that Earth is special. It's part of the atmosphere that protects us from the deadly rays of the sun, while letting in the ones we need."

Jessie nodded. "My dad was telling me that the oxygen in our air is just right. If it were a little less, we wouldn't be able to breath. If there was more, the entire Earth would burst into flames."

"And what about the water cycle?" Jonathan said.

Apollo raised his hand. "Okay, got it. You could also point out the balance of nature, and how plants and animals all work together to survive. But why couldn't there be other planets out there that also provide for life?"

Jonathan folded his arms. "Name one."

Apollo hesitated. "Um, I don't know the names of any."

"That's because we've never found any place else in the universe like our planet. That makes Earth unique, and I believe the Creator made it for us."

Jessie finished her soda and tossed the can into a recycling bin. "Jonathan, Katie, you guys want to do some exploring?"

Jonathan tapped the inside of his right foot against the bottom of the vending machine. Little sparks of pain tingled in his toes. He shrugged.

"Sure."

Katie shook her head. "You go ahead. I want to hang out with these guys."

"Didn't you get enough walking yesterday?" Jonathan asked. "My feet are plotting mutiny, and this retreat center property is about as big as the Grand Canyon."

Jessie waved him on. "I just want to see what's in that barn."

Jonathan sighed. He was usually game for an adventure, but right now he kept thinking about one of those foot whirlpools that spin cold water over your toes. Still, the barn *did* look interesting. It was dilapidated, with peeling red paint and a front wall as gappy as a West Virginia hillbilly's teeth.

"I don't think they use this thing anymore," Jonathan said.

Jessie pointed to the dirt road they were on. "These tire tracks look pretty recent."

The last time Jonathan had seen fresh tire tracks going to a strange place was in Africa, and he had met a lion. There weren't many lions in New Mexico, but this *was* an alien cult. Who knew what they might have hidden?

The door-latch was broken, so they went inside. Enough light came through the doorway and the holes in the walls to see a hay-covered floor with rusty machinery and some stacked hay bales along the far wall.

Jonathan whistled in short blasts.

"What are you doing?" Jessie asked.

"Scanning this alien structure for signs of life."

Jessie tramped through the hay, looking at the rusty machinery and broken-down crates.

"Hey, look at this." Jessie pointed to something in the corner, near the line of hay bales. "We've been farming my whole life, but I've never seen anything like *this* in the fields."

The object had a long nose, wheels, and two wings.

"That's a huge remote-controlled airplane!" Jonathan said.

It looked new and was covered in a shiny black paint, the kind that reflects light. A remote control lay on the closest wing. Jonathan picked it up. It had a retractable antenna, two toggle sticks, and a bunch of other controls. There was also a red button on the bottom that looked like it had been custom added.

"What's that for?" Jessie asked.

"Only one way to find out." Jonathan hit the button.

A swooshing, bell-tingling noise filled the barn. Jonathan nearly dropped the remote control. It was the sound of the UFO!

Something glowed green on the other side of the barn. The kids approached cautiously, not sure what to expect.

Around the corner of the hay bales was a big blobby *thing*, with lights glowing on and off like the rack on a police car and dozens of reflectors which turned the whole thing into a green-glowing mass.

Jessie reached out cautiously and touched the side. "It's papier-mâché!" She gulped. "We'd better get out of here. I don't think we're supposed to see this."

"This must be the UFO we saw."

"I knew it was a fake! But this is small compared to how it looked last night."

Jonathan shook his head. "It just looked bigger because it was against the sky." He walked around it, looking for wheels, or wings, but there weren't any. It was just a big cone, like a rocket. "I wonder how they make it fly."

"Come on, let's go." Jessie pointed to the door.

"In a minute. First, I want to figure this out."

Jessie grabbed his arm. "Jonathan, we need to leave *right* now."

"That's it!" Jonathan pointed to three heavy-duty straps on the bottom of the UFO. "I'll bet these attach to the remote-controlled airplane. It's light enough to work."

A car engine grumbled outside. Tires crunched the loose gravel, and two car doors opened.

Jonathan looked at Jessie. This was not good. The only way out was the doorway, which was where the people from the car were about to enter. Jonathan scanned the barn for anywhere to hide. The only hidden spot was behind the hay bales where the scam UFO was, but that was probably the first place anybody coming in would go. Jonathan looked at the stack of hay bales. There was a chance that the newcomers wouldn't look *up*.

Jonathan formed his hands into a scoop and boosted Jessie up, then clambered after her and crawled to the far end where the bales touched the barn wall. The rough stalks scratched his cheek as he lay flat and tried to burrow into the top layer.

Voices came closer.

"I thought we left this door closed," a man said. It was Andy.

"Wind must have blown it open," Orion said. "So, what time are we going to be at the Convention and Civic Center tonight?"

"Nine should be good. After the UFO flyby we'll still have time to get back for tonight's Parley of Light."

The Utopians were right next to the hay bales, now, and started wheeling the airplane toward the door.

"Andromedus, you're a genius. This UFO idea has really paid off."

"No kidding. In the last six months, our membership has doubled, our donations are up forty percent." Andy's voice rose. "It's like a UFO revival! Just think, Orion, we'll build our following until our re-uniting with the Cosmutans!"

"Remember, we still need a retreat site, and quick."

Andy chuckled. "My kids are working on Katie Park. If we can keep the families here, I think they'll see the Utopian way soon enough."

Jonathan clenched a fistful of hay. So that was their plan. Convince Katie of their lies, and then use her to convert the rest of them. Now that he knew about the fake UFO, he could stop the Utopians—but first he needed to get out of this barn.

More wheels squealed outside.

"Here's the delivery truck."

Orion grunted as he picked up one end of the UFO. "This delivery truck idea is a winner—the truck drops off food and drives away with the UFO. No one the wiser. Good thing the driver is such a committed Utopian."

Another man entered the barn.

"Universal peace!" The man snickered. "You guys won't believe what just happened. I was stopped by the outsiders—they wanted a ride into town."

Andy grunted. He sounded preoccupied. "Helios, help Orion load the UFO. I'll bring the plane later. I'm going to set it just outside until I find the remote control . . . it seems to be missing." His voice snapped back to its usual tones. "What did you tell them, Helios?"

"I told them I had one more stop and then I was heading into town."

"Yes, well, I think you need to just 'forget' to pick them up. I'm not ready for them to leave yet. Besides, you need to get this UFO over to the Roswell Civic Center."

Jonathan clenched his hands tighter, thinking of the surprise he had in store. Then, it happened. The UFO flashed, and the bells began ringing. *Oh no!* He had been holding the remote control in his hand—he must have hit the red button.

"What the—" Andy spun around and looked up. "It's those kids!"

The three Utopians blocked the path to the door. There were no windows. There was only one other way out.

"Jessie, follow me!" Jonathan kicked the wall and smashed through a layer of rotten slats. It was a long jump. "Hold my hands!"

Jonathan grabbed Jessie's hands and lowered her as far as he could. She thudded in the dirt.

Andy was clawing his way up the bales, already almost at the top. Jonathan dug his feet into the hay and leveraged his back against the wall so that he could push. The bale shifted, then began toppling down on Andy. Jonathan didn't wait to see it land, but scrambled through the hole and jumped.

"Let's go!"

The kids ran toward the main retreat center. They had hardly passed the barn door when the three Utopians emerged.

"Load the UFO!" Andy yelled. "I'll get the kids."

Jonathan winced as each step squeezed his blisters. If Orion and Helios loaded the UFO and got away, Andy could deny its existence, and just say that he had an airplane for fun. Speaking of the airplane, Jonathan realized that he still had the remote control in his hand.

Andy's puffing was close behind.

Jonathan gasped. "Faster!"

They were approaching the main building. Surely Andy would stop chasing them before people could see. *Right?*

"Jonathan! Jessie!"

Jonathan and Jessie pounded toward the corner of the building, around which their families had just turned.

Andy's footsteps slowed. "Please, stop! I can explain." His breath came in gasps.

Jonathan collapsed next to his dad. "The UFO is a fake!"

"What?" Dr. Park looked down at Jonathan, then at Andy.

Andy walked up to them, his face red from running, his hands held out as if to stop them from getting the wrong idea. "I think there's been a—a misunderstanding."

"In what way?" Dr. Park asked.

Jonathan planted his palms in the dirt, heaved, and scrambled to his feet. "The UFO we saw is in the back of the delivery truck."

Other Utopians began gathering around. Andy's children ran out to join them.

A cloud of dust roared toward them on the road from the barn. It was the delivery truck, and Helios must have had the gas pedal pushed all the way to the floor mat.

Jessie cupped her hands. "The UFO is a fake, and it's getting away in the back of that truck!"

Andy raised his hands. "It's not true." He tried to laugh. "I have no idea what these kids are talking about."

The truck was coming closer. If it got past them without stopping, there would be no proof. Jonathan gripped the remote.

"Here comes the air force." Jonathan pressed down the toggle stick. It was just like the R/C plane he had at home, only bigger. He pressed the switch for full power.

The plane hurtled toward them, rapidly overtaking the delivery truck. Jonathan focused on the wings, tilting slightly to the left, then right, bringing it in a circle to face the speeding truck.

"What are you doing?" Jessie asked.

"Just a little game of chicken."

Jonathan hit full power again, and this time the plane was headed straight for the truck. Helios didn't have many options—if he drove straight, the plane would smash into his windshield. The truck swerved to the right, left the road, and rammed into a ditch. The wheels spun loose dirt into the air, but the truck didn't move. It was stuck.

"Drive!" Andy yelled.

The engine revved, but it was no good.

Dr. Park ran toward the ditch. "Come on, everyone, I think it's time to take a look in the back of that truck."

The Utopians crowded around the back, waiting for the doors to open. Andy moved as if to block the door, then stopped, folded his arms, and hung his head. The doors swung open.

There was the fake UFO, just a mass of papier-mâché, lights, and reflectors. The Utopians gaped at Andy.

Venus touched Andy's arm. "Father, what's going on?"

Andy sighed. "We have a lot of talking to do."

The Parks and Brenans sat in the police station. Ursula was also there, since she had been the one to drive them into Roswell.

A policeman entered the room. "Dr. Park? Thanks for coming down here." He shook hands with Dr. Park and nodded pleasantly at the rest. "I've got to make a quick call, then I'll be right back. Please, take a seat."

"Ursula, thank you so much for driving us here," Mr. Brenan said.

Ursula nodded. "You're welcome, but please, call me Mary."

"Mary?"

Ursula—or Mary—sighed. "That's my real name. I've been Ursula for the past six months. It all started when I saw the UFO. I had questions, and I thought Androm—Andy had answers."

Katie cleared her throat. Jonathan watched her carefully. He wasn't sure how she had taken these revelations, especially when she found out that converting her had been one of the Utopians' main goals.

"Dad, I need to confess something." Katie looked at the floor. "Even though I believe the Bible, I didn't know how to explain what we saw."

"You mean the UFO?"

Katie nodded. "We saw it with our own eyes, and it seemed so real. It kind of shook me."

"I know what you mean," Mary said. "I fell for it too."

Dr. Park wrapped his arm around Katie's shoulders. "I think this has been a good lesson. Sometimes things look one way, when in reality, the truth is totally different. John 17:17 says: 'Sanctify them through thy truth: thy word is truth.'"

"We can always trust God's Word," Mrs. Park said. "He doesn't lie to us. As humans, we have the tendency to trust our own thinking more than God."

That sounded familiar to Jonathan. He raised his hand. "Isn't that what you say about evolution, Dad?"

"You're right. Science will say one thing and then change later to say just the opposite. That's what scientific theories are all about. It's about doing our best to describe how our world works, and then changing those theories once we find out more about it."

Mrs. Park put her hands on Jonathan's shoulders. "I guess the problem comes when we use man's scientific theories and observations to interpret the Bible, instead of just believing God's word. In the end, God will always be shown to be right."

"Just like our UFO," Dr. Park said. "You saw it with your own eyes, and it seemed real. But when you investigated it, it turned out to be fake. It's the same thing about believing where we came from. Many people want to believe in evolution, so they try to make it fit with the Bible. But when you look at the facts, science shows that evolution is wrong. It's too bad people believe in what they want to, instead of just trusting the Creator."

The policeman came back in, a pen and notepad in his hand. He sat in the swivel chair behind the desk and poised his pen.

"Thanks for waiting. You said you're here to report a UFO fraud by a group called the 'Utopians?'"

"Yes!" Mr. Brenan said. "They held us captive."

The policeman tapped the paper with his pen. "Did they physically keep you from leaving?"

"Well, no, but they wouldn't give us a ride into town."

The policeman nodded sympathetically, but still didn't write anything down. "That's a shame, but unfortunately that isn't considered kidnapping by the law."

"What about the UFO fraud?" Dr. Park asked.

"I'm sad to say, it's just not against the law to fool people."

Mrs. Brenan snorted. "They were tricking people into donating money and joining their little band of alien-wannabes."

The policeman dropped the empty pad onto the table. "I'm sorry. You might want to check with a consumer protection agency to see if they can do anything about it."

Dr. Park raised his hands in disbelief.

The policeman ignored the gesture. "What about you guys? Do you have a way to get home?"

"Yes, Mary here will drive us to a motel for the night, then we're picking up our repaired van in the morning and heading back to Santa Fe."

"Then you're free to go." The policeman extended his hand. "Thanks for stopping by. Drive safely, buckle up, and—universal peace to you."

The Clue from Nineveh

Jonathan squirmed in his seat. Mr. Benefucio's science class was his favorite, but he always dreaded these report days when all the kids got up to spout about evolutionism. It was Rusty's turn, and he was talking about his frog.

Rusty held a plastic cage in one hand and tapped the walls with his other, making the frog leap back and forth.

"He was a tadpole when I caught him, but now he's got frog legs."

Rusty flicked the side again and the frog nearly flipped. Jonathan was sorry for the creature. Rusty would probably skin him alive or poke out his eyes after class.

Mr. Benefucio nodded. "Good, Rusty. Now, tell the class why you chose this for your biology project."

"Because you've been teaching about evolution."

Jonathan snorted. "That's not evolution."

Mr. Benefucio frowned. "Jonathan, this is Rusty's turn." He nodded for Rusty to go on.

"It is *too* evolution, isn't it, Mr. B.?"

The teacher stroked his chin. He was obviously thinking of a way to explain how it wasn't evolution while still teaching more about evolution.

"Rusty, I can understand why it would look that way, but actually—"

Jonathan raised his hand.

"Yes, Jonathan?"

"I can explain why it isn't evolution."

Rusty sneered. "Good for you."

"Take it easy, Rusty." Mr. Benefucio nodded at Jonathan. "Since you were polite enough to raise your hand this time, go ahead and explain to us why this isn't evolution."

"Because tadpoles turn into frogs all the time, but we don't see apes turning into people."

"That is correct. The DNA code of a tadpole already determines that it will become a frog, whereas in the case of apes, no single ape ever changed into a human during his lifetime. Instead, ape-like creatures were the ancestors of humans."

Thad Sherman, leader of the Eagle's Nest, raised his hand. "Not according to the Bible," he said.

Mr. Benefucio's smile stiffened. "We're not discussing the Bible. We're talking about science."

"My dad says science and the Bible go together," Jonathan said.

Eddie nodded. "My dad says that too!"

"And Eddie, he's entitled to that viewpoint. But this isn't Sunday School, and we aren't here to argue religion." Mr. Benefucio's voice softened to its usual tones. "Anyway, Rusty, what we see right now with your changing tadpole could be called growth, or even metamorphosis, but not evolution. Still, it's a fascinating process of nature."

As Rusty walked back to his seat, Jonathan raised his eyebrows at him.

"I told you."

Rusty stopped. "Yeah? Maybe you'd like to explain it to me after school." He leaned over Jonathan's desk, his fist clenched. "We'll see some real evolution, 'cause your nose is gonna turn into a blob of jelly."

"Sit down, Rusty!" Mr. Benefucio said.

Rusty gave one last fist-shake and stomped to his own seat. Jonathan fought the reflex to rub his nose. Rusty usually followed up on those kinds of promises.

Mr. Benefucio rapped his desk. "Who'd like to be next?"

Rusty raised his arm. "Why don't we let the *expert* go next?"

"That's fine with me," Jonathan said.

"Is it?" Mr. Benefucio nodded. "Maybe you should. It will give you a chance to use up some of that excess energy."

Jonathan lifted his two terrariums from under his desk and quickly checked to make sure his lizard was still in the green one. It was sleeping in a pile of grass.

"Instead of an amphibian, I picked a reptile. I brought my pet lizard."

"He probably thinks his lizard was a tadpole once," Rusty said.

Mr. Benefucio frowned Rusty into silence. "Thank you. Okay, Jonathan, I'm sure you enjoy having a pet, but the purpose of this assignment was to show us something interesting or unusual about nature."

Rusty spoke again, louder this time. "Lizards are *only* interesting to my cat. He eats them."

"Rusty, your next comment will send you to the principal's office, understood?"

Rusty nodded.

"Go ahead, Jonathan. What is it about this lizard that you find so interesting?"

Jonathan shrugged. He liked to act nonchalantly when he was about to surprise people.

"He's going to show us a miracle."

"Excuse me?"

"My lizard is going to prove that miracles happen."

School superintendent Barry Brussell dropped his cigarette stub into an ashtray and reentered the office building. His phone was ringing when he reached his desk.

"Yes, Ruth?"

An efficient female voice responded. "Principal Lou Phipps from Painted Dunes Elementary is on line one."

"Thank you, Ruth." Barry stared at the blinking keypad for a moment, then squared his shoulders and hit the button for line one. "Superintendent Brussell here. How can I help you?"

"Superintendent Brussell? My, that sounds so formal. Didn't your secretary tell you it was me?"

Barry's goatee jerked as his jaw-bone flexed. "State your business, Mr. Phipps."

The other man laughed. "Now what kind of a greeting is that? You used to call me Lou. Aren't we on a first name basis anymore?"

"We never were on a first name basis."

"Not originally, no. But after I bailed you out of that little crisis and saved your job—I would say we got pretty chummy after that. Don't you agree?"

Barry balled his fist. "I'm giving you the count of one to get to the point."

"Ouch!" Lou Phipps was still acting pleasantly. "Barry, you need to relax."

"That's all. I'm finished." Barry held the phone away from his ear, ready to slam it down.

"Hang up the phone and you *will* be finished," Lou said.

Barry clenched his teeth and put the phone back to his ear. "I knew it! I knew you'd never be satisfied."

"Just a little more hush money." Mr. Phipps was back to his pleasant, almost coaxing voice.

"You couldn't have spent it that fast!"

"You'd be surprised. There's mortgages, car payments, braces for my girls. You know what an orthodontist charges these days? Well, you remember what it was like *before* you figured out a way to get rich. Just share the wealth a little. No sense forgetting the little people who put you where you are. Time to be fair to your ol' pal Lou."

For a moment, Barry silently tapped the desk with his index finger. "Supposing I decide not to be fair?" he finally asked.

Lou chuckled. "You don't want to disappoint me, Barry. What you want to do is meet me tonight and find out how you can get me out of your hair for good. How about coffee? My treat."

"I'm busy tonight. I've already made plans."

"Aw, change the plans, Barry. Be flexible for ol' Lou. Jenny's Restaurant. Six o'clock. We'll get an early start, so that way you'll still have the rest of the evening free for your lovely family. Jenny's. Got it?"

The phone clicked.

Back in the classroom, Mr. Benefucio was frowning at Jonathan.

"Are you mocking this assignment?" he asked.

"No, sir." Jonathan gulped. "Honest."

"Jonathan, this is a science class, and we know that miracles are a matter of faith."

"I'll prove it, Mr. Benefucio."

Rusty laughed. "Go ahead, Preacher Boy."

Mr. Benefucio turned on him. "You just used up your last chance. Head to the principal's office."

"But—"

"Nothing to discuss."

Rusty paused at the door and wrinkled his long nose at Jonathan. "Hey, Park! When I'm finished with you, they'll need a miracle to put you back together." He slammed the door behind him.

Mr. Benefucio sighed. "All right, Jonathan. I guess I'll just go along with this until we see your demonstration. But I warn you, your grade weighs in the balance."

Jonathan thanked him. "This isn't an ordinary lizard," he explained. "This is a chameleon."

"I see. Well, it's certainly a marvel of nature. Are you going to demonstrate for us how it changes color?"

"Yes, sir." Jonathan tapped the terrariums on his desk. "One of these is full of brown leaves, and one has green grass."

The terrariums were heavy, so the teacher had Thad carry one. Jonathan arranged them on Mr. Benefucio's desk so that the whole class could see the different habitats. He reached into the green one and carefully picked up his lizard, cupping the body in his hand so that the head and tail hung out.

"The lizard is green right now because he was in the grass terrarium. He has the ability to change color to match his surroundings. That way, he blends in and his predators can't find him."

"I wish I could do that," Eddie said. "It would come in handy during hide-and-seek."

Jonathan slid back the door on the brown terrarium and dropped the lizard inside.

"It'll take him a few minutes to change."

Mr. Benefucio nodded. "While he does, maybe you can explain why you call this a miracle. It's a fun thing to watch, and certainly an unusual phenomenon, but there *is* a scientific explanation, so it can't be called a miracle."

"Well, sir, I don't think there's really a scientific explanation."

Mr. Benefucio stared at him, probably trying to decide whether he was being defiant, or just ignorant.

"I just said that there *is* a scientific explanation, Jonathan, and as part of your assignment you are supposed to tell us what it is. You can't just bring a pet into class."

Jonathan stroked the brown terrarium. "I know the explanation, sir, but I think it only sort of explains it."

Mr. Benefucio folded his arms. "Tell us the explanation first, then we can discuss it."

Jonathan breathed deeply. He didn't mind public speaking, thankfully, but he wanted to be sure his logic was right.

"It's kind of like Rusty's tadpole. Just like the DNA code of a tadpole allows it to change into a frog, the DNA code of a chameleon gives it a special kind of skin pigment that allows color changes for the sake of survival."

"Well put, and very interesting, but hardly a miracle."

"Sir, I think it's a miracle because there is no explanation apart from God."

Mr. Benefucio frowned. "Always back to God with you. But you just *gave* us a good explanation."

"Well, we don't know how the DNA works. We know the lizard has it, and we know what it does, but we can't explain *why* the DNA programs it for protection. Not without God, we can't. A program needs a programmer."

"I know your beliefs about God, and you know *my* beliefs about bringing that up in science class."

Jonathan sighed. "Yes, sir."

"Hey!" Eddie jumped to his feet. "He did it! He turned brown!"

Lou Phipps hung the phone up and stared at the wall. He always put on a smooth act when talking to Superintendent Brussell, but his heart felt rotten. As long as he kept a tough outside, no one would know he was soft inside. Anyway, he was providing for his family. Isn't that what good dads do?

The door squeaked open enough to admit a head. Lou recognized the red hair and long nose immediately as Rusty's, his most frequent visitor.

Lou sighed. "What is it, Rusty?"

"Mr. Benefucio told me to come here."

Lou grunted. Biology. He'd probably let a snake loose in lab.

"Sit down, I'll be with you in a moment."

Lou hit the intercom button to his secretary's office. "Marge, call my wife and tell her that I need to meet with Superintendent Brussell tonight. I'll be home as soon as my meeting is over."

Lou swiveled to face Rusty. "What seems to be the trouble?"

Rusty stared at the desk, his wavy hair nearly blocking his eyes. "I dunno."

"You don't know? You must have done something."

Rusty looked at the carpet. "I didn't do nothin."

Lou leaned forward, his elbows on the desk, until Rusty raised his head high enough to look at him.

"Rusty, let me explain to you how this works. I ask you questions and you answer me. Otherwise, you'll be here on Saturday." Lou leaned back. "I have a pile of work to do on Saturday and I'd love to have some company."

Rusty shrugged. "I was talking, that's all."

"Must have been quite a conversation. What were you talking *about*, exactly?"

Rusty scowled. He was sitting up, now, looking straight at the principal.

"I don't remember."

"Oh, yes, memory." Lou flashed his best cold smile. "Tell you what. I've got a good book on refreshing the memory. I'll let you read it on Saturday. It'll help pass the time."

Rusty quailed. "Okay! Okay!"

"Ready to let me in on your little secret?"

"Yeah, all right."

"What a day!" Thad groaned.

Jonathan nodded. "I'm just glad it's over." He threaded the maze of chattering kids with Thad and Jessie tagging behind.

"Sounds like I missed a lot of excitement today," Jessie said.

"Just be thankful you're homeschooled." Jonathan wondered what it would be like to do school at home, without worrying about evolution, and God-haters, and Rusty.

Jessie kept talking. "I'm glad your dad has been doing so much work at the ranch. He's really nice to bring me back with him once in a while, especially when I need to use your school library."

Thad curled his fingers into his palm, like you would to hold a mug-handle, and coughed into his fist. "You may have picked a bad day to walk home with us, Jessie."

Jonathan whacked him with his backpack. "Come on, Thad! You're starting to sound like a scaredy cat."

"I'm warning you, buddy. You need to watch it. Rusty is twice your size."

"No he's not."

Thad frowned. "Fine, he's a hundred and fifty percent of your size."

Jonathan cocked his head, thinking of the percentages. *That sounds about right. Now, his muscles are probably twice my size.*

"I've seen him fight," Thad said. "It was more like a massacre."

And his feet are pretty big. I wonder if he kicks.

"Jonathan Park!" Jessie's shrill voice sliced Jonathan's thoughts. "Are you paying attention?"

Jonathan shrugged. "Rusty doesn't scare me."

"But he had to see Mr. Phipps on account of you," Thad said. "That might make him hate you even more. Mr. Phipps is mean!"

They had gotten away from most of the kids and were passing a small section at the edge of the yard that was nearly hedged off by bushes. A familiar voice sounded from inside the bushes.

"Leave me alone!" Eddie said. He ran out of the bushes, followed by Rusty.

"Get your hands off him!" Jonathan said.

"Hey, Park!" Rusty grinned. "We were just talking about you." He squeezed his right hand into a fist and punched his left palm a couple times.

Jonathan dropped his backpack. "Here I am." He tensed his stomach, trying to stop the knot-tying course inside.

Thad slipped next to Jonathan, his hands held out, palms forward. "Chill out, Rusty. Jessie's getting the yard duty teacher. You could get in trouble."

Rusty growled. "Oh, got your little friend to narc on me, huh?"

"I didn't tell her to call the teacher." Jonathan moved away from Thad. This was his fight, not Thad's.

Rusty raised his fists. "If you really believe in God, you'd better start praying, 'cause you're gonna need all the help you can get."

A whistle shrilled. "Stop that at once!" the yard duty teacher yelled.

Rusty smashed his fists together. "You're lucky. Another second—you'd have been tapioca pudding."

The teacher stalked between the boys and glared at Rusty. "You'd better come with me to the office."

"But I was just *at* the office."

"Then you should know the way. Let's get going."

Rusty looked back over his shoulder. "That means detention on Saturday. You're in big trouble, Park. All of you!"

Jonathan rubbed his forehead. It wasn't hot outside, but he was sweating.

"You look like you need a chocolate bar, or something," Eddie said.

"I'm all right."

Jessie shivered. "Let's get out of here before something else happens!"

Later that afternoon, Kendall Park was driving on the highway in his 4x4 truck when he received a phone call. It was Mr. Benefucio, Jonathan's science teacher. Apparently, Jonathan had participated in what the teacher called a 'disturbance' in class. Mr. Benefucio made clear that 'religion' was not acceptable in his classroom.

"I'm sorry if my son created a problem," Kendall said. "I'm sure that whatever he said about God was from the heart. He has a passion for sharing the gospel."

"Believe me, I know." Mr. Benefucio sighed. "Look, Dr. Park, I'm not asking you to be hard on him, and I'm sure he has good intentions. If he could learn to talk about religion just a little bit less, our classes would run much more smoothly. That's all."

"Jonathan gets that from me, I'm afraid. It's nothing personal, but I do wish that our public schools would show both sides in the field of science."

"Both sides of what?" Mr. Benefucio's voice was still respectful, but it sounded as if he was restraining a laugh. "Dr. Park, I know you're a scientist. Surely you're not suggesting that I get up and read the book of Genesis out loud?"

Kendall grinned at himself in the rear view mirror. "Actually, I think that would be an excellent idea. The Bible is my standard for all things in life. That said, there is much objective data from paleontology and archeology which supports creation—things which are 'scientifically accepted.'"

"That, I'd like to see."

"I'd be happy to come in as a guest speaker any time you want."

"Wait a minute—you know I can't allow religion in the public school."

"I'm afraid I would have to disagree, Mr. Benefucio, as I have a different definition for religion than you, but I could present a talk about creation without even mentioning the Bible."

"How?"

"For starters, I'd establish that creation scientists actually point to observable facts when they make their arguments."

There was a long pause. "Dr. Park, if you can keep religion out of it—then you're on."

Jonathan galloped down the stairs two at a time. Without warning, Katie rounded the corner at the bottom of the stairs and blocked his path. Jonathan tried to spin away from her, tripped, and sprawled across the tile floor.

"Are you okay?" Katie asked.

Jonathan puffed air back into his chest. "Me? I'm fine. My knees?" He winced. "Not so much."

"Dad wants everybody in the living room." Katie helped him up.

"That's where I was going. What's it all about?"

Katie shrugged.

Jonathan's dad and mom and Grandpa Benjamin were already sitting on the couch.

"Is everything okay, Dad?" Jonathan asked.

"Mostly. Take a seat."

Jonathan settled onto the sofa next to Katie and waited. He tried to think of anything he had done wrong recently.

Dr. Park rubbed his knees. "Jonathan, I got a call from your teacher today."

Jonathan gulped. "Why?"

"He liked your experiment, but he didn't like your talking about God."

"Oh. Is he mad?"

"No, not exactly mad, but he doesn't want it to happen again."

Grandpa Benjamin grinned. "Even so, God has used Jonathan's words to give you this opportunity, Kendall."

Jonathan raised an eyebrow.

"I've arranged with Mr. Benefucio," Dr. Park said. "I'm going to teach your class about creation next week."

"But I thought he didn't want to hear about God anymore?"

"He doesn't, and I've agreed to restrain myself to only giving evidence for creation not included in the Bible."

"I have a feeling the Bible will still come up," Mrs. Park said.

"It may. Skeptics generally bring up the Bible themselves when creation is discussed."

"Speaking of the Bible—" Grandpa Benjamin touched his chin with his index finger. That meant a Bible verse was coming. "Romans 8:28 says: 'And we know that all things work together for good to them that love God, to them who are the called according to his purpose.' Jonathan's presentation was used by God to bring Kendall into the class."

All things for good? Jonathan had a vision of red hair and a long nose.

"Grandpa, are all things going to work together with that bully who's picking on every one?"

Mrs. Park cleared her throat. "I believe you've been making that situation worse."

Dr. Park held up his hand. "Wait a minute. I don't approve of fighting as a general rule, but if Jonathan was merely defending himself—"

"Kendall, Jonathan was egging Rusty on in class."

Dr. Park looked sober. "Were you, Son?"

"I . . . guess."

"That isn't like you, Jonathan."

"But Dad, if you could just meet this Rusty. . . ."

"I know you think of this kid as the enemy, but has it occurred to you that Rusty may just be lonely? This is his first year at a new school."

Jonathan tried to picture Rusty as lonely. It wasn't easy to visualize.

"Maybe if he were nicer, he'd make friends easier."

"Jonathan, you're the Christian. You're the one to set the example. Do you remember the verse we looked at in family devotions last week?"

Jonathan sighed. He knew where this was going. "'But I say unto you, love your enemies, bless them that curse you, do good to them that hate you, and pray for them which despitefully use you, and persecute you.' Matthew 5:44."

Mrs. Park nodded. "You've certainly memorized it, but the hard part is learning to apply it."

"It *is* hard, Mom, but there are other parts of the Bible that are easier to obey. I don't mind the part about loving people—most people, that is."

Grandpa Benjamin leaned forward and touched Jonathan's knee. "It's easy to love someone lovable. But God tells us to love our enemies because Jesus wants us to forgive our enemies."

Dr. Park nodded. "Rusty probably isn't learning about God at home. You and your friends may be the only Christian witness he has."

"Remember, Jonathan," Mrs. Park said, "Rusty thinks you're his enemy and is every bit as bothered by the things you've said and done."

"But—"

"Don't tell me he started it, because it doesn't matter. Sin is sin. Jesus has forgiven your sins. Wouldn't you like to help Rusty see his need for a savior?" Jonathan's mom looked into his eyes. "Promise you'll be nicer to him."

She was right. Jonathan nodded slowly. "I'll try, Mom." He tried to smile. "But Rusty is so mad at me, I just hope I don't get hurt being nice."

Jonathan tried to sit perfectly straight with his back pressed against his chair like a ramrod. He grinned at his dad. Not only was Dr. Park teaching, but he was doing an excellent job. Even Jonathan, who had heard all the information before, was fascinated by the presentation.

Dr. Park looked at his watch. "I think now is a good time to review. Somebody explain to me, let's see, microevolution."

Elizabeth raised her hand. She was always attentive, the best student in the class.

"Microevolution means 'small evolution.' Like if colored rabbits were seen by wolves in the snow more easily than white rabbits, after a while, only the white rabbits would survive and their children would be white."

"Exactly. That's microevolution, or what we all know as adaptation. Animal groups can change to adapt to their surrounding environment." Dr. Park pointed to Thad. "Thad, can you explain macroevolution?"

Thad straightened. "Uh, 'big evolution,' meaning that new animals come from—from—" he stopped.

"Macroevolution means that one kind of animal changed into another. Like dinosaurs changing into birds—but we've never seen that happen. Microevolution is completely different from macroevolution. Microevolution is proven by science— we see animals adapt and change for their environment, but no one has actually seen macroevolution, or one animal changing into another."

Mr. Benefucio was sitting at his desk, while Dr. Park stood in front of the blackboard, which was covered with the drawings that Dr. Park had sketched during his talk. Jonathan thought that the teacher seemed twitchy, but he hadn't stopped Dr. Park yet.

"Here's another problem for evolution," Dr. Park said. "Where did life come from in the first place? Evolutionists say that a bunch of chemicals came together by random chance, and then what?"

Eddie raised his hand. "Then those chemicals made molecules and all the plants and animals and everything go back to those original molecules."

"Exactly, but that's the problem. Science tells us that life has to come from life. Now kids, in science, nothing is considered proven unless it is observable. Do we observe any evolution today?"

"Yes!" Rusty said. Because Rusty sat in the seat closest to the door, Jonathan couldn't see his face, but he was pretty sure that the bully had been watching him during the whole class.

"We do," Dr. Park agreed. "And what kind? Do we ever see one kind of animal turn into another? No, we don't. We see microevolution. We see different kinds of dogs, and different kinds of cats, but we don't see a dog evolve into a cat. We don't see life evolve from non-life. You see, evolution from one species to another has never been proven."

Elizabeth raised her hand. "You're saying our science book is wrong?"

Mr. Benefucio stood up quickly. "I'll answer that, Elizabeth. I don't happen to agree with Dr. Park, but I thought it would be fun to hear an alternative viewpoint today. You may choose to believe whichever theory makes more sense to you." He smiled. "Just make sure that on your test, you answer according to what I taught."

Elizabeth wasn't finished. "Maybe we don't see macroevolution, but we didn't see God make the world, either."

Dr. Park nodded. "That's true."

"And we don't see God at all, so God can't be proven."

The rest of the class murmured. Elizabeth's logic had obviously made an impression.

Dr. Park still looked confident. "Science *does* give us evidence for God. Most of what we call 'facts' in life are brought to us on the basis of evidence, not personal experience. For example—how many of you have ever been to Australia?"

Jonathan's classmates looked at each other, but no one raised a hand. Frank, two seats over, always liked to talk about his summers in England, but Australia was all the way on the other side of the globe.

"None of you?" Dr. Park said. "Then here is a question. Does Australia exist?"

"Yes!" Elizabeth said.

"How do you know? You haven't seen it."

Thad raised his hand. "Other people have been there."

"How do you know they aren't lying and making the whole thing up?"

Elizabeth laughed. "Everybody knows about Australia. It's in books, and pictures."

"And movies," Eddie said. "I watched a foodumentary about this weird Australian food paste called Vegemite, and they had all sorts of footage from Australia."

Dr. Park smiled. "What if the pictures are from some other place people just *called* Australia? And you didn't personally see the filmmakers filming. Are you catching on? None of you can prove that Australia exists, but then again, the evidence for Australia's existence is so enormous and obvious, that we accept it."

"But we have no eyewitnesses who saw God create the earth," Mr. Benefucio said.

"We have the witness of nature itself."

"How is that?"

Dr. Park pointed to the far back corner. "Rusty, I hear you did a report on a tadpole. Isn't it incredible that the genetic code of a frog existed in there ahead of time? Isn't it amazing that living creatures have something inside of them that can adapt and survive? Every design must have a designer."

"Yes, and that designer is nature," Mr. Benefucio said. "Dr. Park, you're obviously very knowledgeable, and I respect that, but there are too many stories in the Bible that scientists cannot take seriously."

"Such as?"

The teacher shrugged. "The very first one. Surely, you're not going to defend the story of Adam and Eve living immortally in the Garden of Eden and talking to a snake?"

A loud snicker came from behind Jonathan. It was a patent Rusty snicker.

Dr. Park remained unfazed. "Most definitely. And, there's evidence from archeology."

Mr. Benefucio chuckled. "Really now? I'd love to hear about this 'evidence,' but we're out of time today." He looked at the class. "I think you really made a hit, Dr. Park. Maybe we can prevail on you to come back sometime."

Many of the children applauded.

"I can do better than that," Dr. Park said. He gathered his notes into his briefcase and snapped it shut. "There's a finding from the ancient civilization of Ninevah which offers evidence for the biblical account of creation. This artifact has been in the British Museum for years, and presently is being toured in America." He turned to the class. "Kids, how would you like to take a field trip to our own Santa Fe Museum of Ancient Art to see a special clue from Ninevah?"

Jonathan led the class in a loud cheer.

"Mr. Benefucio?"

Mr. Benefucio tapped his fingers together. "Well—maybe—we'll see."

The desk-phone rang in Lou Phipps' office.

"Not another parent." Lou groaned. He picked up the receiver. "Lou Phipps here."

"Just what's going on at your school, ol' pal Lou?" Superintendent Brussell sounded angry, almost afraid. "I've spoken with two parents today."

Lou opened his eyes wide. "Really? I've spoken with four."

"One dad was absolutely livid. Said he wouldn't stand for his daughter being exposed to religious ideas. He threatened the entire school district with a lawsuit!"

Lou shook his head. "People act like the Gestapo is going to take over the country if the word 'God' is mentioned in the classroom. It all seems rather harmless to me."

"And how harmless will it be if the school district gets sued?"

Lou nodded. So that was the real impetus for the call. He pinched the receiver between his shoulder and neck and leaned back.

"Worried that if the plaintiff takes too careful of a look, they'll find out about your sloppy bookkeeping?"

Barry's voice lowered. "Look, you fool, if they find out about me, you can be sure they'll find out about who helped me cover it up."

Lou's smile stiffened. He sat up straight. "Well, Barry, now *you* sound like the blackmailer. I didn't know you had it in you."

"I had a good teacher."

The intercom buzzed.

"Mr. Benefucio is here, sir," the secretary said.

"Send him in." Lou punched the intercom button off. "The culprit just arrived," he told Barry.

"What?"

"Never mind. I'll take care of this. Nothing to worry about." Lou hung up. So, Mr. Benefucio was here. Well, Mr. Benefucio had some things coming.

The teacher looked nervous as he sat down. People usually looked nervous when they came to his office, Lou thought.

"How has your week been so far?" Lou asked.

"It's been okay." Mr. Benefucio twitched a smile. "And yours?"

"About as well as a principal's week ever goes, I suppose. Mr. Benefucio, I understand there's been a lot of excitement in your classroom lately."

The teacher fumbled his fingers. "I always try to make my classes exciting, sir."

"Yes, I'm sure the kids appreciate it. What most interests me, though, is the little circus you brought into town last Tuesday."

"It was hardly a circus, Mr. Phipps. He's a Ph.D.—a vertebrate paleontologist."

"I don't remember approving any paleontologist, vertebrate or otherwise."

"But—I've brought in guests before. So have a lot of other teachers. And just last week Mrs. Gardner had a mime speak to her drama class—well, I guess he didn't actually speak, but he performed."

Lou slapped the desk. He wanted to make sure that his point was very, very clear.

"I don't care about some mime who pretends to climb a wall! If you ever bring religion into a classroom again, you better just be ready to transfer into the ministry."

"Sir, if you'll permit me to—"

"That will be all, Mr. Benefucio."

"But if I could just—"

"I said that will be *all*, Mr. Benefucio."

After school the next day, Jonathan went looking for his dad to ask him some questions about his new report assignment and found him talking on the phone in his room. Dr. Park gestured that Jonathan could stay.

"Are you sure you won't get in trouble for this, Mr. Benefucio?" Dr. Park asked.

Jonathan wondered why his teacher was on the phone. He tried to think of anything he had done wrong in class, but couldn't.

The phone was in speaker mode, so Mr. Benefucio's voice came through clearly. "This is a voluntary trip, not on school time, so what can Principal Phipps do?"

"A lot. Take it from one who's been in a similar situation. But I do admire your courage."

Mr. Benefucio grunted. "I don't buy into this creation stuff, but your point about letting the kids hear both sides has been nagging me."

"Well, I'll call Mr. Ash, the museum curator, to tell him the trip is on. See you on Saturday!" Dr. Park closed the cellphone. "Good news, Son!"

"I heard! Can I invite Jessie?"

"Of course. Then our whole family should spend some time in prayer. Your teacher is taking quite a risk."

That Saturday, Lou Phipps entered his office late. He liked to sleep in on Saturdays. Really, he'd like the whole day off, but his workload just wouldn't allow for it.

The message button was flashing red on his phone, but before he could even grab a notepad to start taking them down, the phone rang.

"Lou Phipps here."

A shrill voice blared in his ear. He held the receiver a foot away and blinked as a steady stream of words piped through the phone line. The best he could make out, Mr. Benefucio's class was on a field trip to the Museum of Ancient Art with the creationist who had caused such a ruckus earlier in the week.

After about three minutes, Lou took advantage of a brief pause. "Mrs. Lassater, please, as a parent, I understand your concerns—"

"You said it wouldn't happen again, Mr. Phipps!"

Lou held the phone away until he was sure she had finished her sentence, then cautiously brought it back to his ear.

"I did not approve a field trip. Mr. Benefucio has done this entirely apart from my knowledge. It's Saturday. School isn't even in session."

"Well maybe we need a principal who knows what's going on at his school! They're there *right* now."

Lou gritted his teeth. What a way to start a day. "Mrs. Lassater, your son didn't go with them, so no harm has been done."

"Of course my son didn't go with them! I wouldn't let him, and now he feels left out."

"I promise to get to the bottom of this."

The phone clicked.

"Mrs. Lassater? Mrs. Lassater?" Lou hit the intercom. "Marge, get me directions to the Museum of Ancient Art. Fast!"

"Yes, sir. Also, Rusty Mitchell is here to see you."

Lou slapped his forehead. He had forgotten about ordering Saturday detention for Rusty.

"Very well, send him in."

Rusty slouched inside.

"Good morning, Rusty! I hear you're missing out on a little field trip today."

Rusty shrugged. "I didn't even want to go."

"Well, it seems we're both going."

"Huh?"

Lou grabbed his keys and pointed to the door. "I can't leave you here. You're my responsibility for the day. Let's move it, Rusty."

Rusty slouched into his seat and stared out the window, away from Lou. He obviously wasn't enthralled by the chance to spend a day with the principal.

"Rusty?" Lou said.

"Yeah?"

"Doesn't your conscience ever bother you? Don't you ever feel bad, picking on people who are smaller than you?"

Rusty continued to stare out the other window. "I don't care. Survival of the fittest."

"I was a new kid at school once. I know how lonely it can be."

"I don't care."

"Sure you care. If you didn't care, you wouldn't get mad enough to hurt others. But Rusty, when you do that to others, you hurt yourself even more."

Rusty was silent.

"Rusty, look at me."

Rusty's face was hard, and his eyes were glazed, as if he had put up a mental shield. Lou remembered his own days as a schoolkid long ago. He knew what it was like to be inside that glazed look, and he felt sorry for Rusty.

"It's a bad thing to ignore your conscience," Lou said. "If you ignore it too long, it will harden." Lou waited for a response, but nothing came. "You don't know what I'm talking about, do you?"

Lou made his second to last turn and settled down for the last few miles before the museum.

"Rusty, let me tell you a story. It's about a boy your age who belonged to a club that his friends had started." It was Lou's turn to look away. He could sense that Rusty was watching him, but without curiosity. "One day, just by accident, this boy found out that the club president had been keeping some of the membership dues for himself, after they were collected. The club treasurer, he was in on it too. He helped the president cover his tracks by doctoring up the club's account books. But, anyway, this other kid, he finds out about it, see?"

"What did he do when he found out?"

"At first he was going to rat on him to the others, but he didn't want to be a tattletale, so he did something even worse. He made the president pay him money to keep quiet."

"Really? Wow!" Rusty said.

"But he wasn't proud of himself. His conscience bothered him a lot."

"Then why didn't he just give the money back?"

Lou nodded bitterly. "Sounds easy, doesn't it? It might have been, if he'd done it right away. But he got scared. He got scared because now he was in on the secret, and now he was just every bit as guilty."

Lou dug his thumbnails into the steering wheel.

"It started out as greed and it turned into fear. Then, because he was afraid to do the right thing he had to lie to himself and *pretend* he was doing the right thing. It was easy to justify himself because of all of the expenses and needs of his family."

"His family?"

"Well—not his family, his—just try to get the point I'm making. Do you understand? Sometimes people lie, even to themselves, because otherwise their conscience would be too painful."

"Is this a true story, Mr. Phipps?" Rusty asked.

"Yeah. It's true."

"Somehow I get the feeling this story wasn't really about kids in a club. It's something with you, huh?"

Lou pulled into the museum parking lot. "That's not important."

"Did they ever get caught?"

Lou stopped in a parking space. "No." He pulled the key from the ignition. "Not yet."

Inside the museum, Kendall was standing in front of a display in the room dedicated to traveling exhibits. Mr. Benefucio's science class was gathered in a semicircle facing him. There were several other borrowed artifacts from the British Museum displayed around the walls, but the main exhibit was right here where Kendall stood.

"Okay, come close so that everyone can see."

"What is it?" one of the kids asked.

"This is a greenstone cylinder from the Mesopotamia area." Kendall pointed at the details on the cylinder, his index finger hovering just over the glass. "The carving you see is called a 'seal.' Seals depicted stories and events in the ancient world. It was their way of recording history. Pay close attention to what's drawn on the seal, because that's why we're here."

The kids shuffled closer, the shorter ones craning their necks to look.

"Now, who wants to describe it for us?" Kendall asked.

A dozen hands raised.

"You." Kendall pointed to the closest girl. "What's that in the center?"

"A tree."

"And, what's sitting to the right of the tree?" He pointed to another child.

"A man!"

"And to the left? Eddie?"

"A woman," Eddie said. "She's plucking fruit from the tree."

"And what's that standing behind the woman?"

"It looks like a snake."

"But he's standing up," Jessie said.

"Yes he is, Jessie. When we read Genesis, we see God cursing the snake for tempting Eve. Part of that curse was that snakes now wiggle around on the ground. But they weren't like that before."

Jonathan raised his hand. "Is this a picture of the Garden of Eden story?"

"Yes, or more correctly put, this is archeological evidence that it's more than just a story."

Mr. Benefucio folded his arms. "Why do you say that, Dr. Park?"

"If the Bible is really true, then all nations and people descended from Adam and Eve. The history of these events would be handed down by each nation. Some of the details might have changed, as each culture exaggerated and perverted the exact retelling, but the basic story would remain the same. And that's the exciting thing about this stone. It's dated between 2200 and 2100 B.C., possibly around the time of Abraham of the Bible. While the Old Testament tells the story of Eden, this seal came from another people group and tells the same basic story!"

"Is this the only evidence?"

"Of course not. This is just what's on display in the museum today." Kendall looked around for his briefcase. "There's other evidence, such as the Sumerian account of the land of Dilmun. I brought a copy of that, a translation—but I think I accidentally left it in my car."

"Want me to get it for you, Dad?" Jonathan asked.

"If you don't mind." Kendall tossed Jonathan the keys. "It's in the trunk."

Thad raised his hand. "Can I go with him, Mr. Benefucio?"

Mr. Benefucio shook his head. "I want the class to stay together, Thad. Jonathan, you can take your guest, Jessie, with you if you want."

As Jonathan and Jessie walked away, Kendall turned back to the class. "While we're waiting, I'll tell you in my own words about this Sumerian account. It describes Dilmun as a land of perfection, a place where lions and wolves didn't kill, a place where there is no pain or disease or evil at all. . . ."

Lou Phipps and Rusty clattered down a museum hallway.

"Help me look, Rusty." Lou led the way, moving quickly. He wasn't going to let Benefucio get away with going behind his back.

"Hey, Mr. Phipps, I think I just saw Jonathan Park going toward those stairs with his friends." Rusty pointed to a flight of steps in a small hallway to the left.

Lou frowned. "The lady at the front counter said Benefucio's class was down at the end of *this* hall."

"Can I just check real quick?" Rusty edged toward the hallway. "The class might have moved."

"Make it snappy. I'll keep heading down the hall. Meet me there in two minutes sharp, understood?"

Rusty pounded up the stairs to the second floor. Two glass doors led to an open-air walkway that connected with the two-story parking garage. Jonathan and Jessie were walking by the right railing.

"Hey, Mr. Science!" Rusty yelled. "Remember me?"

When Jonathan heard someone yelling, he whirled toward the building. *Rusty?* He blinked.

Jessie gasped. "You're supposed to be at the principal's office!"

"Who do you think I came over with?" Rusty approached, grinning. "Mr. Phipps is here to stop the field trip." He clenched his fists. "You ready to settle things, Park?"

Jessie put her hands on her hips. "Rusty, you're going to be stuck at the principal's office again *next* Saturday, too."

"Big whoop. I'm starting to like Mr. Phipps. He tells cool stories. So now what you gonna do, Park? No teacher to come save your hide this time."

Jonathan's stomach felt completely empty, except perhaps for a few dangling intestines. "I'm not afraid of you," he said.

"Then fight." Rusty swiped his fist in front of Jonathan's nose.

Jonathan stepped back. "I'm a Christian. Christians don't start fights just to fight."

Rusty sneered. "Are Christians chicken?"

"He's not chicken," Jessie said. "He's trying to obey God and love his enemy."

Jonathan thought about this. *That's true, that's what I should be doing.* He took a long breath.

"Look, Rusty. We've both been needling each other, and it's wrong. I'm willing to stop. I'm also willing to ask forgiveness for the wrong things I've done." He put his hand out. "Shake?"

"How 'bout this?" Rusty leaned closer and spit into Jonathan's outstretched hand.

Jonathan swallowed his disgust and wiped the wet glob off on his jeans. "I'm going to ignore that."

"Man, you're even more *spineless* than I thought. How about if I pick on your little friend?" Rusty stepped toward Jessie.

"Leave her alone!" Jonathan said.

Rusty sidestepped him and yanked Jessie's hair.

"Ow!" Jessie screamed. "Get away from me!"

Jonathan grabbed Jessie's arm and pulled her behind him. He wanted to squeeze Rusty's neck.

"I said leave her alone."

Rusty waggled his head. "Make me."

Jessie grabbed Jonathan's shoulder, trying to pull him away. "Stop it, guys! We're here to enjoy the museum, not to fight."

"Sorry, Jessie, but I'm tired of him bullying people."

"Ooh!" Rusty jumped back in mock fear. "Tough guy!"

"Can't you two be friends?" Jessie asked.

Rusty sneered. "I don't need a 'too good for everybody else' for a friend."

Rusty started circling. Jonathan forced himself to breathe through his mouth, hoping the oxygen would steady his racing brain. He also turned, keeping between Rusty and Jessie. Rusty paused with his back to the railing. He raised his fists.

Jonathan tapped his foot, still trying to stay calm. "Rusty, are you going to leave Jessie alone and quit picking on my friends?"

"No, I'm going to settle things with you!" Rusty swung.

The wind popped out of Jonathan's lungs and he doubled over, his stomach feeling flat as a pancake. Rusty poised another fist.

Jonathan lunged, hoping to grab the bully's waist and knock him to the ground. Instead, Rusty spun, and Jonathan slammed into the railing. Something cracked—suddenly there was no railing stopping him, only empty air. He felt like he was floating above a big dark asphalt blur. Then his fingers scraped something metal and he clung.

Jessie screamed.

Jonathan's legs swung free, his whole weight dangling from his hands. A piece of railing had cracked off and he was holding on to a bent piece of piping. There was no crossbar—only slick metal that thinned into nothing.

"Jessie—I'm—slipping," Jonathan gasped.

"Hold on!"

"I didn't mean to knock him through the railing!" Rusty's voice dripped fear.

Jessie grabbed Jonathan's knuckles, but she was too light to pull him up.

"Help him, Rusty! You're stronger."

"N-no way. I'm out of here." Rusty's feet scraped on the cement, then clattered toward the museum.

"Jessie, get someone else!" Jonathan said. "I don't know how long I can hold on!"

His weight kept pulling him down, inch by inch, toward the end of the pipe. *God, help me!*

Back inside the museum, Kendall was still lecturing. He had moved on from the seal and was leading the way around some of the other exhibits, still waiting for Jonathan to come back with the translation of the Sumerian account. It was taking much longer than Kendall expected.

He had asked for examples about things that looked good in nature. Sunsets, seashores, snow-capped mountains—the list was typical.

"Now," Kendall said, are there things in nature that aren't so good?"

Elizabeth's hand went up. "Hurricanes!"

"Very good. Yes, Eddie?"

"Famines and droughts."

"And diseases!" Thad said. "People die."

Kendall nodded. "Excellent illustrations. So in this world we see good things in nature and bad things in nature. Could it be that the world was once a perfect place that was invaded by evil and death?" He paused next to a display about ancient battles. "Genesis explains all of this. It teaches us that when Adam and Eve disobeyed God, paradise was indeed invaded by evil. It fits perfectly with the Bible."

Mr. Benefucio had been looking more and more puzzled as Kendall talked. Now, he raised his own hand, as if he were one of the children.

"Wouldn't God be cruel to allow evil to overcome the world?"

"Cruel by whose standard? God determines what is right and wrong, not man. Because man sinned against God, we deserve punishment. Amazingly, God has given his elect a road back to paradise—forgiveness through His Son, Jesus Christ."

Somewhere down the hallway a door slammed and footsteps clattered toward the traveling exhibit room. Jessie rounded the corner.

For a second, Kendall was shocked to see her running in the museum. Then he saw her face. Something was wrong.

"Dr. Park, Jonathan fell over the railing!"

Adrenaline spiked through Kendall's veins. He ran toward Jessie.

"What's happened?"

Jessie headed for the stairs to the outside. She was panting. "Rusty—and Jonathan—the railing broke."

Kendall flung through the double-doors. He was on an open cement bridge to the parking garage. Iron railings lined both sides, except for one gap on the right where there was no railing. A man he didn't recognize was laying on the cement, his hands wrapped around the legs of a boy. The boy had red hair—it wasn't Jonathan.

After Jessie left, Jonathan kept praying and gripping with all his might. He tried to hold his body as stiff as he could, because every wiggle made him slide farther toward the end of the pipe. The veins running from his wrist to his elbow bulged in a sickening blue maze.

"Are you still there?" someone whispered.

"Yes!" Jonathan slipped another inch. "Help me!"

Rusty's head peered over the side. His eyes were wide. His lips twitched.

"Park, please, I'm sorry—"

"Rusty, help!"

The pipe creaked. Jonathan couldn't hold on any longer. He slipped toward the sharp pipe-edge and closed his eyes.

"Got you!"

Hands clasped his wrists and stopped his fall as the pipe slipped through the air. Jonathan clutched at the hands and locked his fingers with Rusty's.

"You're—heavy." Rusty grunted. He started lowering Jonathan toward the ground.

"What are you doing?" Jonathan said. "I'm too high up!"

"My legs are slipping. I'm slipping, Park! I'm falling! Help!" Rusty yelled.

Footsteps pounded on the cement. "What's going on?" It was Principal Phipps. "That girl said someone fell. Rusty, what are you doing?"

"Help!" Rusty yelled again.

Jonathan was staring up at the sky, and for a second he saw Mr. Phipps' face framed through the railing. Then Rusty stopped slipping.

"I've got you, Rusty," Mr. Phipps said. "Now pull him up higher."

"My fingers—I can't hold on much longer!"

"Come on, do it, pull him up."

Jonathan felt Rusty's fingers weakening. His own were losing feeling after clenching the pipe so long. They felt like ten little bones poking upward.

"Rusty, you can't drop him," Mr. Phipps said. "You hear me? You're thinking it will look like an accident."

"I'm not!" Rusty screamed.

Rusty's hands jerked Jonathan up, then, as he hung suspended for a moment before plunging back down, strong hands grasped his shoulders and pulled him over the edge. He groveled on the hot cement, his face pressed into the grit, tears of relief wetting his cheeks. *Thank you, God.*

"Jonathan!"

The hands released him, and then his dad was at his side, hugging him tight.

Someone was crying. Jonathan sat up, his head still giddy from the fright. He thought it was Jessie crying, but it wasn't—it was Rusty. He was sobbing into Mr. Phipps' shoulder, and Mr. Phipps' eyes were also wet as he bent over him.

"It's okay, kid. Everything's okay."

Dr. Park reached out his hand. "Mr. Phipps, I'm very much in your debt."

"Forget it." The principal cleared his throat and pulled Rusty to his feet. "About time one of us principals earned his pay. Jonathan, did Rusty push you over that railing?"

Jonathan shook his head. "No—not exactly. Truth is, sir, we've both been pretty mean to each other lately. I'm sorry, Dad. Rusty started picking on Jessie, and I couldn't let it go."

"He was fighting for me, Dr. Park," Jessie said.

Rusty wiped his nose on his sleeve. "If it makes any difference, Park, I didn't mean to knock you off."

"Thanks, Rusty. And you too, Mr. Phipps. I think you're a nice principal."

Mr. Phipps blinked. "Nice? Oh. Well—let's just say I'm a nicer principal today than I was yesterday."

"Sounds like you had quite an adventure in the museum."

"It was." Lou Phipps was walking on the path outside of the school so that no one could hear his conversation. "Yeah, Barry, it was, but that's not why I'm calling. You keep trying to change the subject."

"All right, Lou. What's the catch?"

"No catch. I'm giving you back every cent I blackmailed you out of." There was silence on the other end. Lou chuckled. "Barry, you still there?"

"Yeah. Yeah—all right—and the other money?"

"Other money?" Lou asked. "Oh, you mean the money *you* stole. Relax, Barry. I'm giving that back too."

"What do you mean *you're* giving it back?"

"I mean that I'm making a special donation to the school district."

"And just what do you hope to accomplish?"

Lou stopped walking. That was a good question. One that had stumped him. "I guess—I guess so that I can look at myself in the mirror again."

"But you don't have that kind of income. How can you afford it?"

Lou smiled a little bitterly at the bushes. "I can't, really. You can help me out if you want. Otherwise, I'll take out a loan."

"Have you lost your mind?" Barry still sounded shocked. Lou imagined him sitting in his office, his eyes as round as quarters. Either that, or they were squinted nearly shut with suspicion. "What do you expect me to say?" Barry asked.

"Well, how about 'wow, Lou! What a nice person you turned out to be.' Something along those lines, maybe?"

"Quite frankly, your change of heart concerns me. Usually people with a change of heart start talking."

"I'm not quite ready to incriminate myself," Lou said. "Now, I can't promise what will happen if they ever take a closer look at our books. However, in the meantime, you won't have any trouble from me."

"Lou? Seriously—what happened?"

Lou picked up a stick with his free hand and poked at a bunch of dead leaves in the bushes.

"Somebody called me a nice principal. I liked the sound of it, but it was a title I wasn't living up to. I've kind of gotten re-acquainted with my conscience. I've even—" Lou gulped. "I've even started thinking about God."

On Monday, the news came from Mr. Benefucio. Mr. Phipps was going to overlook the museum incident. Jonathan was ecstatic.

"I've talked with Mr. Phipps a couple times at school. He seems like a different person." Jonathan grabbed another cookie from the fresh plate on the counter.

"A person in the process of being called by God, I would suggest," Grandpa Benjamin said.

Jessie tsk-tsked as Jonathan reached for a third cookie. "I just wish Rusty were a different person," she said.

Jonathan agreed. "At least he hasn't been quite as bad since the museum. I think it scared him."

Grandpa Benjamin leaned on the counter. "Well, Jonathan, now what do you think about God's command to love your enemies? Can you see the good that came out of obeying God, even when you didn't completely understand?"

"I think so, Grandpa."

Mrs. Park lifted the last plate of cookies from the oven and slipped out of her oven mitts. "It may affect Rusty some day too. His story isn't over."

"The important thing," Dr. Park said, "is that you did what was right, Son. That's its own reward."

Once the cookies were devoured, everyone split up, and Jonathan and Jessie headed for the living room.

"Jonathan," Jessie said, "thanks for watching out for me in the museum."

"No problem, Jess." Jonathan grinned. "That's what I'm here for."

The Adventure Continues!

Read *Jonathan Park: The Adventure Begins Part 3...*